MODERN HUMANITIES RESEARCH ASSOCIATION

TUDOR & STUART TRANSLATIONS

VOLUME 4(I)

General Editors
ANDREW HADFIELD
NEIL RHODES

OVID IN ENGLISH, 1480–1625

PART 1

METAMORPHOSES

OVID IN ENGLISH, 1480–1625
PART 1

METAMORPHOSES

Edited by

Sarah Annes Brown and Andrew Taylor

MODERN HUMANITIES RESEARCH ASSOCIATION
2013

Published by
The Modern Humanities Research Association,
1 Carlton House Terrace
London SW1Y 5AF

© The Modern Humanities Research Association, 2013

Sarah Annes Brown and Andrew Taylor have asserted their rights under the Copyright, Designs and Patents Act 1988 to be identified as the authors of this work.

Parts of this work may be reproduced as permitted under legal provisions for fair dealing (or fair use) for the purposes of research, private study, criticism, or review, or when a relevant collective licensing agreement is in place. All other production requires the written permission of the copyright holder who may be contacted at rights@mhra.org.uk

First published 2013

ISBN (Hardback) 978–0–947623–92–0
ISBN (Paperback) 978–0–78188–100–2

Copies may be ordered from www.tudor.mhra.org.uk

MHRA TUDOR AND STUART TRANSLATIONS

GENERAL EDITORS

Andrew Hadfield (University of Sussex)
Neil Rhodes (University of St Andrews)

ASSOCIATE EDITORS

Guyda Armstrong (University of Manchester)
Fred Schurink (University of Northumbria)
Louise Wilson (University of St Andrews)

ADVISORY BOARD

Warren Boutcher (Queen Mary, University of London); Colin Burrow (All Souls College, Oxford); A. E. B. Coldiron (Florida State University); José María Pérez Fernández (University of Granada); Robert S. Miola (Loyola College, Maryland); Alessandra Petrina (University of Padua); Anne Lake Prescott (Barnard College, Columbia University); Quentin Skinner (Queen Mary, London); Alan Stewart (Columbia University)

For details of published and forthcoming volumes please visit our website:

www.tudor.mhra.org.uk

TABLE OF CONTENTS

General Editors' Foreword	viii
Preface	ix
Illustrations	x
List of Illustrations	xi
Introduction	1
William Caxton, ECHO AND NARCISSUS (1480)	17
T. H., THE FABLE OF OVID TREATING OF NARCISSUS (1560)	25
Thomas Hedley, THE JUDGEMENT OF MIDAS (*c.* 1552)	59
Arthur Golding, SALMACIS AND HERMAPHRODITUS (1565)	65
Thomas Peend, THE PLEASANT FABLE OF HERMAPHRODITUS AND SALMACIS (1565)	73
William Barksted, MYRRHA, THE MOTHER OF ADONIS (1607)	93
H. A., THE SCOURGE OF VENUS (1613)	125
James Gresham, THE PICTURE OF INCEST (1626)	155
Dunstan Gale, PYRAMUS AND THISBE (1617)	175
Thomas Heywood, JUPITER AND CALLISTO (1609)	193
George Sandys, JUPITER AND CALLISTO (1621)	215
Textual Notes	225
Bibliography	233

GENERAL EDITORS' FOREWORD

The aim of the *MHRA Tudor & Stuart Translations* is to create a representative library of works translated into English during the early modern period for the use of scholars, students and the wider public. The series will include both substantial single works and selections of texts from major authors, with the emphasis being on the works that were most familiar to early modern readers. The texts themselves will be newly edited with substantial introductions, notes, and glossaries, and will be published both in print and online.

The series aims to restore to view a major part of English Renaissance literature which has become relatively inaccessible and to present these texts as literary works in their own right. For that reason it will follow the same principle of modernisation adopted by other scholarly editions of canonical literature from the period. The series will have a similar scope to that of the original *Tudor Translations* published early in the last century, and while the great majority of the works presented will be from the sixteenth century, like the original series it will not be rigidly bound by the end-date of 1603. There will, however, be a very different range of texts with new and substantial scholarly apparatus.

The *MHRA Tudor & Stuart Translations* will extend our understanding of the English Renaissance through its representation of the process of cultural transmission from the classical to the early modern world and the process of cultural exchange within the early modern world.

Andrew Hadfield
Neil Rhodes

PREFACE

This is the first of two volumes dedicated to Ovid's works. We decided to devote an entire volume to translations of the *Metamorphoses* because of that poem's great popularity and impact. Part 2, *Poems of Love and Exile*, will cover all of Ovid's remaining works.

In accordance with the policy for the series as a whole, the texts presented here follow modern conventions for spelling and punctuation. STC numbers of the early editions are identified for readers who wish to consult the original texts.

EEBO facsimiles have been used as the basis for most texts, although original copies have been consulted to clarify ambiguities.

We are grateful for the advice of the series editors, Neil Rhodes and Andrew Hadfield, and for the valuable assistance of MHRA Research Associate Louise Wilson. Richard Moll made several helpful suggestions when we were preparing the Caxton extract. We would particularly like to thank both Colin Burrow and Mandy Green for their judicious advice on several aspects of the edition.

The editors are grateful to the Master and Fellows of Trinity College, Cambridge for permission to reproduce images from the copies of Dolce's *Le Trasformationi* (1553) and Sprengius's *Metamorphoses Ovidii* (1563) held in the Wren Library.

ABBREVIATIONS

The following abbreviations have been used in this edition:

ODNB   Oxford Dictionary of National Biography

OED   Oxford English Dictionary

STC   Short Title Catalogue

ILLUSTRATIONS

Le trasformationi di M. Lodovico Dolce. Di nvovo ristampate, e da lui ricorrette, & in diuersi luoghi ampliate. Con la tauola delle Fauole (Venetia: Appresso Gabriel Giolito de Ferrari e fratel., 1553), Cambridge, Trinity College, Butler 6.

Lodovico Dolce (b. 1508/10–68), a Venetian friend of the painter Titian, was a prolific author, editor and translator associated with the Venetian press of Gabriel Giolito de Ferrari. His compositions include treatises on painting, for example, *Dialogo della pittura* (1557), language, and gems; he edited the major Italian poets and much besides. The freedom of his translations into Italian of Greek and Latin poets and dramatists soon attracted criticism. His version of Ovid's *Metamorphoses* is typical, showing clearly the influence of Ariosto's *Orlando Furioso*, with Dolce converting Ovid's fifteen books of hexameter into thirty cantos of ottava rima. The woodcuts attributed to Giovanni Antonio (Gianantonio) Rusconi (1511–87) found in Dolce's *Trasformationi* (1553) register the shift towards a classical style of representing mythological scenes.[1] Rusconi was the illustrator of *Della architettura [. . .] secondo i precetti di Vitruvio [. . .] libri dieci* (1590), which consisted of 160 illustrations — his work on these may have commenced as early as 1553 — and accompanying Italian summaries of Vitruvius's text.

Metamorphoses Ovidii / argmentis qvidem soluta oratione, enarrationibus autem & allegorijs elegiaco uersu accuratissimè expositæ, summaq[ue] diligentia ac studio illustratæ, per M. Iohan Sprengivm avgvstan ; vnà cum uiuis singularum transformationum iconibus, à Vergilio Solis, eximio pictore, delineatis (Impressvm Francofvrti : Apvd Georgivm Corvinvm, Sigismundum Feyerabent, & hæredes VVygandi Galli, 1563), Cambridge, Trinity College, Z.8.168.

The arguments, and paraphrastic and allegorical interpretations (in elegiacs) of Ovid's *Metamorphoses* offered by Joannes Sprengius (Johannes Spreng, 1524–1601) in this work were illustrated with 178 woodcuts by the famous Nuremberg engraver Virgil Solis (1514–62) in the German mannerist tradition.[2] In fact, these follow the same 178 fables illustrated by the Lyonese artist Bernard Salomon for *La Metamorphose d'Ovide figurée* (Lyon: Jean de Tournes, 1557), with Solis reversing and enlarging the images. Salomon was earlier responsible for the illustrations in Alciati's *Emblematum libri duo* (1547). The woodcut blocks of Solis's influential illustrations for Ovid were used for 25 successive editions, in Dutch, Flemish, German and Spanish, as well as Latin, between 1563 and 1652. English Renaissance translations of Ovid generally lack such programmes of illustration.

---

[1] Luba Freedman, *Classical Myths in Italian Renaissance Painting* (Cambridge: Cambridge University Press, 2011), p. 55.
[2] On Sprengius's Ovid, see Ann Moss, *Ovid in Renaissance France: A Survey of the Latin Editions of Ovid and Commentaries Printed in France before 1600*, Warburg Institute Surveys, VIII (London: The Warburg Institute, 1982), pp. 44–48.

LIST OF ILLUSTRATIONS

Lodovico Dolce, *Le trasformationi* (1553), p. 72 .... *page* 19
Sprengius, *Metamorphoses Ovidii* (1563), p. 43^r 27
Sprengius, *Metamorphoses Ovidii* (1563), p. 135^r 61
Lodovico Dolce, *Le trasformationi* (1553), p. 92 67
Sprengius, *Metamorphoses Ovidii* (1563), p. 51^r 75
Lodovico Dolce, *Le trasformationi* (1553), p. 216 95
Sprengius, *Metamorphoses Ovidii* (1563), p. 125^r 108
Sprengius, *Metamorphoses Ovidii* (1563), p. 49^r 123
Sprengius, *Metamorphoses Ovidii* (1563), p. 126^r 127
Sprengius, *Metamorphoses Ovidii* (1563), 127^r 157
Sprengius, *Metamorphoses Ovidii* (1563), p. 48^r 177
Sprengius, *Metamorphoses Ovidii* (1563), p. 47^r 184
Lodovico Dolce, *Le trasformationi* (1553), p. 85 189
Lodovico Dolce, *Le trasformationi* (1553), p. 46 195
Sprengius, *Metamorphoses Ovidii* (1563), p. 25^r 217
Sprengius, *Metamorphoses Ovidii* (1563), p. 26^r 221
Sprengius, *Metamorphoses Ovidii* (1563), p. 27^r 223

INTRODUCTION

Ovid may not be the most consistently revered classical author, but he has some claim to being the most influential. Publius Ovidius Naso was born in 43 BCE, in Sulmo, a town in central Italy. His boyhood years were a golden age for Roman literature. Among the best known poets of the time were Horace (65 BCE–8 BCE), Propertius (*c.* 50 BCE–15 BCE), Tibullus (*c.* 55 BCE–19 BCE) and, of course, Virgil (70 BCE–19 BCE). As a member of the noble equestrian class, Ovid would have been expected to pursue a career in public life, yet, despite apparent opposition from his father, he abandoned law and politics for poetry.[1] His first published work was the *Amores* (16 BCE), three volumes of love elegies charting the narrator's relationship with 'Corinna'. More controversial was his *Ars Amatoria*, in which the poet offers rather cynical advice to both male and female lovers. The *Remedia Amoris*, by contrast, purports to cure those afflicted by love. Disappointed love is the focus of most of the *Heroides*, fictional letters from a series of mythical and historical women, many of them betrayed or abandoned.

Around 2 CE Ovid began work on two rather different poems. One was the *Fasti*, loosely based around the Roman calendar, and the myths and deities associated with its holidays. The other was his acknowledged masterpiece, the *Metamorphoses*, a fifteen-book epic — although it does not in fact fit stably into any single genre — charting the (largely mythical) history of the world from its creation to the deification of Julius Caesar. It is his most influential work, and the chief source for many myths which are still being retold and adapted today — the stories of Daphne and Apollo, Actaeon, Arachne and Pygmalion, for example. While still working on the *Metamorphoses*, in 8 CE, the Emperor Augustus sentenced Ovid to 'relegation' — a form of exile which did not strip him of his property or all his civil rights. Ovid attributed his fall from favour to two causes — 'carmen et error' — a poem and a mistake.[2] The poem was certainly the rather salacious *Ars Amatoria*, although the fact that it first appeared in 1 BCE, several years before Augustus took action, might suggest that this was not the real reason for the Emperor's displeasure. The nature of the 'error' is unknown, although many have speculated whether there might be some link between Ovid's disgrace and the exile of Augustus's scandalous granddaughter Julia. Ovid's place of exile was Tomis (now Constanta in Romania), a coastal town on the shores of the Black Sea. It was here that he composed his *Tristia* and *Epistulae ex Ponto*, both collections of elegiac epistles, some addressed to friends in Rome deploring his changed circumstances and expressing his longing to return home. Another late work was a curious short poem of invective, *Ibis*. He died in exile in 17 or 18 CE.

Ovid's literary reputation seems to have been unaffected by his troubled later years, and the reception of his works can be traced in an unbroken tradition. He influenced both his immediate successors, including 'Silver Age' poets such as Statius (*c.* 45 CE–*c.* 96 CE), and later Roman poets, such as Claudian (*c.* 370 CE–*c.* 410 CE).[3] Although there are few references to Ovid in the early centuries following the decline of Rome, his continuous influence is attested by the series of manuscript copies which ensured the survival of most of his works, although some (such as a play based on the story of Medea) have been lost. The ninth-century writer, Modoin, Bishop of Autun, chose to style himself 'Naso' while casting the Emperor Charlemagne as a new Augustus. The eleventh-century cleric and poet Baudri of Bourgeuil was another self-

---

[1] Ovid, *Tristia, Ex Ponto*, trans. by Arthur Leslie Wheeler, 2nd edn, rev. by G. P. Goold (Cambridge, MA: Harvard University Press, 1988), *Tristia*, IV. 10. 21.
[2] *Tristia*, II. 1. 207.
[3] See Michael Dewar, 'Siquid habent vei vatum praesagia: Ovid in the 1st–5th Centuries A.D.', in *Brill's Companion to Ovid*, ed. by Barbara Weiden Boyd (Leiden: Brill, 2002), pp. 383–412.

consciously Ovidian writer, who seems to have modelled his vision of the bedchamber of Adela, daughter of William the Conqueror, on Ovid's own ecphrastic set pieces.[4] Ovid's works were read with renewed attention in the twelfth century, which also saw the burgeoning of the important moralizing commentary tradition that would prove influential for several centuries. This tradition has affinities with Biblical exegesis, in that both aim to identify hidden, multiple meanings behind apparently straightforward narratives. Arnulf of Orléans's *Allegoriae super Ovidii Metamorphosin* (c. 1175), which recast myths of dubious morality as spiritually uplifting allegories, was an important influence on this developing commentary tradition.

As well as interpreting Ovid in ways which may now seem curious, earlier translators of Ovid apparently had different views from modern readers about the relative interest and importance of the poet's varied works. Surviving manuscripts give a good indication of which poems were most admired. The pre-eminence of the *Metamorphoses* seems never to have been in dispute, and thirty four twelfth-century manuscripts of the poem have survived. Apparently Ovid's next most popular works were the *Fasti* and the *Epistulae ex Ponto*.[5] The much lower numbers of surviving copies of the erotic poems reflect their unsuitability for pedagogic purposes, and their lack of amenability to Christian or moralizing readings.

In the thirteenth and fourteenth centuries poets writing in the emerging vernaculars turned to Ovid with enthusiasm. The continuing influence of figures such as Petrarch, Dante, Machaut and Chaucer on their successors helped ensure that Ovid's star remained undiminished. Chaucer's use of Ovid well illustrates the varied uses to which his works, particularly the *Metamorphoses*, could be put, anticipating the equally varied responses to Ovid in this volume.[6] To take just three examples: Chaucer updates the tale of Coronis as a bawdy fabliau in *The Manciple's Tale*, includes the poignant story of Ceyx and Alcyone to illustrate the grief of John of Gaunt for his dead wife Blanche in *The Book of the Duchess*, and draws on Ovid's description of Fama, the goddess of rumour, as the starting point for a philosophical exploration of ideas about poetry, truth and authority in *The House of Fame*. The commentary tradition also continued to develop. Significant moralized versions include the early fourteenth-century anonymous *Ovide Moralisé* and Pierre Bersuire's *Ovidius Moralizatus* (1362). The first printed editions of Ovid's works appeared in 1471. In 1493 Raphael Regius published an edition which included an influential commentary as well as the Latin text. Among the many subsequent editions, the second Aldine edition (1515–16), edited by Andreas Naugerius (Andrea Navagero), stands out, as it offered a more scholarly and systematic attempt to retrieve the best readings of the texts from the various manuscript traditions, and to explain its editorial methodology to readers.

The practice of translation underwent a somewhat similar process of professionalization. Much changed between Caxton's 1480 version of Ovid, which now exists only in manuscript form although it may also have been printed, and the publication of Sandys's complete translation of the *Metamorphoses* in 1626.[7] In the earlier decades translation was usually bound up with a moralizing and often specifically Christian commentary. Although the broad outlines of Ovid's narrative are generally left intact, the translator is as anxious to inform readers of the various possible interpretations which might be assayed as to communicate the stories

---

[4] Neil Wright, 'Creation and Recreation: Medieval Responses to *Metamorphoses* I. 5–88', in *Ovidian Transformations: Essays on Ovid's Metamorphoses and its Reception*, ed. by Philip Hardie, Alessandro Barchiesi and Stephen Hinds (Cambridge: Cambridge Philological Society, 1999), pp. 68–84.

[5] Peter E. Knox, 'Commenting on Ovid', in *A Companion to Ovid*, ed. by Peter E. Knox (London: Wiley-Blackwell, 2009), pp. 327–40 (p. 330).

[6] See more broadly, John M. Fyler, *Chaucer and Ovid* (New Haven, CT: Yale University Press, 1979).

[7] For a concise overview, see Gordon Braden, 'Epic Kinds', in *The Oxford History of Literary Translation in English: Volume 2, 1550–1660*, ed. by Gordon Braden, Robert Cummings and Stuart Gillespie (Oxford: Oxford University Press, 2010), pp. 167–93 (pp. 174–79).

themselves. These earlier writers may, at least at first, seem out of tune with the distinctive atmosphere and qualities of Ovid's verse, particularly with his urbanity and humour. But in the later period commentary became less obtrusive, and writers seem keener to reproduce or indeed embellish Ovid's wit. If commentary is present it is usually briefer, and increasingly factual and scholarly in nature rather than moral or allegorical — in other words, closer to what we would expect from a modern edition.

Yet it is important not to overlook or underestimate the earlier responses to Ovid. Although moralizing commentary does not immediately appeal to most modern readers, it is sometimes itself almost Ovidian in its incongruous inventiveness and openness to contradictory interpretations. Thus because the word 'cerf', stag, sounds like 'serf', it was sometimes suggested that Actaeon represents Christ, the suffering servant. Yet Actaeon could also be seen as a spendthrift, destroyed by his obsession with hunting dogs.[8] (The tradition of identifying such unexpected meanings in the poems can be traced back to Ovid himself who found in the unfortunate, if slightly ambiguous, figure of Actaeon, an emblem for his own fate, exiled for an unwitting error.) This creative and playful aspect of earlier Ovidian commentary seems to mutate in later, more secular, Tudor literature, into the taste for much looser adaptations of Ovid, which freely cut and embellished the original, even adding entirely new characters and episodes. The translator's own original contribution to the tradition, once offered as a discrete commentary, is now woven into the story itself. The rather arbitrary contradictions of *in bono* and *in malo* Christian exegesis — the repetition or analysis of images in good and bad senses — become the more subtle and organic tensions which so fascinated later Renaissance writers whose education would have included the practice of debating on both sides — *in utramque partem* — of a question. Heather James notes a nice representation of this complex reading practice in Drayton's *Mortemeriados* (1596): 'As [Mortimer and Isabella] lie 'imparadiz'd (6.30) in her chamber, the lovers puzzle over the meanings of Phaethon's tale (she laments his fall; he praises the ambition)'.[9] Here the contradictory readings arise naturally out of the story, just as they do in a play such as *Dr Faustus*, and do not rest on the ingenious and slightly forced contrivances of the moralizers. The moralizing tradition may seem quintessentially old-fashioned; however in its lack of concern for authorial intention, its readiness to find meanings which defy common sense, and its privileging of ideology, it sometimes seems almost to anticipate strands within later twentieth-century critical exegesis.

The purposes as well as the styles of Ovidian translation differed greatly. At one extreme can be found works such as H. A.'s *The scourge of Venus* (1613), a retelling of the story of Myrrha. The initial choice of a tale of transgressive desire, and the subsequent exaggeration and embellishment of all the racier elements of the story, testify to the poet's erotic purpose, as does the conscious debt to Shakespeare's lushly sensuous *Venus and Adonis*, which a character from the anonymous late sixteenth-century play *The Pilgrimage to Parnassus* vowed to lay under his pillow at night. At the other extreme, we find texts which remind us of Ovid's important role within pedagogy. Schoolboys would be required to memorize and imitate selections from the *Metamorphoses*, *Fasti*, *Heroides* and *Tristia*, and in John Brinsley's *The Grammar Schoole* (1612) Ovid is recommended as a particularly suitable poet for classroom use.[10] Brinsley's translation of the *Metamorphoses* (1618) reflects the poem's centrality within the curriculum. It is laid out in four columns: the original, a literal translation, and two further layers of annotation, designed to help the student of Latin hone his linguistic skills. Florilegia, anthologies of carefully selected rhetorical 'flowers' from Ovid and other poets, were also useful within a

---

[8] Renate Blumenfeld-Kosinski, *Reading Myth: Classical Mythology and its Interpretations in Medieval French Literature* (Stanford, CA: Stanford University Press, 1997), p. 120.

[9] Heather James, 'Ovid in Renaissance English Literature', in *A Companion to Ovid*, ed. by Peter E. Knox (London: Wiley-Blackwell, 2009), pp. 423–41 (p. 436).

[10] See Jonathan Bate, *Shakespeare and Ovid* (Oxford: Clarendon Press, 1994), pp. 20–22.

pedagogic context, as they allowed the compiler to weed out any more scurrilous passages. There is some debate as to the possible use of translations, such as Golding's, in the classroom.[11]

In selecting texts and extracts for inclusion here, the editors have tried to showcase the variety of Tudor and early Stuart Ovidianism, and offer the modern reader works which have been largely overlooked except by specialists, yet which repay further attention. Thus writers such as Golding and Sandys, whose works have been more widely studied and discussed, and which are available in modern editions, are represented only by brief extracts.[12] Where possible, works have been reprinted in full even though this has limited the number of writers represented here. We wished to invite readers to compare different treatments of the same myth, and paired versions of the stories of Callisto, Echo and Narcissus and Salmacis and Hermaphroditus are thus included, as well as three versions of the story of Cinyras and Myrrha. These very different responses to Ovid's tale of Myrrha's doomed love for her father are all interesting in their own right, and the inclusion of all three versions allows the reader to consider the ways in which translators drew on each other as well as on Ovid himself. Because the story functions as a 'prequel' to that of Venus's love for Myrrha's son Adonis, these three versions of her tale also testify to the great influence exerted by Shakespeare's *Venus and Adonis*. The impulse to adapt the story of Myrrha may partly have been spurred by the uneasy reminders of that tale in *Venus and Adonis* itself. Shakespeare's Venus has a matronly quality, whereas Adonis behaves like a petulant child. Jonathan Bate observes of the poem that its juxtapositions 'of sexuality and parenting suggest Adonis is forced to re-enact, with gender and generational roles reversed, his mother's incestuous affair'.[13]

Many of the texts included in this volume go beyond what might normally be termed translation. Yet translation at this time was an inherently hybrid practice, and to omit moralizing commentaries, such as Peend's (1565), the incorporation of translation into a larger encyclopaedic project such as Heywood's (1613), freer adaptations such as H. A.'s *The scourge of Venus* (1613), which weaves translations of two Ovidian tales together to form a new whole, or Barksted's *Mirrha, the Mother of Adonis* (1607), which introduces entirely new episodes into the story, would be to mis- or at least under-represent the sheer variety of Ovidian translation during this period. It would also prevent an appreciation of the contrast between the earlier period's more fluid approach to the category of translation and the modern tendency to view translation and original writing as two discrete activities. All these different versions of translation are central to our understanding of early modern Ovidianism; they both reflected and helped shape each generation's relationship with Ovid's works.

The earliest text included in this volume, the story of Echo and Narcissus from William Caxton's *Ovyde hys Booke of Methamorphose* (1480), may immediately confound the expectations of a modern reader because it is not a direct translation of Ovid, but of a moralized version of the poem in French prose. Yet, despite this fact, and even though it predates the beginning of the Tudor period by five years, Caxton offers an appropriate starting point for our edition because his is the first full-length English version of the *Metamorphoses*. William Caxton's name is probably, to the general reader, the most familiar in the volume; however, despite his pioneering role as a printer and publisher, he has found few to champion his skills as a writer with any great enthusiasm. Yet texts which appear stylistically crude, and which approach translation (and criticism) in unfamiliar ways, can offer rewards to today's readers. Reading Caxton's Ovid is a useful reminder of the very different ways in which people encountered classical texts in

---

[11] Anthony Brian Taylor argues that there is little evidence for their widespread use. See 'Golding's Ovid, Shakespeare's "Small Latin", and the Real Object of Mockery in "Pyramus and Thisbe"', *Shakespeare Survey*, 42 (1990), 53–64.

[12] *Ovid's Metamorphoses*, trans. by Arthur Golding, ed. by Madeleine Forey (London: Penguin, 2002); *Ovid's Metamorphosis Englished, Mythologiz'd, and Represented in Figures. An Essay to the Translation of Virgil's Æneis [Bk I]*, trans. by George Sandys (New York: Garland, 1976).

[13] Bate, *Shakespeare and Ovid*, p. 54.

this period. In the intervening centuries systematic scholarship and research have established, for moderately educated readers, a sense of the differences between the classical world (whether historical or mythical) and our own, which, though perhaps not entirely accurate, is at least quite clearly defined. But the atmosphere of Caxton's Ovid seems little different from that of an Arthurian romance. This is not simply a matter of diction; the stories are subtly adjusted to fit a rather different horizon of expectations. The characters in the story of Echo, for example, are more clearly simply human than they are in Ovid. Liriope, Narcissus's mother, is a 'damsel of great kindred' rather than a nymph; Echo, similarly, is 'a fair maid and a wise'. This slight shift might reflect Caxton's Christian frame of reference, which could not so readily accommodate minor woodland deities. Similarly, in the moralization which follows the story, the writer imposes his own religious perspective onto the original tale, which now appears to have taken place in a Christian world:

> Many ladies used their life in great sorrow for his love, of which it may well be that some of them prayed our lord that he would give to them such form that he might prove and preve [suffer] and feel such pain and martyre as they do that love without parity, and that he might love without having love thereof. God might well hear this request for it was reasonable, and fortune suffered it as ye shall after hear in this history.

Even a fairly casual reader would be likely to note that the Christianized vocabulary has not been derived from Ovid. A more careful comparison with Ovid reveals that Narcissus's male admirers — it is a rejected youth who prays that he may be afflicted with unrequited love in Ovid — have been airbrushed from the story. Reading Caxton is a little like looking at the pictures of everyday life to be found in medieval illuminated manuscripts. The artistry is not always technically impressive but there is still plenty of interest and appeal in the picturesque detail. The now unfamiliar Anglo-Norman words, in particular, add colour to the text: 'renardy', 'jangleress', 'truffs', 'papelardy'. Caxton likes to stick closely to his French source, and was writing at a time when, although no longer the first language of the upper classes, French was still widely used for official purposes in England.

In some ways the second text in this volume, T. H.'s *The fable of Ouid treting of Narcissus* (1560) may seem still more rebarbative to modern ears than Caxton. Although it was published much later than Caxton, and contains fewer unfamiliar words, its opaque language and, in particular, its knotty syntax, make it more difficult to read. The poem is dismissed by C. S. Lewis as 'beneath criticism'.[14] T. H. was writing at a time when English poetry was still finding, as it were, its feet, and he does not seem to have been well served by his printer. But, as is the case with many of the writers included in this volume, he appears to have been a thoughtful reader of Ovid, if not a very good poet. For example, he adds an authentically reflexive refinement to Ovid's 'quae simul adspexit [. . .] non tulit ulterius', 'as soon as he saw this [. . .] he could bear it no more' (*Met.*, III. 486–87), translating this as 'No longer could he dure the pain he saw he suffered there' (l. 166). Narcissus's pain, in this translation, is more explicitly experienced at one remove.

Although both are extremely unsophisticated by the standards of later Elizabethan Ovidianism, there are important differences between T. H. and Caxton. T. H. seems to have a far surer sense of the cultural gap which separates him from Ovid. The story itself is not Christianized; the scorned youth prays to the gods rather than to God that Narcissus should get his comeuppance. Whereas Caxton asserts that 'Echo signifieth good renomee', T. H. sometimes offers various possible readings, and even when he provides only a single gloss, this is tentative and often qualified. For example, Daphne's metamorphosis signifies 'as I ween' the honour due to virtuous virginity (l. 279), and he later suggests that we compare Tiresias to a

---

[14] C. S. Lewis, *English Literature in the Sixteenth Century Excluding Drama* (Oxford: Oxford University Press, 1954), p. 250.

disinterested and incorruptible adviser (l. 305), without insisting upon this interpretation. He treats other readers' interpretations with respect:

> Now will I show that erst I said I would,
> Of this same talk in some comparing sort,
> What I conceive, the which not as I should
> If I declare, and that my wits resort
> Without the reck of wisdom's sober port;
> Now of the learnèd I do crave,
> And of my judgement here the sense you have. (ll. 563–69)

At first glance, Thomas Peend's *The Pleasant fable of Hermaphroditus and Salmacis* (1565) seems a rather similar production, for it too comprises a translation followed by a moralizing commentary. Peend aspired to produce a complete translation of the *Metamorphoses*, yet was prevented by the appearance of the first four books of Golding's memorably exuberant and English Ovid in the same year. There is nothing in Peend to match passages such as this description of Diana with her nymphs:

> The Theban lady Crocale more cunning than the rest,
> Did truss her tresses handsomely which hung behind undressed.
> And yet her own hung waving still. Then Niphe neat and clean,
> With Hiale glistering like the grass in beauty fresh and sheen,
> And Rhanis clearer of her skin than are the rainy drops,
> And little bibbling Phyale, and Pseke that pretty mops,
> Poured water into vessels large to wash their lady with. (III. 198–204)

Peend's was a much slighter talent than Golding's, yet there are a few touches in his poem which anticipate the epyllia of the 1590s. An epyllion, or little epic, is an extended poetic treatment of a myth, usually one with an erotic theme, which embroiders the classical source with new incidents and characters. Although, unlike Shakespeare in *Venus and Adonis* (1593), or indeed Francis Beaumont in his own later *Salmacis and Hermaphroditus* (1602), Peend does not add entirely new episodes, he does venture some fairly substantial additions to Ovid's text. One significant addition, coupled with a possibly significant small absence, anticipates the atmosphere of Marlowe's epyllion *Hero and Leander*. Peend compares Hermaphroditus with a series of other beautiful youths:

> The Phrygian boy, by th'eagle caught on Jove t'attend and wait,
> Liriope's son, Narcissus fair, nymph Echo her dainty bait,
> Not Attis fine, which was some time accepted well with Jove,
> Nor yet the boy in incest got, which Venus so did love,
> All these were not to be compared with young Hermaphrodite.
> Nor Cupid sure, his brother blind, if poets truly write,
> Might not with him in shape compare. (ll. 15–21)

Ovid's account of Salmacis's beauty, by contrast, is truncated by Peend. Although *The Pleasant fable of Hermaphroditus and Salmacis* lacks the heady homoeroticism of Marlowe's *Hero and Leander* (first published in 1598, five years after the writer's death), there is an interesting parallel between Peend's heightened interest in his male lead and the way Marlowe lingers on Leander while keeping a certain distance from Hero.

As well as adding a few new elements and observations, Peend shows some originality in his engagement with Ovid's own propensity for witty wordplay. Sometimes he seems to play with the transformative power of language: the myth's central metamorphosis is reflected in its linguistic texture. Salmacis is described as a 'nicey nymph' (l. 128) a few lines before we are told that she *appeared* 'nice and fine' (l. 130). Nice, or nicey, although it has become an anodyne adjective, may mean here both wanton and fastidious, and seems to switch meanings over the course of a few lines. (Golding, whose translation Peend certainly knew, describes the indolent nymph lying down 'nicely' in the grass at l. 34.) Twelve lines after reproaching Salmacis for her 'wanton tricks' (l. 80), Hermaphroditus is himself compared to a 'wanton kid' (l. 86), yet when applied to the innocent youth, the word means not 'lewd' but 'frisky'.

Peend describes himself as one who daren't speculate about why Venus married ugly Vulcan because he is not 'exempt from Venus' might' (l. 348). Given the intellectually and culturally sophisticated environment he worked in, the Inns of Court, where young men trained to become lawyers, it is hard to imagine that Peend or his readers were narrowly prudish, despite the apparent message of the poem. Critics take different views of Peend's attitude towards his source. R. W. Maslen draws a useful comparison with George Pettie's use of dual address in his version of the myth of Scylla's transgressive passion for her father's enemy Minos. Pettie offers a stern warning to children never to disobey their parents and then, pretending that his older readers have left the room, advises young people to imitate Scylla's example.[15] Although the ambiguities in *The Pleasant fable of Hermaphroditus and Salmacis* are less controlled than this, it does seem likely that Peend enjoyed the tale's titillating qualities despite his apparently severe moralization.

J. H. Runsdorf suggests that the poem's moral goes somewhat against the grain of Ovid because it implies that Hermaphroditus is secretly attracted to Salmacis.[16] A still more un-Ovidian meaning may be revealed if we look more closely at the role of Tiresias in the poem. Sophie Chiari observes that the translator's implicit identification with Tiresias is significant, suggesting that 'the blind prophet stands for the translator himself', particularly when he expresses anxiety about pronouncing judgement on the gods (ll. 316–36).[17] The prophet, like Hermaphroditus, famously underwent gender realignment and his bisexual nature is an odd 'absent presence', not just in the poem but in the glossary as well. Some of the entries here are expansive, and Peend seems to assume very little knowledge of myth. Yet the entry for Tiresias is brief and elliptical: 'Tiresias: an old prophet of the city Thebes in Boetia, a country in Attica, and is now called Vandalia'. It is almost as though Peend is staging an anxiety about disclosing too much about Tiresias, replacing the true facts of his story with a stuttering accumulation of superfluous geographical detail, replacing the prophet's sex change with a region's name change.

The poem's refusal to identify Tiresias's bisexual identity, when coupled with the fact that the poet seems to feel an affinity with the prophet, may encourage the reader to look again both at the actual moment of metamorphosis in Peend's poem, and at the effects of the closing 'curse':

Their parents heard the plaint the which their double-shapèd son
Had made, and so with virtue strange the spring was spread anon,
Thus both in wish they did agree, and now contented well they be. (ll. 164–66)

Peend employs a more neutral vocabulary than Ovid to describe both the coalescence of Hermaphroditus with Salmacis and the subsequent transformation of the waters. In the *Metamorphoses* the waters are changed 'incesto [...] medicamine' (IV. 388), a phrase which might be translated 'by an impure drug', and Golding communicates this tainted quality when he describes the waters as 'Infected with an unknown strength' (l. 135), just hinting at a paradox,

---

[15] R. W. Maslen, 'Myths Exploited: The Metamorphoses of Ovid in Early Elizabethan England', in *Shakespeare's Ovid: The 'Metamorphoses' in the Plays and Poems*, ed. by A. B. Taylor (Cambridge: Cambridge University Press, 2000), pp. 15–30 (p. 24).
[16] J. H. Runsdorf, 'Transforming Ovid in the 1560s: Thomas Peend's *Pleasant Fable*', *American Notes and Queries*, 5 (1992), 124–27.
[17] Sophie Chiari, ed., *Renaissance Tales of Desire* (Cambridge: Cambridge Scholars Publishing, 2009), p.14.

given that the waters' 'strength', or power, is in fact to weaken. Peend however describes how 'with virtue strange the spring was spread anon' (l. 165). Even though the resonances of the word 'virtue' were less unequivocally positive in the sixteenth century the wording used by Peend still seems softer than its Latin equivalent. The recasting of a curse into a blessing appears to be confirmed when Peend wraps up the story: 'Thus both in wish they did agree, and now contented well they be' (l. 166). The tone of calm content seems at odds with the stern moralizing which follows. Peend warns young men against being drowned in 'filthy sin' and paints a picture of a bitter fallen youth who will spitefully 'joy to see his wish, on others in like sort' (l. 198). J. H. Runsdorf ascribes *Schadenfreude* to Peend's Hermaphroditus, but this is in fact only evident in the commentary. In the translation itself it seems entirely possible that Hermaphroditus means to bless rather than curse the pool. It is as though, rather as is the case with the final Salmacis-Hermaphroditus compound itself, there are two voices in the poem struggling for mastery: one which disapproves of sexual looseness and ambiguity; the other which finds the teasing liminality of the myth rather alluring.

If this is the case, it is interesting to note that Francis Beaumont carries this 'Tiresian' attraction to androgyny one step further in his own *Salmacis and Hermaphroditus* (1602), an epyllion whose most obvious debt is to Shakespeare's *Venus and Adonis*. In his prefatory poem, 'The Author to the Reader', he implies that this is a story of star-crossed lovers:

I sing the fortunes of a lucklesse payre,
Whose spotlesse soules now in one body be[18]

and implies a playful endorsement of androgyny:

I hope my poeme is so lively writ,
That thou wilt turne halfe-mayd with reading it.[19]

And at the very end of the poem Beaumont states that Hermaphroditus's parents 'with that great power [. . .] the fountaine blest.'[20] It is uncertain whether Beaumont's apparent metamorphosis of Ovid's tale into a celebration of a fluid and polymorphous sexual identity was directly derived from his less well known predecessor. Like Peend, Beaumont touches on the unequal match between Venus and Vulcan, describing, in the course of a long interlude about Jove's passion for Salmacis, how Venus sued to Astraea for support against her bullying husband. But this may be no more than a coincidence, and it is hard to make a cast-iron case that Beaumont was influenced by, or even read, Peend, despite the occasional use of a similar phrase or rhyme.

Another early Ovidian piece perhaps issues a similar invitation to interpret against the grain of the narrative — and to identify an unexpected bond between the poet and one of his characters. Thomas Hedley's broadside, 'The Judgement of Midas' (1552), is an intervention into a lively and generically diverse 'flyting' which took place between Thomas Churchyard, a poet whose works included the first English translation of Ovid's *Tristia* (1572), and Thomas Camel. The contest was sparked by Churchyard's satirical criticisms of the policies — enclosure, among others — of the Lord Protector, John Dudley, Duke of Northumberland. The originator of the spat, Thomas Churchyard, adopted the persona of 'David Dicar', a Piers Plowman-like figure, whose verse is both archaic and rustic.[21] This of course allows Hedley to align him with Pan. Thomas Camel, a socially conservative poet who liked to emphasize his pretensions to learning, fits the role of Apollo. Balladeer William Elderton intervened in the

---

[18] *Elizabethan Narrative Verse*, ed. by Nigel Alexander (London: Edward Arnold, 1967), p. 168.
[19] *Ibid.*, p. 168.
[20] *Ibid.*, p. 191.
[21] John N. King places the flyting within the context of a vogue for *Piers Plowman*, following the publication of William Crowley's edition of the poem in 1550. *English Reformation Literature: The Tudor Origins of the Protestant Tradition* (Princeton, NJ: Princeton University Press, 1982), pp. 339–40.

flyting when he published his own poem, 'A Decree betwene Churchyarde and Camell'. He defended Churchyard's satire, although he deplored the fact that both poets had resorted to mudslinging. This prompted Hedley, as a supporter of Camel, to cast him as Midas, the foolish judge. 'The Judgement of Midas' is rarely discussed by those interested in translations of Ovid, perhaps because its political purpose and context of publication don't fit modern views about the function and nature of translation. Chris Boswell, for example, asserts that 'the translation is only really of interest here as an allegorical warning to the protagonists about the risks of flyting over such sensitive political matters, and its implicit suggestion that they might perhaps end up having their ears cropped for their trouble'.[22] However, of all the many pieces which make up the flyting, Hedley's is by far the least enmeshed in the quarrel and may quite easily be read independently as an adaptation of an Ovidian myth by a poet who seems to have read the *Metamorphoses* with some care, even though he is happy to cut or elaborate the Latin.

Hedley simplifies Ovid's narrative in some respects, omitting the figure of Tmolus, a mountain god who acts as the official judge in the contest between Pan and Apollo. In the *Metamorphoses* Midas only intervenes after Tmolus has decided in favour of Apollo, whereas Hedley casts him as the presiding judge from the start. For readers who note the omission of Tmolus an interesting further question is raised by Hedley's adaptation. Midas's problems begin, in Ovid, when he questions the wisdom of a judge. Although this is not true of Hedley's Midas, it *is* true of Hedley himself who intervenes, to chastise not Churchyard directly, but the judgement of Churchyard's supporter, Elderton. Both Midas and Hedley reverse the decisions of earlier judges. Perhaps it would be going too far to suggest that Hedley was deliberately undermining the message of his poem and his own ostensible 'judgement' on the flyting, planting a seed of subversion for the Ovidian reader in an ostensibly conservative intervention into a controversial debate. But such an interpretation would certainly fit well with the atmosphere of uncertainty and pain which surrounds so many of Ovid's depictions of judgements and contests. The flaying of Marsyas and the transformation of Arachne into a spider, in particular, seem unwarranted.

If Hedley, or his text at least, invites the reader to identify him with an ostensibly faulty figure in Ovid's narrative, a later poet seems to insert himself within the story as an entirely new character. This is William Barksted in his adaptation of the story of Myrrha's incestuous passion for her father Cinyras (1607), the first of three versions of this tale included in this volume. After the identity of his mistress has been discovered by the horrified Cinyras, Myrrha flees to Panchaia[23] where she encounters a satyr:

> There was a satyr, rough and barbarous,
>   Pleasing his palate at a trembling spring,
> Under a beech with boughs frondiferous,
>   Thought he had seen a nymph, or rarer thing
> Than flesh and blood, for in the calmèd stream
> He saw her eyes, like stars, whose rays did gleam
>   'Bove Phoebus far, and so amazèd stood,
>   As if she had been goddess of that flood. (ll. 585–92)

Jim Ellis suggests that the satyr, Poplar, represents the Petrarchan poet.[24] But one might go further than this and suggest that Poplar is the author himself whose name, like the satyr's, is

---

[22] Chris Boswell, 'The Culture and Rhetoric of the Answer Poem: 1485–1626' (unpublished doctoral thesis, University of Exeter, 2004), p. 138.
[23] *Panchaia* (meaning 'all good things') is a fabulous island in the 'utopian' tradition, sited somewhere in the Erythrœan Sea, east of Arabia (i.e. an undiscoverable part of *Arabia Felix*), rich in precious stones, incense, myrrh, etc. (See Virgil, *Georgics*, II. 139; *Met.*, X. 307–10).
[24] Jim Ellis, *Sexuality and Citizenship: Metamorphosis in Elizabethan Erotic Verse* (Toronto: University of Toronto Press, 2003), p. 137.

somewhat arboreal. Whereas Io and, more memorably, Narcissus, see themselves reflected in water, Poplar sees the face of another, standing over him. Perhaps this is a hint that the mirrored Myrrha is his own poetic creation, a creature who exists inside his own mind. Poplar's unexpected Petrarchan eloquence acquires a fresh significance if we think of him as an avatar of the poet. He is immediately smitten with passion for Myrrha:

> Thus he begins: 'Fairer than Venus far,
>   If Venus be, or if she be 'tis thee;
> Lovely as lilies, brighter than the star
>   That is to earth the morning's Mercury;
> Softer than roses, sweeter breathed than they,
> Blushed 'bove Aurora, better clothed than May,
>   Lipped like a cherry, but of rarer taste,
>   Divine as Diana, and as fully chaste. (ll. 601–08)

If Poplar is Barksted there is a comic mixture of self-deprecation and vanity in his account of how Myrrha feels she might almost have succumbed to his eloquence despite his great ugliness (ll. 617–20). But the moment which hints most intriguingly at the real identity of Poplar comes in this stanza, which creates confusion as to who is speaking, the poet or the satyr:

> Thou did'st deceive me, Myrrha, when I said
>   Thou flew'st for fear; thou gav'st me cause to fear,
> And I might justly have this 'gainst thee laid —
>   Thou wentest wide by paths that were so near;
> Who begin ill, most often end in ill,
> And she that doth her first pure youth so spill,
>   In lawless lust, though made a wife to one,
>   Remains like wax for each impression. (ll. 633–40)

Although the fourth line is slightly obscure, the speaker seems to imply that Myrrha was just playing hard to get, that she was not really afraid; he also alludes to the fact that incest is a transgression which involves staying too close to home. The fanciful conceit of the poet being misled by his own enticing creation, a woman who has deceived him as to her real 'intentions', is still more effective if we see the poet's voice speaking in unison with that of Poplar, deceived by her lovely appearance into assuming that she is modest. The goddess Diana intervenes at this point and turns him into a tree:

> Having thus said, the satyr vanished so,
>   As men's prospect, that from a mirror go. (ll. 663–64)

This striking prologue to the moment of metamorphosis seems to be a final teasing clue that Poplar is the poet's own mirror image.

As well as perhaps including himself in the poem, Barksted reveals an enthusiastic determination to refer to every celebrated character and incident from the *Metamorphoses* in the space of one brief narrative, alluding to sundry canonical stories as though to shore up the authority of the new one. Diana notes, when she interrupts Poplar's chase, that this is the exact same spot where Actaeon saw her naked:

> 'And even there', quoth she, and then did point,
>   'Revenged, I saw his hounds tear joint from joint.' (ll. 671–72)

In the opening section of the poem, Myrrha is described as going to hear Orpheus sing. This episode in itself of course conflates two separate Ovidian tales, but Barksted is determined to bring in still more characters, cramming them into the poem like the figures in the busy frontispieces which precede each book of Sandys's *Metamorphoses*, engravings in which every significant character is shown inhabiting a single crowded landscape:

> Such passion it did strike upon the earth,
>   That Daphne's root groaned for Apollo's wrong;
> Hermaphrodite wept showers, and wished his birth
>   Had never been, or that he more had clung
> To Salmacis, and Clytie grieved in vain
> Leucothoë's wrong, the occasion of her bane.
>   'My wilful eye', this should the burden be,
>   'Hath robbed me of twice slain Eurydice.' (ll. 41–48)

Barksted's allusive procedures may be contrasted with Peend's rather uninventive name-checking of other Ovidian stories in the catalogue of handsome youths whom he compares with Hermaphroditus, prompted, Raphael Lyne suggests, by the fact that he had been working on a translation of the entire poem before being anticipated by Golding.[25] Barksted employs the more inventive device of placing additional characters (some of them in metamorphosed form presumably) in the landscape of his poem as well as in the reader's mind.

Barksted's decision to focus on Myrrha, the mother of Adonis, was probably partly dictated by the popularity of *Venus and Adonis*. Barksted invokes the earlier poem directly in the text, reminding himself, in the final stanza, that he must not trespass on Shakespeare's turf, that 'dear loved [. . .] neighbour' (l. 890), by continuing the story beyond Adonis's infancy. H. A, whose *The scourge of Venus*, the second of this volume's three treatments of Myrrha, was published in 1613, does not refer to Shakespeare directly, but signals his debt by his use of the same stanza form (an iambic pentameter quatrain followed by a couplet: ababcc) and also, perhaps, in the poem's first line, 'Whilst that the sun was climbing up in haste', which seems to echo the first line of *Venus and Adonis*: 'even as the sun with purple-colour'd face'.

In *The scourge of Venus* H. A. strays well beyond the bounds of his chosen story. He makes effective use of his own wider knowledge of the *Metamorphoses*, incorporating elements from the parallel tale of Byblis's passion for her brother into his poem.[26] In a scene closely modelled on the Byblis tale, H. A.'s Myrrha writes her father a letter in which she declares her love:

> 'Father', she writes, yet shame did blot it out;
> Then thus she writes, and casts away all doubt. (ll. 101–02)

In Ovid's original story the letter is delivered and the brother disgusted. Here, however, just as she has given the letter to a trusted servant, Cinyras enters to ask Myrrha which one of her suitors she favours and the letter is never read. Like T. H. and Caxton, H. A. is clearly very aware of the relationships between Ovid's stories, the way in which they accrue many of their resonances only when read within the context of the poem as a whole. The alert reader of Ovid will almost certainly notice the parallels between the two stories of incest. Just as with Ovidian metamorphoses, the surface of the story has been transformed, yet some deeper resemblances remain.

A still more subtle awareness of the rich intratextuality of the *Metamorphoses* and the complex patterns of affinity between its tales is apparent in the final adaptation of Myrrha's story, James Gresham's *The picture of incest* (1626). In the middle of the account of her transformation into a tree, Gresham seems to bring a third substance, stone, into the equation:

---

[25] Raphael Lyne, *Ovid's Changing Worlds: English Metamorphoses 1567–1632* (Oxford: Oxford University Press, 2001), p. 40.
[26] *Met.*, IX. 454–665.

> Those goodly pillars, which but erst did grace
> Her stately moving fabric, in their place
> Were so involved within the humid earth,
> As if they only there had had their birth (ll. 595–98)

The metaphor associates Myrrha with a building, as does the word 'fabric' in the next line. This rather curious interplay between wood and stone at the moment of her transformation from woman to tree, creates an effect of shimmering instability, of metamorphic flux, which literalizes the metaphors of the blazon tradition and might possibly gesture back to her ancestress, Pygmalion's statue. (Centuries later, Ted Hughes would hit on the same device as Gresham in his own account of Myrrha's metamorphosis into a tree: 'She swayed | Living statuary on a tree's foundations'.[27]) A few lines later Gresham explains that within Myrrha's 'metamorphosed sapphire veins, | The life-maintaining marrowy-sap remains' (ll. 605–06). The reference to a hard mineral substance, sapphire, again perhaps nods back to the story of Pygmalion's statue. It is also a very neat Englishing of Ovid's play on the word *medulla* which means both marrow and sap. English can't replicate that particular instance of wordplay but by finding 'sap' within 'sapphire' Gresham cleverly compensates for the loss of the Latin pun. It may have been Shakespeare's *Venus and Adonis* which gave Gresham the idea of echoing the tale of Myrrha's stony ancestress. Here Venus reproaches Myrrha's son, the indifferent Adonis:

> Fie, lifeless picture, cold and senseless stone,
> Well-painted idol, image dun and dead,
> Statue contenting but the eye alone,
> Thing like a man, but of no woman bred! (ll. 211–14)

Venus and Adonis's influence was not limited to these three 'prequels' — its impact can be traced in many later mythological poems, and is particularly apparent in Dunstan Gale's *Pyramus and Thisbe*. This poem was probably written in 1596 although the earliest surviving edition was published in 1617. Here Venus and Cupid appear as characters influencing the action, and we learn that Pyramus reminds Venus of Adonis, although she dismisses Thisbe as 'but brown, as common women are' (l. 78). On Thisbe's scarf there is even an illustration of Shakespeare's poem:

> Love-wounded Venus in the bushy grove,
> Where she entreated, Adon scorned her love. (ll. 165–66)

Gale's description may also be indebted to a similar garment worn by Marlowe's Hero. *Hero and Leander* was not published until 1598, but had already been widely circulated in manuscript by the time Gale wrote *Pyramus and Thisbe*.

Although Venus is in a sense the villain of Gale's poem, as she makes Cupid enflame the hearts of Pyramus and Thisbe in a fit of malice, Shakespeare's Venus provides a model for Pyramus's plangent grief when he thinks Thisbe has been killed. The supposed 'death' of Thisbe echoes that of Adonis, for the savage lioness who frightens Ovid's Thisbe has become an admiring male, whose feelings towards Thisbe, if not as erotic as those Shakespeare's Venus ascribed to the boar who kills Adonis, are certainly affectionate:

> Yet still it came, to welcome her it came,
> And not to hurt, yet fearful is the name,
> The name more than the lion her dismayed,
> For in her lap the lion would have played,
> Nor meant the beast to spill her guiltless blood (ll. 205–09)

---

[27] Ted Hughes, *Tales from Ovid* (London: Faber & Faber, 1997), p. 128.

INTRODUCTION

When he discovers her bloodied garment Pyramus, like Shakespeare's love-struck Venus, is 'sick-thoughted';[28] still more significantly, he is described as 'sick-thoughted like a mother' (l. 251), reinforcing the echo of the relationship between Shakespeare's predatorily maternal Venus and childish Adonis. This odd reversal of both gender and generation is continued in the comparison which follows:

> Or who hath seen a mournful doe lament
> For her young kid, in piecemeal torn and rent,
> And by the poor remainders sit and mourn,
> For love of that which, out alas, is gone?
> Let him behold sad Pyramus, and say,
> Her loss, his love, doth equal every way. (ll. 253–58)

These Shakespearean traces in the works of the later poets in our period are a reminder that the Ovidian tradition in English is a cumulative process, and that translators and adapters of Ovid are influenced by each other as well as by the *Metamorphoses* itself.[29]

It might seem, from a modern perspective, as though Ovidian translation progressed smoothly through the period covered in this volume, becoming gradually more sophisticated and more amenable to the tastes and expectations of today's readers. But the story is a little more complicated than this. Although at first glance it seems as though Christianity is a much more decisive and visible influence on Ovidian translation in the earlier period, one of the latest poets included in the volume, H. A., writing in 1613, interrupts his retelling of Myrrha's story to offer up a prayer that the world may be kept free of such perverse sinners:

> So God preserve it, if it be his will,
> And let the Gospel ever flourish here;
> Yet I do fear we have some yet as ill —
> The pleasing fools do with their folly bear;
> In Paradise I see we cannot live,
> But we shall find some foul seducing Eve. (ll. 241–46)

Although the later translations lack the distracting moralizing apparatus of the earlier period, they can still communicate a strongly felt Christian sensibility.

Thomas Heywood's *Troia Britanica*, from which his version of the Callisto myth included here is taken, also disrupts the sense of Ovidianism's 'progress', as it harks back to a much earlier phase of Ovidian appropriation even though it was published in 1613. At first glance *Troia Britanica* seems as distant from modern literary tastes as the early moralizing tradition represented in this volume. Much of the material in Heywood's long poem is derived from Raoul Lefèvre's *Le Recueil des histoires de Troyes* (1464), which was translated and printed by William Caxton in 1473 as the *Recuyell of the Historyes of Troy*, the first book to be printed in English. Heywood, following his source, approaches history in a way which modern readers are likely to find bizarre. The idea that Britain was founded by Trojans is invoked in the dedicatory poem to the Earl of Worcester, and *Troia Britanica* is premised on a view of world history which reconciles events in the Old Testament with other religions and mythologies. The gods of Greek legends are stripped of most of their powers, and reinvented as mighty kings, early descendents of Japhet, son of Noah. This view of history, which was fairly widespread at the time, can be traced back to earlier scholars such as Annius of Viterbo, whose *Antiquitatum Variarum Auctores* (1498) was supposedly based on ancient writings which Annius found at Mantua (it was in fact a fabrication).

---

[28] Goran R. Stanivukovic, 'Shakespeare, Dunstan Gale, and Golding', *Notes and Queries*, 239.1 (1994), 35–37 (p. 36).
[29] See Maggie Kilgour, *Milton and the Metamorphosis of Ovid* (Oxford: Oxford University Press, 2012).

Whether or not Heywood actually believed that the Greek myths were records of real events, only slightly exaggerated or distorted, his treatment of his material is decidedly sophisticated. And although his historiography is medieval, the poem's execution is characterized by a control, a witty urbanity, which matches that of his contemporaries. He appears to enjoy some of the alterations to the Ovidian material associated with euhemerism (an interpretive mode which offered mundane explanations of myths' miraculous events), such as the fact that Jupiter cannot actually metamorphose himself into a nymph but must dress in drag and practise behaving like a woman:

> Diana Jove in every part surveys,
> Who simpers by himself, and stands demurely,
> His youth, his face, his stature she doth praise,
> A brave virago she supposed him surely.
> 'Were all my train of this large size', she says,
> 'Within these forests we might dwell securely,
> 'Mongst all that stand or kneel upon the grass,
> I spy not such another manly lass.' (ll. 297–304)

Heywood's camp Jove and enthusiastic but naïve Diana anticipate other memorable moments in which cross-dressed men infiltrate an all-female world, the invasion of the female academy in Gilbert and Sullivan's *Princess Ida* (1884) or the introduction of 'Daphne' and 'Josephine' into an all-girl band in Billy Wilder's classic screen comedy *Some Like It Hot* (1959), for example. In transplanting magical myths into a more everyday environment Heywood discovers additional scope for humour and liveliness. It seems likely that *Troia Britanica* has been neglected partly for reasons of genre. Tragedies, lyrics, sonnets and epics slot far more neatly into our generic expectations and teaching needs than Heywood's long and miscellaneous history which weaves stories from various sources with ancient and modern history. Yet in fact the *Metamorphoses* is characterized by much the same generic unruliness.

George Sandys's complete translation of the *Metamorphoses* appeared in 1626, but the first five books were published in 1621, and it is from that early edition that the extract included here, the story of Callisto, is taken. At first glance this conforms much more closely to modern expectations of a translation than many of the other examples in this volume. It is complete, close to the original Latin, and includes no obtrusive moralizing passages. However, in the notes added to the 1632 edition, Sandys offers elaborate allegorical readings, as well as scholarly glosses, and in fact provides a unique compendium of the enduring moral and allegorical readings of the *Metamorphoses* still current well into the seventeenth century. And even though Sandys looks forward to the metrical smoothness and sophistication of the coming Augustan neoclassicism, there are some slightly archaizing Englished touches. Juno insists that the sea gods keep the newly stellified Callisto and Arcas out of their waters:

> Command you that the seven Triones keep
> Their lazy wain out of your sacred deep. (ll. 143–44)

'Wain', as well as being a rustic English word for wagon, which remained in later use as a poetic archaism, is also short for 'Charles's Wain', a non-classical appellation for the seven brightest stars of Ursa Major, perhaps now best known as the Plough. Another slightly anomalous moment is a reference to Callisto as 'a squire of Phoebe's' (l. 16). 'Squire', translating *miles*, strongly connotes the northern European Middle Ages, and disrupts the otherwise carefully classicized atmosphere of Sandys's scholarly translation, albeit not so obtrusively as Caxton's medievalisms. It is not only when straying into the territory of imitation, introducing characters, incidents or interpretations which are quite absent from the *Metamorphoses*, that a translation reveals the stamp of its author and its age.

INTRODUCTION

Having suggested that traces of older approaches linger in the vocabulary of Sandys, the pious Christian asides of H. A. and the approach to world history adopted by Heywood, it is salutary to go back a hundred years before our volume begins, and discover, by contrast, a sophisticated 'modernity' in *The Manciple's Tale*, where the gods' affairs are treated like those of bourgeois householders. It is clear from works such as *The Knight's Tale* that Chaucer is fully capable of adapting mythical material in a more decorously classical fashion, and that he has chosen not to do so here in order to create a particular effect:

> And so bifel, when Phebus was absent,
> His wyf anon hath for hir lemman sent.
> Hir lemman? Certes, this is a knavyssh speche!
> Foryeveth it me, and that I yow biseche.[30]

Ovid's crow is here a caged pet, which doesn't mince his words:

> For all thy waityng, blered is thyn ye
> With oon of litel reputacioun,
> Noght worth to thee, as in comparisoun,
> The montance of a gnat, so moote I thryve!
> For on thy bed thy wyf I saugh him swyve.[31]

To underline the reader's probable sense that Chaucer is in control of the incongruously modern and mundane atmosphere of his tale, the manciple, its narrator, explains that he is a 'boistous' man, and not 'textuel'. The tale's conscious lack of sophistication is itself part of a sophisticated overarching purpose, the creation of a distinctive narrating voice.

The modern reader who surveys different versions of Ovid is likely to be more conscious of the preoccupations and assumptions which govern the translator's or adapter's approach to the poet than of the equally contingent circumstances in which he or she is reading. When we think we are trying to find the voice which is most faithful, or most interestingly unfaithful, to Ovid, it is in fact just one 'Ovid', the Ovid of our own era, who is being used as a yardstick. Reflecting on our own reactions to earlier responses to Ovid may encourage us to become more aware of our own assumptions. Why do we tend to assume that Caxton's anachronisms are naïve, whereas Ovid, that most sophisticated poet, delights in equally anachronistic romanizing detail? Why are we distracted by Heywood's 'mistaken' sense of history but scarcely notice Ovid's own failure to disentangle history from myth? These early translations may not simply teach us about a moment in literary history — they may encourage us to look at Ovid himself with fresh eyes.

---

[30] *The Riverside Chaucer*, ed. by Larry D. Benson (Oxford: Oxford University Press, 2008), ll. 203–06.
[31] *Ibid.*, ll. 252–55.

WILLIAM CAXTON
ECHO AND NARCISSUS
from
OVYDE HYS BOOKE OF METHAMORPHOSE (1480)

WILLIAM CAXTON

ECHO AND NARCISSUS

from

OVYDE HYS BOOK OF METAMORPHOSE (1480)

[*Metamorphoses*, III. 339–406]

Lodovico Dolce, *Le trasformationi* (1553), p. 72

Caxton's translation exists in a single manuscript, which may have been prepared from a printed copy, although no trace of such an edition survives. It reflects the great influence of the moralizing, allegorical tradition, and was based on a Middle French version of the *Ovide moralisé en prose*, rather than on the Latin text.

William Caxton (*c*. 1420–1492) started his career as an apprentice in the Mercers' Company, and became a leading merchant in Bruges. In 1471 he moved to Cologne where he acquired a printing press. In either 1473 or 1474 his *Recuyell of the Historyes of Troye*, translated from the French of Raoul Lefevre, became the first book to be printed in English. Shortly afterwards he returned to England where he set up a printing press near Westminster Abbey. Here the first book he published was the *editio princeps* of the *Canterbury Tales*. Caxton enjoyed the patronage of prominent figures such as Margaret, Duchess of Burgundy, and Anthony Woodville, the 2nd Earl Rivers, brother-in-law of Edward IV, whose *Dictes and Sayings of the Philosophers* was printed by Caxton in 1477. Caxton's translation of Ovid seems to have been designed partly with this kind of aristocratic audience in mind; in his prologue to *The Golden Legend* (1483), he explains that he embarked on the project at the request of 'certeyn lords, ladyes and gentylmen'.

Two existing French texts of the *Ovide moralisé en prose*, a 1484 edition 'translaté et compilé par Colard Mansion' and an unpublished manuscript held by the British Library (MS Royal 17. E. iv), bear the closest relation to Caxton's text, and thus to his likely source. Mansion, who produced the first of these texts, was a Flemish printer who collaborated with Caxton in Bruges. The French provenance of Caxton's Ovid is strongly reflected in its vocabulary and syntax. Yet although Caxton tends to stick closely to his source, his translation reveals some influence from other texts, including Gower's *Confessio Amantis*.[1] For many years only part of the manuscript, that containing books X–XV, was thought to have survived. This shorter second half was owned by Pepys and is now held in the Pepysian Library in Magdalene College, Cambridge. The missing first nine books were discovered among the papers of Sir Thomas Phillipps in 1964. Four illuminations are included in the Phillipps manuscript, and there are spaces for other illustrations which remain blank.

For Caxton, metamorphosis is not simply his text's subject matter. He is alert to the subtle, reflexive patterns at work, both in the *Metamorphoses* itself and in his own relationship with Ovid, describing both the transitions between tales and later readers' interpretations of the myths as varieties of metamorphosis.[2] There was no printed edition of the Pepys manuscript until 1819, and thus Caxton never exerted any direct influence on later English writers. Yet the *Booke of Methamorphose* is an important moment in the history of Ovidian translation, and a significant example of a Christian, moralizing approach to the *Metamorphoses*.

EDITIONS

William Caxton, trans., *Six bookes of Metamorphoseos in whyche ben conteyned the fables of Ovyde*, ed. by George Hibbert (London: Shakespeare Press, 1819).

—, *Ovyde hys booke of Methamorphose Books X-XV*, ed. by Stephen Gaselee and H. F. B. Brett-Smith (Oxford: Basil Blackwell, 1924).

—, *The Metamorphoses of Ovid*, 2 vols (New York: G. Braziller, 1968).

FURTHER READING

J. A. W. Bennett, 'Caxton's Ovid', *Times Literary Supplement*, 2 November 1966, p. 1108.

N. F. Blake, *William Caxton* (Aldershot: Variorum, 1996).

Gertrude C. Drake, 'Ovid's *Metamorphoses*: The Facsimile of the Caxton MS, and Sandys's 1632 Version', *Papers on Language and Literature*, 7 (1971), 313–35.

Alexandra Gillespie, 'Caxton and the Invention of Printing', *Tudor Literature, 1485–1603*, ed. by Mike Pincombe and Cathy Shrank (Oxford: Oxford University Press, 2009), pp. 21–36.

Liz Oakley-Brown, *Ovid and the Cultural Politics of Translation in Early Modern England* (Aldershot: Ashgate, 2006).

ECHO AND NARCISSUS

Now I have told you of Tiresias that became a woman, and by Juno lost his sight, and after by Jupiter[3] became a diviner in such wise that he could let the people have knowledge of their doubt. It happed on a day that a damsel of great kindred named Liriope, wife of a puissant[4]

---

[1] Liz Oakley-Brown, *Ovid and the Cultural Politics of Translation in Early Modern England* (Aldershot: Ashgate, 2006), pp. 171–72.
[2] *Ibid.*, p. 167.
[3] by Jupiter] through the intervention of Jupiter
[4] puissant] powerful

man named Cephisus, came to Tiresias to know of him the truth of a doubt, and proved[5] him first in this wise. This lady had newly childed, and was delivered of a fair son, the fairest that ever was seen. The child was named Narcissus, and for his great beauty every[6] loved and desired him, would he or none.[7] The mother, that loved him entirely, came to Tiresias for to know his destiny, and specially for to know if he might live long. The diviner said he should live long if he were kept[8] seeing of himself. They that heard this dark answer held him for vain and a fool, and mocked him. But in the end he was found veritable and true. It happed that 21 year after this Narcissus had the fame and renomee[9] in all countries nigh and far, that he was the fairest man of all the world. And the voice ran all about that many ladies and damsels loved him paramours,[10] but he was so fierce[11] and so proud that he never deigned to love none, but set all his cure[12] and courage[13] in hunting and chassery.[14] On a day, by adventure,[15] Echo saw him, which was a fair maid and a wise at that time. But now she is nothing but a sound. She had at that time other usage of speaking than she hath now. She was a jangleress[16] and a speaker, but she may not now begin any reason,[17] and if any had spoken a word she would resound the end of the word emprised.[18] This thing happed to her by Juno that had reprised[19] her of a fault done to her when Juno espied the nymphs which lay with her husband Jupiter. And she was by them at the point to take them with the trespass. But Echo made her to understand the contrary by truffs[20] and by jangling, and said so much that the nymphs fled tofore[21] her and hid them in such wise that she could not find them, but if she had taken in the plain feat. And when Juno apperceived this, she said to her: 'Echo, often times thou hast abused me by thy filed tongue. But thou shalt no more abuse me'. Then Juno abridged her speech in such wise that never after she began any reason, but whosoever beginneth, she recordeth and finisheth the last word, as she that cannot yet be still.

Echo by adventure saw the fair Narcissus on a day going alone in places out of the way. He seemed to her so fair and so honest[22] that she was all esprised[23] of his love and she began to follow him secretly in such wise that Narcissus took none heed. And the more she saw and beheld him, the more she was enflamed in her courage[24] of love, and had gladly resounded and spoken to him if she had might. But as it is said tofore, she might not begin any reason, but she rehearsed[25] well the end of the reason said.

Echo put all her intent for to follow the youngling and to await if she might hear him say any word by which she might answer. Narcissus, that by adventure was alone and far within

---

[5] proved] tested
[6] every] everyone (*OED* 6)
[7] would he or none] whether he wanted [them to] or not
[8] kept] kept from
[9] renomee] renown. This is one of many Anglo-Norman words used by Caxton.
[10] paramours] sexually, romantically
[11] fierce] Here 'proud' (*OED* 3), derived from the French 'fier'
[12] cure] care
[13] courage] inclination (*OED* 2) or energy (*OED* 3)
[14] chassery] This word is not listed in the *OED* but seems clearly derived from the French 'chasse', hunting.
[15] by aventure] chance
[16] jangleress] female chatterer, idle talker
[17] reason] speech
[18] emprised] undertaken
[19] reprised] retaliated against, taken revenge on
[20] truffs] idle tales, trifles
[21] tofore] before
[22] honest] perhaps 'comely' here (*OED* 2.c)
[23] esprised] enflamed
[24] courage] heart, as seat of emotions
[25] but she rehearsed] unless she repeated

the boscage,[26] escryed[27] his fellows and said on high, 'Hoowh[28] come'. And she answered nothing, but 'Come'. Narcissus heard the voice and returned, but he saw nobody, whereof he was much abashed.[29] He began again to cry 'Come hither', and she answered 'Come hither'. Narcissus returned for to see him or her that he had heard. But he saw nothing, and he was abashed, and cried 'Why fleest thou?'. And Echo answered 'Why fleest thou?'. Narcissus, that had hereof great marvel, tarried and abode all still and looked about him, but he saw nothing. He had then more wonder than he had tofore and cried again 'Let us assemble'. And Echo answered 'Assemble'.[30] Narcissus heard never voice that so much pleased him, and then issued out of the wood and came into the plain. Echo appeared then tofore him, and drew toward him, weening to have embraced him. But he, as fierce and disdainous for his great beauty, refused her and said to her, 'I am not so foul ne[31] so abandoned that ever thou shalt have of me copy.'[32] Echo was then so ashamed and so sorrowful of this word that she could not answer for anger but 'copy'. Echo for shame leapt into the wood, into a ditch, and never after would issue for shame. But nevertheless for that, she removed not her heart, but loved alway more and more Narcissus, and her sorrow and anguish increased alway by cause he had refused her. Love wax and pained her so much that she, all discomforted, went in exile and came to nought and lost all humidity, for her bones great and small became stones, and her abideth nothing but the voice, which is heard in the woods and valleys customably. Her voice liveth pardurably,[33] but she shall never be fonden ne seen.

Sense allegorical to the foresaid fable

Echo signifieth good renomee, by which Juno was amazed[34] which signifieth the world that espieth and weeneth to take them that trespass and find them in their faults and trespasses. She found many whom she left not to destroy for the praising or good fame of the world,[35] and many there be full of deceit and renardy[36] that make them self seem, by false hypocrisy and papelardy,[37] humble, simple and piteous,[38] and do abstinences so openly and great that to the world they been authorized[39] and renomed of holiness, and thus deceive the simple people of the world by the shadow of their false dissimulation, in such wise as there is none other talking but of them and of their good life. But under false coverture they been full of malice, when they been thereas they may execute it, and else not in other place where they should been espied or known.[40] For their good renomee covereth and hideth all their malice in such wise that they be not reprehended nor taken[41] in such malice as they do.

---

[26] boscage] thicket
[27] escryed] called out to
[28] Hoowh] a hunting call, to gather scattered hunters together
[29] abashed] surprised
[30] assemble] possibly both to meet and to couple sexually (*OED* 3.b)
[31] ne] nor
[32] copy] fullness, plenitude. (Compare the Latin *copia*.) Caxton uses the word in a similarly erotic context in his translation of Aesop, cited in the *OED*: 'Requyrynge hym that she might haue the copye of his loue' (*OED* 1.b). There may also be a play on the idea of reproduction.
[33] pardurably] eternally
[34] amazed] puzzled, perplexed
[35] The meaning seems to be that Juno does not spare people simply because they enjoy a good reputation.
[36] renardy] cunning, like a fox, 'reynard'. The form 'renaldry' is recorded in the *OED* (first usage 1612).
[37] papelardy] hypocrisy
[38] piteous] here probably meaning 'pious' (*OED* 3)
[39] authorized] highly esteemed
[40] Hypocrites are careful only to behave badly when they are sure they won't get found out, for example when no one they know is near.
[41] taken] caught out

Echo ne[42] reasoneth any man but that other first reason her,[43] for good renomee ne fame may not be raised ne had of any creature but if he have done first any good work which hath been tofore recited and rehearsed abroad in the world of which they been praised and allowed among the people. Narcissus had had great renomee and fame of his beauty if he would have loved Echo but he was so proud and surquidrous[44] that he lost the grace of the world; he would despise and dispraise every man by cause of his great beauty, and thereby he minished and lessed much his good renomee. Echo was turned into pure sound, for sound without body is to understand renomee and fame, which may have no body for it ne is but word published and pronounced tofore it be heard in the woods or in the vallies. For thoo places been heard redound[45] when one cryeth. It seemeth that a voice issueth out of the woods or vallies which endeth and finisheth the word tofore said, like as the fable reciteth. Narcissus despised Echo and many other damsels to whom he would in no wise grant their request ne never enjoyed any of them of his love. Many ladies used[46] their life in great sorrow for his love, of which it may well be that some of them prayed our lord that he would give to them such form that he might prove and preve[47] and feel such pain and martyre[48] as they do that love without party,[49] and that he might love without having love thereof. God might well hear this request for it was reasonable, and fortune suffered it as ye shall after hear in this history.

---

[42] Ne] 'Ne' before a verb indicates a negative.

[43] reason] The *OED* only lists usages pertaining to argument and debate for the verb 'reason', but Caxton seems to be using the word in a sense linked to more neutral meaning of the noun 'reason': remark, utterance (*OED* 3.a). 'Address' is perhaps the best gloss here.

[44] surquidrous] arrogant

[45] redound] '(of a place) to resound or reverberate' (*OED* 5.b)

[46] used] spent

[47] preve] This seems to be simply a variant spelling of 'prove', here used to mean to have experience of, to suffer (*OED* 7).

[48] martyre] torment

[49] party] The women are imagined regretting the fact their love is not reciprocated. In Ovid it is a young man who, having been spurned by Narcissus, wishes him a similar fate.

T. H.

THE FABLE OF OVID TREATING OF NARCISSUS (1560)

T. H.

THE FABLE OF OVID TREATING OF NARCISSUS (1560)

[*Metamorphoses*, III. 339–510]

Sprengius, *Metamorphoses Ovidii* (1563), p. 43ʳ

This poem, which comprises a comparatively close translation of Ovid's tale and a much longer discursive moralization, has the distinction of being the first Elizabethan treatment of the *Metamorphoses*. The identity of T. H. remains uncertain. One candidate is the book's own publisher, Thomas Hackett.[1] However there are significant differences between *Narcissus* and the more formal, elaborate and, indeed, more clearly written works which Hackett is known to have authored. T. H. has also been identified with Thomas Howell. Joseph Ritson first made this suggestion,[2] and it now seems to have been fairly widely accepted.[3] But, once again, the known works by this writer don't resemble *Narcissus*; they are far simpler, clearer and more conventional. A further reason for rejecting both these candidates is the internal linguistic evidence that the poem seems to have been composed significantly before its publication date.[4]

---

[1] Both Ducke and Melnikoff seem to assume that Hackett is the author. Joseph Ducke, 'Shakespeare's *Macbeth* and the 'Fable of Ovid Treting of Narcissus' by Thomas Hackett' (2007) http://www.grin.com/e-book/110628/about-shakespeare-s-macbeth-and-the-fable-of-ovid-treting-of-narcissus [accessed 21 January 2010]; Kirk Melnikoff, 'Thomas Hacket and the Ventures of an Elizabethan Publisher', *The Library*, 7th ser., 10 (2009), 257–71.

[2] Joseph Ritson, *Biographia Poetica: A Catalogue of the English Poets* (London: C. Roworth, 1802), p. 250.

[3] Boas, Bate and Lyne, amongst others, associate T. H. with Howell. Frederick S. Boas, *Queen Elizabeth in Drama and Related Studies* (London: George Allen & Unwin, 1950), p. 104; Jonathan Bate, *Shakespeare and Ovid*, (Oxford: Clarendon Press, 1994), p. 28; Raphael Lyne, *Ovid's Changing Worlds: English Metamorphoses 1567–1632* (Oxford: Oxford University Press, 2001), p. 35.

[4] Thomas Warton suggests convincingly that the poem, because its language is so archaic, seems to have been written some time before it was published (*The History of English Poetry*, 4 vols (London: Reeves and Turner, 1871), IV, p. 298).

Because of the uncertainties surrounding the poem's authorship we will refer to the poet only as T. H.

The translation is written in poulter's measure, that is, alternating Alexandrines and Fourteeners, to form a poem of twelve- and fourteen-syllabled lines. The moralization is in rhyme royal stanzas of seven lines. It is probable that T. H. was using Raphael Regius's influential edition of the *Metamorphoses* (1518),[5] reprinted many times over the course of the sixteenth century, as well as several other commentaries on the poem. Lee T. Pearcy notes that he sometimes seems to misunderstand the meaning of the Latin.[6] Many have expressed frustration at the poem's clumsiness and obscurity. Although the general thrust of each stanza is generally clear, the word order is frequently counterintuitive; the syntax, in particular, can be very knotty, sometimes failing to yield a fully satisfactory meaning. Some of the poem's difficulty may probably be ascribed to the printer's incompetence as there seem to be careless errors, as well as to some apparent misunderstanding of the original. One example of the compositor's confusion can be seen in line 50. The text reads '"Whistlest thou me", quod he, who heard her answer even the same'. It seems certain that T. H. wrote 'Why fliest thou me', translating Ovid's 'quid [. . .] me fugis?' (*Met.*, III. 383–84). Because the syntax is often elliptical, it is harder to rule readings of words in — or out. Gordon Braden describes *Narcissus* as 'almost literally unreadable' and observes that 'It is possible to kill Ovid's stories, as is proved by Golding's immediate predecessor in the field'.[7]

But some recent critics have found the poem more rewarding. Liz Oakley-Brown offers a Lacanian reading of *Narcissus* as an expression of early modern subjectivity,[8] and R. W. Maslen praises the poet's ingenious wordplay in an extended discussion of the poem.[9] There is also something engaging about the poet's anxiety to please and his receptivity to a range of very different readings of the myth. T. H. articulates an enthusiastic appreciation for Ovid, whom he describes as 'sure divine' (l. 214), and he identifies the witty transitions between the tales of the *Metamorphoses* as especially praiseworthy (ll. 221–27). Raphael Lyne notes that this emphasis on transitions, and thus on the work as a whole rather than on individual episodes, 'contrasts with a common view of reading in general in this period [. . .] that readers expected and were expected to approach texts not as wholes but as parts to be scanned for their beneficial meanings and then redeployed'.[10] As well as explicitly articulating his alertness to transitional moments, in the moralizing section T. H. reveals his sequential approach to reading the *Metamorphoses* by picking out the main elements of Book I in their correct order (ll. 263–90).

The poem was not reprinted until the twentieth century, and does not seem to have exerted a strong direct influence on later writers, although it has been suggested that Golding and Peend might have known *Narcissus*.[11] Only W. E. Buckley's 1882 edition of the poems of Thomas Edwards, which includes *Narcissus* as an appendix, retains the long moralizing commentary.

---

[5] See note 29.

[6] *The Mediated Muse: English Translations of Ovid, 1560–1700* (Hamden, CT: Archon, 1985), pp. 3–4.

[7] Gordon Braden, *The Classics and English Renaissance Poetry: Three Case Studies* (New Haven, CT: Yale University Press, 1978), p. 49.

[8] Liz Oakley-Brown, 'Translating the Subject: Ovid's *Metamorphoses* in England, 1560–7', in *Translation and Nation: Towards a Cultural Politics of Englishness*, ed. by Roger Ellis and Liz Oakley-Brown (Bristol: Multilingual Matters, 2001), pp. 48–84 (pp. 55–60).

[9] R. W. Maslen, 'Myths Exploited: The Metamorphoses of Ovid in Early Elizabethan England', in *Shakespeare's Ovid: The 'Metamorphoses' in the Plays and Poems*, ed. by A. B. Taylor (Cambridge: Cambridge University Press, 2000), pp. 15–30 (pp. 19–22).

[10] Lyne, *Ovid's Changing Worlds*, p. 36.

[11] Arthur Golding, *Shakespeare's Ovid: Being Arthur Golding's Translation of the 'Metamorphoses'*, ed. by W. H. D. Rouse (London: De La More Press, 1904), p. ii; Maslen, 'Myths Exploited', p. 22.

EDITIONS

T. H., *The Fable of Ovid treting of Narcissus translated out of Latin into English metre with a moral thereunto, very pleasant to read. MDLX* (London: Thomas Hackett, 1560), STC 18970.

Thomas Edwards, *Cephalus and Procris: Narcissus: From the Unique Copy in the Cathedral Library, Peterborough*, ed. by Rev. W. E. Buckley (London: Nichols, 1882).

Nigel Alexander, *Elizabethan Narrative Verse* (London: Edward Arnold, 1967).

O. L. Jiriczek, *Specimens of Tudor Translations from the Classics* (Heidelberg: Carl Winter's Universitätsbuchhandlung, 1923).

FURTHER READING

Frederick S. Boas, *Queen Elizabeth in Drama and Related Studies* (London: George Allen & Unwin, 1950).

Joseph Ducke, 'Shakespeare's *Macbeth* and the 'Fable of Ovid Treting of Narcissus' by Thomas Hackett' (2007) http://www.grin.com/e-book/110628/about-shakespeare-s-macbeth-and-thefable-of-ovid-treting-of-narcissus [accessed 21 January 2010].

R. W. Maslen, 'Myths Exploited: The Metamorphoses of Ovid in Early Elizabethan England', in *Shakespeare's Ovid: The 'Metamorphoses' in the Plays and Poems*, ed. by A. B. Taylor (Cambridge: Cambridge University Press, 2000), pp. 15–30.

Kirk Melnikoff, 'Thomas Hacket and the Ventures of an Elizabethan Publisher', *The Library*, 7th ser., 10 (2009), 257–71.

Liz Oakley-Brown, 'Translating the Subject: Ovid's *Metamorphoses* in England, 1560–7', in *Translation and Nation: Towards a Cultural Politics of Englishness*, ed. by Roger Ellis and Liz Oakley-Brown (Bristol: Multilingual Matters, 2001), pp 48–84.

Lee T. Pearcy, *The Mediated Muse: English Translations of Ovid, 1560–1700* (Hamden, CT: Archon, 1985).

Anthony Brian Taylor, 'Narcissus, Olivia, and a Greek Tradition', *Notes and Queries*, 44 (1997), 58–61.

THE FABLE OF OVID TREATING OF NARCISSUS

God resisteth the proud in every place,
But unto the humble he giveth his grace.
Therefore trust not to riches, beauty nor strength,
All these be vain, and shall consume at length.[12]   *waste away*

Imprinted at London by Thomas Hackett, and are to be sold at his shop in Cannon Street, over against the three cranes.

---

[12] length] These lines appear on the title page of the 1560 edition.

The printer to the book

Go little book, do thy endeavour	*do your utmost*
To all estates that vice doth refuse;	*ranks*
In thee may be learnèd how to persever	*continue*
Sin to abhor, virtue to use.	
The wise the author will excuse,	
Because he inveigheth against sin and pride,	
Who causeth many a one perilously to slide.	*go wrong*

In thee may the wise learn virtue in deed,
In thee may the strong man of himself know,
In thee may the rich man of himself read
How to gather his riches, or them to bestow.
With most worthy matter in thee doth flow,
Who seeketh in thee for profit and gain,
Of excellent matter soon shall attain.

The argument of the fable

Liriope had a son by Cephisus named Narcissus, whose continuance of life Tiresias, a prophet, affirmed to be long if the knowledge of himself procured not the contrary, whose sentence[13] hear now. Echo, the calling imp[14] from whom Juno had bereft the right use of speech, so loved this Narcissus that through the thought and care that she sustained for the getting his good will that ever despised her, she consumed the relics,[15] of which consumed carcase were turned into stones. The great disdain of Narcissus, herein Rhamnusia[16] strangely revenged, for he, heated through hunting, by the drinking of a well (supposing to quench his thirst) espied therein the shadow of his face, wherewith he was so ravished that, having no power to leave his blind desire for the attaining of an impossibility, there he starved.[17] For the preparation whose burial the nymphs had ordained such furniture as thereunto appertained, and had. Returned to the solemn earthing and burial of such a carcase, they found instead of the dead corpse a yellow flower which with us beareth the name of a daffadilly.

The end of the argument

Liriope, whom once Cephisus did embrace,	
And ravish in his crooked flood where she was shut from grace,[18]	
Did travail and bring forth, when time of birth befell,	*labour*
A child even then whom love had likèd well,	
And him Narcissus named, of whom the lot[19] to learn,	

---

[13] sentence] punishment

[14] imp] The original 'impe' appears to be an error for 'nimphe'. 'Imp' has a range of meanings, including scion, devil or youth, but is rarely used of women.

[15] consumed the relics] wasted away

[16] Rhamnusia] The goddess Nemesis, whose sanctuary was at Rhamnous

[17] starved] died, pined away

[18] 1–2] The indentation follows *1560*, where the first line to be indented is line 3.

[19] of whom the lot to learn] The sense seems incomplete. 'She sought' is presumably to be understood.

If he should number many years and perfect age discern.
　　The reader of his fate, Tiresias, 'Yea', did say,
If that the knowledge of himself his life did not decay.　　*destroy*
　　Full long a vain pronounce this seemèd till his death,
10　By fury quaint, did make it good and unseen loss of breath.　　*cunning, unfamiliar*
　　For twenty years and one, Narcissus death escaped,
What time no child was seen so fair, nor young man better shaped;
　　A number both of men and maids did him desire,
But beauty blent[20] with proud disdain had set him so on fire　　*blended*
　　That neither those whom youth in years had made his make,　　*companion*
Nor pleasant damsels fresh of hue could with him pleasure take.
　　This man, the fearful harts enforcing to his nets,
The calling nymph one day beheld, that neither ever lets　　*fails*
　　To talk to those that spake, nor yet hath power of speech
20　Before; by Echo this I mean, the doubler of screech.
　　A body and no voice was Echo yet, but how[21]
The blab had then none other use of speech than she hath now,
　　The latter end to give of every sense or clause,
Whereof the wife of Jupiter was first and chief the cause;
　　For that when she did seek the silly nymphs to take,
That oft she knew within the hills had lodgèd with her make,
　　This Echo with a tale the goddess kept so long,
That well the nymphs might her escape; but when she saw this wrong:
　　'This tongue', quoth she, 'wherewith so oft thou did'st deceive
30　The goddess Juno, little use of speech shall erst[22] receive.'
　　And so her threatenings prove; yet Echo endeth speech　　*to this day*
With doubling sound the words she heareth and sendeth again with screech.
　　Thus when Cephisus' son, the deserts[23] walking fast
With wandering pace, she had espied, her love and on him cast,[24]
　　With stealing steps she followeth fast her hot desire,
And still the nearer that she comes, the hotter is her fire,
　　None otherwise than as the nearer fire doth lie
To brimstone, matters meet to burn to flame doth more apply;　　*incline*
　　How oft, oh, would she fain with pleasant words him glad,　　*gladden*
40　And fawn on him with prayers sweet, but nature it forbad,
　　And letteth her to begin but that she doth permit.[25]
Full pressed is Echo to perform according to her wit,　　*driven*
　　In listing for to hear some sound his mouth escape　　*listening*
Whereto her words she might apply, and him an answer shape.
　　By chance Narcissus, led from company alone,

---

[20] blent] *1560* 'bent'

[21] but how] This seems to be the prelude for an explanation of Echo's condition. This is supplied; however, 'but how' seems to be lost sight of within the sentence.

[22] erst] The usual meaning is 'first' or 'earlier'. It may be a misprint for 'hence'.

[23] deserts] Previously used of any wild, uninhabited region. 'Deserts' translates the Latin *rura* (*rus*), lands, countryside (*Met.*, III. 370).

[24] 33–34] The poet's use of *anastrophe* (inversion of normal word order) here and elsewhere creates difficulties for the reader. The more natural word order would be: 'Thus when she had espied Cephisus' son walking [in] the deserts fast with wandering pace and cast her love on him'.

[25] 41] 'And prevents her from beginning to say anything but that allowed by nature', i.e. to echo or repeat the words of others

Did say, 'Is any here?', to whom she answereth her anon.
　　　　He museth, and amazed doth look on every side,
　　And calling loud, 'Come near', he saith, whom she bids eke abide.
　　　　Again he looketh about, and seeing none that came,
50　'Why fliest thou me?', quod he, who heard her answer even the same.
　　　　He stayeth and, not knowing whose this sound should be,
　　'Come hither, let us meet', he said, and 'Let us meet', quoth she.
　　　　Then with so good a will, as though she never heard
　　A sound that liked her half so well to answer afterward　　　　　　　　　　　　　*pleased*
　　　　And to perform her words, the woods she soon forsook,
　　And to embrace that she desired, about the neck him took.
　　　　He flieth fast away; her folded arms that spread
　　About his neck he cast away, and ever as he fled,
　　　　'Death would I choose ere thou hast power of me', quoth he,
60　Whom she none other answer made but, 'Thou hast power of me';
　　　　And after that, with leaves, she hid her shamefast face,
　　Within the woods in hollow caves maketh her dwelling place;
　　　　Yet love doth no whit more decrease, but with her smart
　　Augmenteth still, and watching cares consumeth her wretched heart.
　　　　By leanness eke her skin is dried, and to air
　　Her blood consumeth, so hath she nought but voice and bones to spare,　　　　　*evaporates*
　　　　Wherereof is nothing left but voice, for all her bones
　　They say, as to her likest shape, were turnèd into stones;
　　　　And since the woods hath been her home, herself to hide
70　From every hill,[26] and nought but sound in her doth now abide;
　　　　Thus her, thus other[27] nymphs, of woods and waters born,
　　Had he deceived, and young men eke, a number had in scorn,
　　　　At last with hands lift up, so one[28] to the gods did plain,
　　That so his hap might be to love and not be loved again.
　　　　Whereto it seemèd well Rhamnusia gave ear,
　　And sought to grant this just request, it after did appear.
　　　　A spring there was, so fair, that streams like silver had,
　　Which neither shepherds hap to find, nor goats that upward gad
　　　　Upon the rocky hills, nor other kind of beast,
80　With flashing feet to foul the same, or trouble at the least,　　　　　　　　　　　*splashing*
　　　　Wherein, themselves to bathe, no birds had made repair,
　　Nor leaf had fallen from any tree, the water to appair;　　　　　　　　　　　　　　*sully*
　　　　About the which the ground had made some herbs to grow,
　　And eke the trees had kept the sun from coming down so low;
　　　　Narcissus there, through heat and weary hunter's game,
　　Glad to take rest, did lie him down and fast beheld the same,
　　　　And as he thought to drink, his fervent thirst to slake,
　　A drier far desire him took, by looking in the lake;　　　　　　　　　　　　　　　　*thirstier*
　　　　For seeing as he drank the image of his grace,
90　Therewith he, rapt, fell straight in love with shadow of his face,

---

[26] herself to hide from every hill] In order to complete the sense here a phrase such as 'she resolved' needs to be understood before these words.
[27] thus other] *1560* 'they other'. It seems likely that the printer misunderstood the poet's (accurate) translation of 'sic hanc, sic alias' (*Met.*, III. 402).
[28] so one] *1560* 'soone'. Ovid refers here to 'aliquis despectus' (*Met.*, III. 404), 'one scorned [youth]'.

    And museth at himself, with which astonied cheer,   *stupefied*
As image made of marble white his countenance did appear.
    Like stars he seeth his eyes, and Bacchus' fingers[29] sweet;
He thought he had on golden hairs for Phoebus not unmeet;
    A neck like ivory white, a mouth with savour good,
A face with skin as white as snow, well colourèd with blood.
    All which he wonders at, and that he liketh well
Is even himself, that wonder makes with small advice to dwell;   *prudence, tarry*
    He sees that he doth ask, again doth him desire,
100 Together he doth burn himself and kindle eke the fire.
    The well that him deceived, how oft kissed he in vain,
How oft therein his arms he drowned, in hope for to attain
    The neck that he desired so much to embrace,
And yet himself he could not catch in that unhappy place;
    Not knowing what he seeth, therewith he is in love,
And those same eyes that error blinds, to error doth him move.
    Ah fool, why dost thou seek the shape that will not bide,
Nor being hath, for turn thy face away and it will slide;
    The shadow of thyself it is that thou dost see,
110 And hath no substance of itself, but comes and bides with thee,
    If thou can'st go away, with thee it will depart.
Yet neither care for meat or sleep could make him thus astart,   *start up*
    But in that shadow place, beside the well, he lies,
Where he beheld his feignèd shape with uncontented[30] eyes,
    And lifting up those eyes, that his destruction made,
Unto the trees that stood about he raught his arms and said: *reached out*
    'Hath ever love, oh woods, dealt crueller with man;
You know that hiding place hath been to lovers now and then;
    Now can you call to mind, you that such worlds have last,   *lasted*
120 That ever any pinèd so by love in ages past?
    I see and like it well, but that I like and see
Yet find I not; such error, lo, this love doth bring to me.
    And to increase my grief, no sea nor irksome way,
No hills nor valleys with closed gates doth say our meeting nay;
    A little water here doth sever us in twain;
He seeketh, I see, that I desire, to be embraced as fain,
    For look, how oft my lips I move to kiss the lake,
So oft he showeth his mouth, content full well the same to take;
    To touch thee might full well, a man would think, be done,[31]
130 It is the least of other things that lovers ought to shun.[32]
    What so thou be, come forth, why dost thou me deceive?
Why fliest thou him that thee so much desireth to receive?
    My beauty and mine age, truly methinks I see,
It is not that thou dost mislike for nymphs have lovèd me;

---

[29] fingers] Fingers translates *digitos*. In some editions *digitos* is replaced with *dignos*: 'et dignos Baccho, dignos et Apolline crines', 'and hair worthy of both Bacchus and Apollo' (*Met.*, III. 421). The Regius edition of Ovid has *digitos*.

[30] uncontented] This usage predates the first occurrence listed in the *OED*.

[31] done] *1560* 'dime'.

[32] shun] *1560* 'shine'. The couplet makes little sense in *1560*, so we have adjusted the final words of both lines.

       Thou promisèd to me a hope, I wot not how,
With friendly cheer, and to mine arms the same thou dost unbow.
       Thou smilest when I laugh, and eke thy trickling tears,
When I do weep, I oft espy, with signs thy countenance stirs
       By moving of thy lips; and, as I guess, I learn
140   Thou speakest words the sense whereof mine ears cannot discern;
       Even this I am I see, my proper shape I know,
With loving of myself I burn, I moan, and bear the glow.
       What shall I do, and if I ask, what shall I crave?
Abundance brings me want; with me it is that I would crave.
       Oh would to God I might depart my body fro,
In him loves this that wish is strong, his liking to forgo;[33]
       But now my strength through pain is fled, and my years
Full soon are like to end; thus death away my youth it bears.
       Yet death that endeth my woes, to me it is not so sour,
150   He whom I love right fain I would might live a longer hour;
       Now to one', quoth he, 'together let us die'.
In evil estate,[34] and to his shape returneth by and by,
       And with his gushing tears, so up the water start,
His shape that thereby darkened was, which when he saw depart:
       'Now whither dost thou go? Abide!', he crièd fast,
'Forsake him not so cruelly, his love that on thee cast;
       Though thee I may not touch, my sorrows to assuage,
Yet may I look relief to give unto my wretched rage.'
       And whilst he thus torments, he barèd all his chest
160   Before the well, with stony fists and[35] beats his naked breast,
       With a carnation hue, by strokes thereon did leave,
None otherwise than apples white with ruddy sides receive,
       Or as the growing grape, on sundry clusters, stripe
A purple colour as we see, or ever they be ripe.   *before*
       Which, as he did espy, within the water clear,
No longer could he dure the pain he saw he suffered there;
       But as by fire to wax a melting doth ensue,
And as by heat the rising sun consumeth the morning dew,
       So feebled by love, to waste he doth begin,
170   At length, and quite consumeth by heat of hiding fire within;
       And neither hath he now hue of red and white,
No liveliness nor lusty strength that erst did eyes delight,   *formerly*
       Nor yet the corpse remains, that Echo once had loved,
Which though with angry mind she viewed, to sorrow she was moved;
       And look how oft 'Alas' out of his mouth did pass,
So oft again with bounding words she cried 'Alas, alas',   *rebounding*
       And when that he his sides with reckless hands did strike,
She also then was heard to make a sound lamenting-like.
       Thus looking in the well, the last he spake was this:
180   'Alas, thou lad too much in vain beloved of me amiss',
       Which self same words again this Echo straight did yell,

---

[33] 145–46] He wishes (unlike most lovers) to be separated from the object of his love.
[34] In evil estate] This translates the Latin 'male sanus' (*Met.*, III. 474). 'He is' is to be understood.
[35] and] Frequently, as here, 'and' is delayed beyond its natural position in the sentence.

And as Narcissus took his leave, she bade him eke farewell.
  His head, that him abused, under the grass he thrust,
And death shut up those eyes that on their master musèd fast,
  And when he was received into that helly place,
He eke within the ugly Styx[36] beheld his wretched face.
  The wood and watery nymphs, that all his sistren were,
Bewails his lot as is their wont, with cutting of their hair,
  Whose wailing Echo's sound did mourningly declare;
190 For grave pomp, a bier with lights and fire they did prepare,
  Then body was there none, but growing on the ground
A yellow flower with lily leaves instead thereof they found.

FINIS FABULE[37]

The moralisation of the fable in Ovid of Narcissus

  A tale wherein some wisdom may be found
May be allowed, of such as lies refuse;[38]
Hereon I mean not that my wit can ground   *establish*
A matter fit for all men to use,
The praise thereof I utterly refuse,
And humbly them beseech to read the same,
Me to excuse or, by their judgement, blame.[39]

200   For neither I presume, by youthful years,
To claim the skill that elder folks do want,   *lack*
Nor undertake that wiser often fears,[40]
To venture on my spites, then would pant;[41]
Right well I know my wits be all too scant;
But I, by your correction, mean to try
If that my head to reason can apply.

  I mean to show, according to my wit,   *ability*
That Ovid by this tale no folly meant,
But sought to show the doings far unfit
210 Of sundry folk whom nature gifts hath lent,
In divers wise to use with good intent,
And how the bounty turneth to their pain,
That lack the knowledge of so good a gain.   *advantage*

---

[36] Styx] *1560* 'Stype'. (The poet may have written 'Styge'.)
[37] Finis fabule] 'End of the tale'. *Fabulae* is the more normal genitive form, but in Medieval Latin 'ae' is frequently replaced with 'e'.
[38] 193–94] Even those with reservations about fictions ('lies') might still tolerate such a tale if it contained a useful moral.
[39] 195–99] He doesn't claim to offer a reading which will satisfy everyone but invites people to judge for themselves. This is consistent with his readiness to include lengthy descriptions of other commentators' readings of the myth.
[40] 202] He doesn't undertake to do something which wiser men generally fear to do.
[41] 203] 'To dare to aim to do something despite my inability and then suffer for it'

Which Ovid now, this poet sure divine,[42]
Doth colour in so wonderful a sort,
That such as twice refuse to read a line
With good advice, to make their wit resort *judgement*
To reason's school, their lessons to report,
Shall never gather Ovid's meaning strange,
220 That wisdom hideth with some pleasant change. *diverting metamorphosis*

His tales do join in such a goodly wise,
That one doth hang upon another's end,
As who should say, a man should not despise
To look before which way his work will bend,
And after how he may the same amend;
Thus Ovid bids his readers for to know
The things above as well as those below.[43]

The fable that he treated of before,
Is how that Juno fell in argument
230 With Jupiter, which after leisure more,
To write at large, than time convenient,
For such a cause have in different:[44]
But to be short; Tiresias was their judge,
Whose sentence Juno seemèd for to grudge.

For she, because he said not as she would,
Bereft him of his eyes and made him blind,
As one unfit to view the world, that could
No better judge, unto a woman's mind;
Redress whereof none Jupiter could find,
240 But with some honour to relieve his woe,
Each thing to come he made him surely know.[45]

The foremost proof whereof, in this same tale,
Liriope, the nymph, receivèd now,
That did demand an answer not to fail
If that her child, to whom her liking vow
Even at the first, was given him to allow,[46]
Should not perfect years and many grow.
'Yea, yea', quod he, 'himself if he not know.'

---

[42] divine] Although 'divine' may mean simply pre-eminently gifted rather than godlike, it is still a striking epithet.
[43] 221–27] The translator admires Ovid's clever transitions. He suggests that they help remind the reader that one should think about the consequences of one's actions and then reflect whether one might improve one's behaviour. This, he says, indicates that Ovid had heavenly as well as earthly matters in his mind. The interpretation seems rather strained.
[44] in different] in dispute. Here, as elsewhere, the syntax is unclear. It would seem that T. H. is saying that he would like to say more about the quarrel between Jove and Juno but he doesn't have enough time. Assuming this *is* the intended meaning the poet is being rather coy as Jove and Juno were quarrelling about whether women or men enjoyed sex more (*Met.*, III. 316–38).
[45] 239–41] Jove gives Tiresias the gift of prophecy in compensation for his blindness.
[46] 245–46] The meaning is not fully clear but seems to translate 'iam tunc qui posset amari', 'who might even now be loved' (*Met.*, III. 345).

      Here, as I said, appeareth that the end
250 Of every tale another doth begin;
      Here likewise may we see the poet bend
      To bid us look his meaning here within,
      Supposing that their wits be very thin,
      That will behold the scabbard of the blade,
      And not the knife wherefore the sheath was made.

      For if that Ovid's meaning was to write,
      But how Narcissus, drinking of a well,
      With shade of himself did so delight,
      That there till death he thought to starve and dwell,
260 Both him a fool, a lie in verse to tell,
      The wise might think, and those that read the same
      To be unwise and merit greater blame.

      The turning of Lycaon[47] to a beast
      Doth well declare that to the wicked sort
      Full heinous plagues preparèd be at last,
      Of God, that to their doings will resort,   *turn His attention*
      With justice hand at home they cannot sport,
      But if they seek for to withstand his will,
      They find to work themselves a way to spill.[48]

270 By saving eke of Pyrrha and her make,   *mate*
      Deucalion,[49] from the consuming flood,
      What else is meant but God above doth take
      An order ever to preserve the good
      From peril still, in times that they be wood,[50]
      That few or none, but such as God doth choose,
      Can happy live, or them from harm excuse.   *shelter*

      And Daphne,[51] changing to the laurel green,
      Whose leaves in winter never lost their hue,
      Doth well to us betoken, as I ween,
280 That such as to virginity be true
      Mortal glory ever shall ensue,[52]
      And, as the laurel lives in winter's rage,
      So shall their praise, though death devour their age.

      Of Phaëthon[53] eke, Apollo's wretched son,
      That would presume his father's cart to guide,

---

[47] Lycaon] Cf. *Met.*, I. 199–242. The poet now traces in order a sequence of narratives from the first two books of the *Metamorphoses*.
[48] 269] They contrive to behave in a way which will bring about their own deaths.
[49] Pyrrha and her make, Deucalion] Cf. *Met.*, I. 313–416.
[50] wood] mad. The epithet qualifies the times rather than the good people.
[51] Daphne] Cf. *Met.*, I. 452–567.
[52] ensue] Here used transitively with 'such' as the object.
[53] Phaëthon] Cf. *Met.*, II. 1–328.

	Of courage more than counsel well begone,	*furnished*
	What may be thought but such as will abide,	*persist*
	With small advice, not from their will to slide,⁵⁴	*wisdom*
	And do refuse their fathers' counsel sure,	
290	There helpless harms unto themselves procure.	*remediless*

    What needeth me⁵⁵ examples to rehearse,
Since I do take another thing in hand;
These show that poets colour under verse
Such wisdom as they cannot understand
That lightly list to look on learning's land;⁵⁶   *wish*
But such as with advice will view the same   *wisdom*
Shall lessons find thereby their lives to frame.

    And now to turn unto the tale I mean
To treat upon: when that the doom was read
300 Of this Cephisus' son, by one that clean
Had lost the sight of all that nature bred,
A vain pronounce it seemèd that he spread,   *declaration*
Whose sentence: himself did not know,   *meaning*
To perfect age his life he shall bestow.

    Tiriesias here, whom may we like unto
Even such a man as hath no mind to gain,
With righteous lips that seek no wrong to do,
That yield to riches for no manner of pain,
Nor yet the truth in anything will lain,   *hide*
310 Which shall (as he was blind for justice sake)
Be quite bereft of all that he can make.⁵⁷

    For he that will not Juno's servant be,
I mean not now the pleasing of the stout
And mighty dames that would have all agree
Unto their fancies that they go about,
But he, I say, and proof doth put no doubt,
That will not seek the rich folk to please,
Through hate and wrong hath often little ease.⁵⁸

    Yet when they lack this use of worldly sight,
320 That little have they left on earth to see,
And that by wrong another hath their right,
Because to will⁵⁹ their wits would not agree,
By loss hereof they got a greater fee,

---

⁵⁴ 287–8] Phaëthon represents those who persist in an ill-considered course of action in defiance of good advice.
⁵⁵ me] Perhaps 'mo' (more) is intended here.
⁵⁶ 294–95] Readers who only engage superficially with learning cannot understand the full meaning of a subtle poem.
⁵⁷ 305–11] Here the poet makes a parallel between the honest man, who will lose all the money he might potentially have earned if he'd been less frank, and Tiresias, who lost his sight through his own honesty.
⁵⁸ 313–18] The poet explains that he does not mean to signify, by Juno, wealthy and capricious women in particular, but the rich more generally.
⁵⁹ will] (another's) desire or command

For God of good doth give them knowledge more
Than all the gain of earth could them restore.

For where their eyes be cast from worldly wealth,
And have respect to things that be above,
In much more perfect wise the certain health
Shall they discern, than such as have a love
330 To vain desires that rise for to remove,[60]
And further be they able to avow
Of hidden things than worldly folk allow.

But as Tiresias' judgement seemèd vain,
In the fore-reading of Narcissus' fate,   *foretelling*
So foolish folk from credit will refrain   *belief*
Of wisdom's voice, that seldom comes too late;
They only mark the present earthly state,
Without regard of anything at all,
What in this life or after may befall.

340 And eke again regard how Ovid here
Of prophecies doth show the doubtfulness,
Whose meaning never plainly doth appear,[61]
In doubtful words that hath a hid pretence   *purpose*
Whereon we guess, but great experience
Full oft we find, and proving of the same
Doth well declare our judgements be by aim.[62]

Wherefore we neither ought to make too light,
By the depining[63] of a skilful voice,
Nor yet presume so far above our might
350 As of the certain scanning to rejoice,[64]
Of hidden things that reach beyond our choice;
For who can surely say it will be so,
Or disallow the thing they do not know.

Tiresias' voice did Pentheus despise,
In counting false the things that he foresaw,
Yet of his death the[65] guess did seem too wise
Which he foretold by his divining law;[66]
And Pirechus'[67] judgement eke appearèd vain,
That would presume of doubtful speech to make,
360 A certain sense the meaning to mistake.

---

[60] 330] Such desires rise only to disappear, 'remove'.
[61] 342] The meaning is clearer if we imagine 'but rather' prefacing the next line.
[62] by aim] by conjecture. The poet seems to be saying that our guesses often prove to be wrong.
[63] depining] 'despising' is perhaps intended.
[64] 349–50] We shouldn't complacently assume that the correct interpretation has been reached.
[65] The] *1560* 'they'
[66] 356–57] 'But the prophecy relating to Pentheus's death, which Tiresias foretold using his powers of divination, would prove to have been only too well founded'.
[67] Pirechus] Perhaps this is a reference to Pyrrhus of Epirus who was told he would die if he saw a wolf and a bull fighting, and failed to escape this fate despite the warning.

     So that hereby right well we may regard
What hap they have that work by doubtful guess   *fate*
To scorning folk,[68] and eke the evil reward
That often falleth, the poet doth express;
Thus two extremes he teacheth to redress,
And by Narcissus warneth us to beware
Of the mishap that pride doth still repair.   *deliver*

     For well Narcissus may betoken here
Such one as hath that other members want,
370 As strength and power, a cause of weaker's fear,
A passing wit above the ignorant,
Of beauty fair, in riches nothing scant,
And to conclude, from chief of nature's pack,
That hath the choice that other thousands lack.

     Who, being deckèd with so goodly gifts,
Shall have a number that will much require
Of the acquaintance, for the divers drifts   *impulses*
Which fancy craveth to content desire;
But if he have the same abusèd fier,[69]   *proudly*
380 That this Cephisus' son did here receive
Example take: himself he shall deceive.

     The man that thinks himself to have no make,   *equal*
Each offered friendship, straight, will quite refuse;
For so Narcissus carèd not to take
The fellowship of such as sought to choose
His company above the rest to use;
But as by pride he grew in great disdain,
So for reward his end was full of pain.

     Whose[70] strength is such that it can much prevail,
390 Yet cannot say, 'I am the most of right',
Whose heaps of gold be of full high avail,   *value*
Yet need not brag to be the richest wight,
Whose beauty eke full pleasant is in sight,
Yet hath no cause to say above the rest,
'I all despise for nature made me best.'

     No creature hath ever yet been such
That can justly say 'I most excel';
God thought hereof the pride was very much,
When Lucifer he cast from heaven to hell,
400 In showing where presuming folks should dwell.

---

[68] 361–63] It seems that the poet is criticizing two distinct groups, those who ignore prophecies out of pride and those who (also out of pride) presume they know exactly how to interpret a prophecy. But the syntax is unclear.
[69] fier] an Anglo-Norman usage
[70] Whose] The poet moves away from the specific example of Narcissus to warn men more generally not to overrate their gifts.

None ought to trust to riches or to strength,
To power or beauty; all consumeth at length.

    The rich, and proud, disdainful, wealthy man[71]
That Lazarus forbade the crumbs to eat,
Which from his board should fall, might after ban   *curse*
His much abundance and his dainty meat,
Which was the cause of all his torment great;
Yet if he could have usèd well his gain,
He little should have had of all his pain.

410   Now Croesus eke, the wealthy king of Lide,   *Lydia*
Whose sums of gold were passing to be told,
Did see at last his riches would not bide,
As Solon[72] said, his end that did behold;
Wherefore we prove, who putteth their trust in gold,
Or slipper wealth, are seen in care to dwell,   *unstable*
And lose at last the good they like so well.

    Of strength again, who will himself avaunt   *boast*
Shall see that conquest goes not all by might;
This David[73] made the Philistines to grant,   *yield*
420 That slew their giant Goliath, their knight,
Against the which no man then thought too wight;[74]
For all his pride, yet saw they at the last
Him overthrown, and dead by David's cast.

    Now Sampson's strength, that causèd all this woe,
I overpass, and Milo's[75] might so strange,
That could endure a furlong well to go,
And on his back an ox to bear the range;   *the entire length*
For all his might to weak estate did change
When that his strength did bring his latter hour,
430 To show the end of might and mortal power.

    Sennacherib, the strong Assyrian king,
Did put his whole affiance in his power;   *faith*
Yet Hezekiah's prayers good did bring
His sore destruction in a sudden hour;
By night the angel did his host devour
With death, whereby Sennacherib might know
That God full soon his might could make full low.[76]

---

[71] wealthy man] Dives (Luke 16:19–31)
[72] Solon] According to Herodotus (*Histories*, I. 29–33), Solon advised Croesus that other men had known greater happiness than him.
[73] See 1 Samuel.
[74] wight] powerful and mighty, particularly within the context of warfare. The line might be paraphrased 'in comparison with whom no man seemed so mighty'. But it is also possible that 'to(o) wight' is a printer's error for 'to fight'.
[75] Milo's] Milo of Croton, a sixth-century BCE athelete, met his end when attempting to rend a tree asunder. His hands became trapped, and he was killed by wolves.
[76] 431–37] The details of this encounter are recorded in 2 Kings and 2 Chronicles.

  Darius' flight, which Ferres[77] overthrew,
  And Tereus'[78] slaughter by the Scythian queen,
440 Be fit examples, for to let us know,
  That who to power will put their trust, and ween   *think*
  By only might to vanquish, all be seen
  Of this their purpose oftentimes to feel,[79]
  When Fortune list to turn her happy wheel.

  That beauty's babes must bide the hard prepare,   *hardship, prepared*
  That oft is sent to bate their jolly cheer,   *diminish*
  Among the rest doth Absalom[80] declare,
  When, notwithstanding all his beauty clear,
  And eke his fair and yellow golden hair,
450 Between the boughs did hang, till that his foes,
  With death's despatch, did rid him of his woes.

  The sorrows great of Menelaus' wife,[81]
  Whose beauty fair so far to see was sought,
  The wretched end of Cleopatra's life,
  Whose rich array was all too dearly bought,
  Doth plainly show that all was vain and nought;
  Thus riches, strength and power, confess we must,
  With beauty eke, too slipper be to trust.

  Again we see each mortal thing decay,
460 A damage by displeasure hath the rich,[82]
  And beauty's blooms full soon are blown away;
  The strong by sickness feels a feeble stitch,   *pain*
  From weal to woe, thus by promise pitch,[83]
  Our time is tossed, with such unsureties' change,   *uncertainties*
  As to behold, advice may think full strange.[84]   *seem*

  Yet some there be, so puffèd up with pride,
  And, as Narcissus, drownèd in disdain,
  That light regard they have what will abide,   *happen*
  So far unaware of their ensuing pain;

---

[77] Ferres] Perhaps the printer's misreading of 'Bessus', a Satrap who killed Darius III.
[78] Tereus] This does not seem to be a reference to the most famous Tereus, who was metamorphosed into a bird after raping his sister-in-law (*Met.*, VI. 424–674). It might be a reference to a companion of Aeneas who was killed by Camilla. Camilla was a Volscian, rather than a Scythian, but perhaps the poet is confusing her with another celebrated female warrior, Penthesilea.
[79] feel] Presumably 'fail' is the intended meaning here.
[80] Absalom] The third son of David, Absalom was killed when his hair was caught in the branches of a tree (2 Samuel).
[81] Menelaus' wife] Helen of Troy
[82] 460] Although the general meaning of the line is clear enough, it is rather oddly expressed and there may be printer's errors here. Perhaps the first four words represent a misunderstanding of some phrase ending in the word 'treasure'.
[83] 463] He appears to be saying that the fortunate are hurled (pitched) low. The precise force of 'promise' seems uncertain.
[84] advice may think full strange] It may seem odd to offer advice (given the unpredictability of events and the impossibility of guarding against reversals).

470	Of other folk unrecking they remain,	*careless*
	As though they thought, 'who worthy were to be	
	A mate full meet and fellow fit for me?'	

    To whom it haps as to Cephisus' son
It chancèd here, which Echo did despise;
The calling nymph, which earnest love begun
In hasty sort, did end in woeful wise,
Not much unlike the vain desires that rise
By fruitless thoughts to get some foolish thing,
Which harm or else repentance far will bring.   *extreme*

480   But by this fable some there be suppose
That Ovid meant to show the fawning sort
Of flattering folk,[85] whose usage is to glose,   *flatter*
With prayers sweet, the men of greatest port,   *social standing*
And most of wealth, to whom they still resort
In hope to get, refusing nought to lie,   *acquire wealth*
The end of speech as Echo they apply.[86]

    For if the men by whom they ween to gain
Shall say, 'Me thinketh that this is very well',
Even 'Very well' they answer straight again,
490 As though advice had bid them so to tell,
When 'Very naught' they same might reason spell;[87]
The end of every fortune's darling's voice,
Thus they repeat without a further choice.

    Now if a tyrant say 'It shall be so',
None other thing but 'so' they have to speak,
Although it turn a thousand unto woe;
The strong may sup, to wrack may go the weak;
So they the rich may please, they nothing reck;   *care*
The same they say they answer afterward,
500 As though it twice were worthy to be heard.

    And, lest I seem to overskip the sense
Of any writer worthy to be known,
Whereby the poet's wise and hid pretence   *Ovid's*
Which other wits, by travail great, great hath sown,[88]
To show what good of Ovid's seed is grown,
Through my default may scannèd be amiss,[89]
Upon this fable Bocace writeth this.[90]   *Boccaccio*

---

[85] flattering folk] Bersuire offers flattery as one possible interpretation of Echo's role.
[86] 482–86] Such people echo the ideas of others in order to curry favour.
[87] 491] 'When they might, with good reason, say "very bad"'
[88] sown] Perhaps an error for shown, possibly prompted by the reference to 'seeds' in the line which follows.
[89] 506] 'Through my failure (to include accounts of other commentators) Ovid may be misinterpreted'
[90] 507] Giovanni Boccaccio, *Genealogia Deorum Gentilium*, VII. 59

    By Echo, which doth spoken words repeat,
And else is dumb, I fame do understand
510 That mortal folk doth love with fervent heat,
And followeth fast in every place and land,
As things whereon her being all doth stand,
And yet the same a number will forsake,
And light esteem for foolish pleasure's sake.

    Within whose well of shining, gay delights,
That we may like unto a water cold,
That sliding is some time, as Bocace writes,   *flowing*
Themselves, that is, their glory, they behold,
And are so sure in lust and pleasure cold,
520 That rapt therewith, not able to astart   *start up*
From thence they be, or from their madness part.

    And there at last they die which fame forsook,
That them so much desired to embrace,
Whose life so lost for little praise did look
Of virtue's voice, that bides in every place,
And biddeth fame to every coast to chase
Their praises great, that cause well deserve,
Not with their corpse to let their name to starve.[91]

    But such as will make light the love of fame
530 For lickerous lust that liketh them so well,   *wanton*
By good deserts[92] and recks for no good name,
How much in wit or beauty they excel,
How strong or rich soever they shall dwell,
Their dainty joys, their body, name and all,
They lose at once, which death their life doth call.

    And if perhaps that nature did bestow
More good of them in life than of the rest,
And that thereby some remembrance grow
Of nature's bounty, given them for the best,
540 Even like a fading flower, this fleeting guest
It may resemble, which is fresh today,
And yet ere[93] night is weathered clean away.   *before*

    What Bocace meant, thus somewhat have I told,
The scanning too of others' guess herein   *conjecture*
I have, and will at last at large unfold,
But where I left, now first I will begin,

---

[91] 522–28] Those whose names are not allowed to die are contrasted with those, described at the beginning of the stanza, who reject fame.

[92] by good deserts] This seems to mean 'according to his just deserts', although this phrase would make more sense a little later in the stanza.

[93] ere] *1560* 'or'. This archaic spelling of 'ere' as 'or' is one indication that the poem may have been composed some time before the publication date.

To show how much the hasty sort shall win
By their disdain, the which Narcissus here
Doth represent to me as doth appear.

550   For first who was[94] his beauty and his shape
Therewith, and notes of others his disdain,
And then shall mark of his end and his mishap,
Who blinded was with his too good a gain,
As in a glass shall see the picture plain
Of a full proud and overweening wight   *person*
That Nature's gifts disdain to use aright.

And sith I have declarèd here before   *since*
What little trust of right we ought to have
To that which we receive, for to restore
560   To him that first our pleasing treasures gave,
To sure to joy, but when he list to crave
The good he sent, the same he taketh away,
Ere we be ware our hap so soon decay.[95]   *aware, good fortune*

Now will I show that erst I said I would,
Of this same talk in some comparing sort,
What I conceive, the which not as I should
If I declare, and that my wits resort
Without the reck of wisdom's sober port;[96]   *bearing*
Now of the learnèd I do crave,[97]
570   And of my judgement here the sense you have.

I feign a man, to have a goodly wit,
The self same years that this Narcissus had,
With like disdain of others far unfit,[98]
And then imagine one that would be glad
With council good to cause him for to know,
To make his wit both sober wise and sad,
That pride's reward is to be made full low.

And this same one I Echo presuppose,   *postulate*
By whom I guess that good advice is meant,
580   Which is full loth a goodly wit to lose,
And sorry much to see the same ill-spent;
She followeth him therefore for this intent:
To make him mark and well regard the end
Of everything that he doth once intend.

---

[94] was] As a witness of the story of Narcissus is being invoked, 'was' is perhaps an error for another verb such as 'saw'.
[95] 557–63] There is some lack of clarity here, but the essential point is that God lends us our gifts and they may be taken from us at any time.
[96] 566–68] Again, there is some local unclarity, but the poet seems to be assuring the reader that he isn't being too assertive, and that he is not relying on his own wits, careless of what other wise people have said.
[97] crave] It is probable that the word 'pardon' has been omitted from this line, as it is two syllables short.
[98] unfit] The disdain is 'unfit', unsuitable, rather than the friends.

Her nature is not to be full of talk,
Not to devise, but to advise full well; *invent*
Words that spring from youthful thoughts at walk,
Not greeing still to reason's sober spell, *agreeing, speech*
The ending sense whereof she aye doth yell,
590 As who should say, 'we ought to regard the cause
And end of speech oft spoke with little pause'.[99]

For sith each words and doing ought of right
To be referred unto some reason's end,
Without respect whereof, little might
Our doings rest[100] which to no purpose bend,
To sharpest wits advice her love doth send,
As fittest folks to gain her great good will,
If they receive the good she proffers still.

Now how she woos this man that hath this wit
600 I need not tell, sith Ovid doth declare,
But him she followeth as she thinks it fit,
Till that she see him void of wanton care;
To shape an answer then she doth prepare,
To every sense that he shall speak or sound,
To cause him mark thereof the certain ground. *basis*

The end of every sentence[101] she repeats,
Whereby for what he spake he may discern;[102]
But he that on the vanes of pleasure beats,[103] *sails*
His wanton ship without a steady stern,
610 Of good advice shall nothing reck to learn,
But her refuse when she would him embrace,
Affection so away doth reason chase.

So this same man whom Nature wit hath lent,
A virtue great to them that use it well,
Advice, perhaps, can be content
To hear, and listen what her words can spell,
But when he once espies she thinketh to dwell
Continually with him to be his make,
Her offered friendship straight he doth forsake.

---

[99] 585–91] Rather than make her a flatterer who literally repeats what she hears, the poet suggests that she represents a counsellor who expounds what the 'end' (conclusion or result) will be of careless words. Compare the poet's earlier discussion of Ovid's clever transitions between tales (ll. 221–27).
[100] little might | Our doing rest] 'Our actions have little chance of having any lasting result'
[101] sentence] *1560* 'sense'
[102] 607] 'In order that he can clearly understand (the full implications of) his words'
[103] 608–09] It is difficult to be certain how these lines should be read. A 'vane' might be a weather vane. However as the plural form is used perhaps 'vane' signifies the web of a feather. ('Van' can also mean wing, although the first usage listed in *OED* is 1667.) 'Beat' is also ambiguous. It might invoke flying, which would be consistent with the possible reference to feathers. But it is often used in a nautical context so might possibly take 'ship' as its object. But as 'beat' doesn't seem to have been used in this transitive sense until the nineteenth century, it seems more likely that the second line stands in apposition to the first.

620	To live by loss his good he doth refuse,	
	Unbridled will, oh whither wilt thou train	*lead*
	This wandering wit that hath no power to choose	
	The ready way to such a perfect gain;	
	But as the blind to passage right doth pain	
	Himself no more than when he goeth amiss,	
	To win thy voice as much thy travail is.[104]	

    But why accuse I will, that may be charmed
By good advice, if thou had'st not disdain;
Thy pride, thy pride, hath worst of all thee harmed,
630   That puffs thee up upon presumptions vain,
Which maketh those continue that would be fain
Of thy good will to make thy wits full wise,
Whose love thou hast the profit, to despise.[105]

	This wit refusing good advice, love,[106]	
	And wandering fast to will's uncertain reach,	
	Doth let her starve that sought a way to move;	
	Then happy end, that proof doth plainly teach,	*fitting*
	Is full prepared, disdainful folk to appeach,	*charge with a crime*
	Whose pride is such as puts away the sight	
640	Of council good and every judgement right.	

	And so advice I leave forsaken quite,	
	As Echo was, for all her great good will,	
	And will declare wit's rash and mad despite,	
	Of such a friend neglect for lack of skill,	
	Whereby he fast procures himself to spill,	*destroy*
	As one unware of all his woes to come,	
	Whose reckless life receiveth a wretched doom.	

    A careless life thus led in youthful years
A wilful way beseemeth well to take;
650   So this same wit, as wild desire him stirs
Unconstantly, for lust and pleasure's sake,
From this to that his vain inventions wake,
A restless time in needless work doth spend,
Till that hereof he finds the foolish end.

	Then weary quite of all this wanton sport,	
	And trusting much to taste a more stable drink,	
	To praise well because he doth resort,	*on that account*

---

[104] 624–26] The poet states that a blind man takes no more trouble if he follows, by chance, the right path than if he takes the wrong turning. But the force of the final line is not clear. Perhaps 'thy voice' should be glossed 'will's voice', which is no more nor less trouble to secure than the voice of good advice.

[105] 631–33] The syntax seems confusing here, but should perhaps be glossed: 'Pride, which makes you despise all those people who desire your good opinion in order to sharpen your wits and whose love is an advantage (profit) to you'.

[106] good advice love] 'good advice's love' or 'good advice to love' is perhaps intended.

  (Whereby mishap he rather comes I think)
  Whose pleasant fare and sweet delighting drink
660 Who shall approach will think a thousand year
  Till they have seen there in the water clear.[107]

  Which hath in it no foul nor ugly sight,
  Nor loathsome looking thereabout to stand,
  The silver streams so shining be, and bright,
  As can delight the greatest lord in land;
  The ladies eke, full fair, with hand in hand,
  Will fast repair unto this pleasant well,
  Where, with advice, I wish them all to dwell.

  Which for because that[108] wit did quite despise,
670 Now mark his harm and hard predestined woe;
  This well he fast beholds in musing wise,
  And lies to drink where more his thirst doth grow;
  Alas for that himself he doth not know,
  For there he seeth the image of his grace,
  His shape and eke proportion of his face.

  His wits, his strength and every other gift
  That may be thought a virtue any way,
  Appeareth there with every sundry shift *device*
  That Nature sendeth to make the carcase gay,
680 And eke that Fortune lends for each assay; *attempt*
  There nought is hid that is worthy praise to pike, *obtain*
  Nor aught is seen that men might well mislike.

  Whereon the faster that his eyes be cast, *more firmly fixed*
  Thereat the more his marvel doth increase,
  And eke the more his marvel thus doth last,
  The less he seeks his blind desire to cease,
  Which forceth love to put himself in press *trouble*
  To like the thing that better were to lack,
  Than by such love to bring himself to wrack.

690 For who so covets that he cannot catch,
  And most alloweth that needeth most amends, *approves*
  With so good will, and still desires to watch,
  Such wretched joys, a cursèd life that spends,
  As proof doth teach, unto destruction bends,
  Delighted so with that he should refuse,
  And quite forsaking that he ought to choose.

  But of his love, such is the blind respect,
  And such the sweet, delighting, wretched plight,

---

[107] 655–61] The poet suggests that the proud man wearies of frivolity and seeks praise, but praise only brings him bad luck. He goes on to explain that praise can be beneficial when accompanied by advice.
[108] that] 'that' (advice) is the object, 'wit' the subject, of despise.

	That his avail he blindly doth neglect,	
700	To help himself, as one that hath no might,	
	So ravished is he with the pleasing sight	
	Of that to him which little pleasure gains,	
	Unless we count the winning good of pains.	

    For in this well too well he views the form
Of every gift and grace, that nature gave
To him for that he chiefly should perform
With good, much good, his good thereby to save;
Yet by his good, as sure is evil to have,
He gains the loss that other never feel,
710 Which have not won such wealth by Fortune's wheel.

    And why because he deems not as he ought, *judges*
Each virtue liketh value of the same,
His face, the best that ever was wrought,
And shape he thinks deserveth no manner blame;
By wit he weens full wondrous things to frame, *conceives*
And what he hath he thinks all the best,
Besides himself despising all the rest.

    Although indeed, he neither be so fair,
So well proportioned, nor so surely wise,
720 Nor yet in strength be able to compare
With half the number that he did despise,
Above them all he thinks himself to prize,
Which overweening wins him all his woe, *arrogance*
A simple gain I count, that hurts me so. *poor*

    For rapt so fast, through his abusèd eyes,
Even on himself, whereof he doth delight,
Within this well no faults he ever spies,
Whereby himself he any way might spite,
But as each face appeareth fair and white
730 (Though it be foul) within the flattering glass,
This lying lake shows every gift to pass. *excel*

    Whereto he straight consents by judgement blind,
And grants to have as much as seemeth, and more,
So easy, lo, self love is now to kind
So some is had;[109] so sweet a grievous sore,
So glad he is to keep his harms in store,
And much desirous for to abide[110] his woe,
And eke so loth his mischief to forgo.

---

[109] 734–35] 'So mild and forgiving (easy) is self-love to our natural inclinations, provided that you have just a little of it.'
[110] abide] used here to mean 'retain' or 'stand by'

	Which causeth this, because of nature all	
740	Be pleasèd well, well of themselves to hear,	
	And yet the wise, with good advice, will call	*appeal*
	Unto themselves if they deserve to bear	
	The praises great, which seem so true and clear	
	By others' mouths, which ever talk the best,	
	Of them they see in good estate to rest.[111]	

    Now wit, that wants all that wisdom wills
The wise to have, is void of this respect,[112]   *consideration*
For what he hath he thinks it greatly skills,   *avails*
But what he is the whilst he doth neglect;
750 Thus joy to have so much doth him infect,
That care to be so good as he appears
He quite forsaketh, so blindly love him blears.   *blurs his sight*

    Through which he loseth every virtuous strength,
And lacks the skill so godly gifts to use,
So every good doth turn to bad at length,
And he consumeth himself that doth abuse,
This lot is sent to him that will refuse
Advice's love, to light on praise's[113] well,
Where till he starve he still delights to dwell.

760   To starve,[114] I mean, the good he hath to lose,
To which I think himself he sure doth bind,
That of himself more good doth presuppose,
(By looking in this present well so blind)   *misleading*
Than in himself a wiser man can find;
For who doth covet himself of wiser school   *learning*
Than deeds him show, doth prove himself a fool.

    Who thinks he hath more than he doth possess,
In this not only is deceivèd quite,
But hath so much of that he hath the less,
770 Of wit I mean, wherein who shall delight
More than he ought, himself doth this despite,
Unwitting clean; the more he thinks he hath,   *completely*
Even by so much hath less, as Plato[115] sayth.

    So he that deems his wit above the rest,
So much the less than others hath hereby,
And he that thinks his one of all the best,
'The worst of all', it reason will reply,[116]

---

[111] 744–45] People tend to praise those who enjoy wealth and social standing.
[112] 746–47] Such foolish people don't stop to think whether they deserve the praise they receive.
[113] praise's] *1560* 'prayseth'. It seems likely that the printer read 'praise's' as a verb and changed it to an alternative form of the third person singular.
[114] starve] In the last line of the previous stanza 'starve' is used to mean 'die' but is now being used in its transitive sense of 'kill' or 'destroy'.
[115] Plato] Perhaps a reference to *Philebus*, 48a–50a.
[116] 776–77] The poet seems to be saying that reason, semi-personified, will assert that the man who thinks his wit the best in fact has the worst wit.

Although the same he never can espy,
Because he trusteth the lying well of praise,
780 Whereby his wit and all he hath decays.

For sith the well of praise as well consists — *depends*
Upon the springs of unadvisèd talk,
As of the voice of wisdom, that resists
The speeches of fools, whose tongues awry will walk
Besides the path, of reason's guiding balk, — *away from, refuse*
It may well be that such themselves deceive,
As of untruth a certain truths conceive.

Thus what hath made this wit to starve we see,
Self love, the very hid consuming sore
790 Of goodly wits, that else could well agree
To every sense of wisdom's present lore;
And now — to show the very cause wherefore
They lose the strength of this so good a gain,
And leave advice — forsooth, it is disdain.

This envious heir, disdain, this dainty thing, — *offspring*
When it begins to harbour in the breast
Of any man, this harm it first doth bring:
Contempt of those in better state that rest
Than he is in, that counteth to be best,
800 So that his faults, who fain would have him know, — *gladly*
And be his friend, he counts him as his foe.

Then of contempts proceedeth haughty pride,
The which who gets shall never lightly leave,
So great an evil so fast as seen to bide, — *firmly, continue*
Even to the best when it beginneth to cleave,
That honour, wit, or any gift receive,
This of disdain, contempt, whereof proceeds
The poison pride, this same self-love that breeds.[117]

Whereto hereby I may conclude aright,
810 That as contempt did cause Narcissus quail, — *waste away*
So, by disdain, each wight doth lose his might,
And every virtue through this same doth fail,
As well Narcissus proveth in this same tale,
Who lost through love each thing he most did like,
For his disdain who worse revenge could pike?[118]

Can greater woe to any man betide
Than that to lose wherein he most delights?
No sure, and yet to surquedry and pride — *arrogance*
This is the just revenge that still requites

---

[117] 802–08] The syntax here is characteristically obscure although the main thrust of the stanza, that contempt breeds pride which infects even the gifted with self-love, is clear enough.
[118] pike] a variant spelling of 'pick', select

820　　Their great disdain and all their old despites:
　　　To lack of that, at last, they like so well,
　　　Which want, abundance makes with them to dwell.[119]

　　　　This sense is strange, and yet as true as quaint, *judgement, curious*
　　　That plenty should be cause of greater lack;[120]
　　　A man in health can never lightly faint, *easily*
　　　The happy man no misery doth smack,
　　　The rich, by riches, feels no needy wrack,
　　　Again, who sits in honour's shining chair,
　　　Is far enough from wretched people's share.

830　　　And what can hap thus harm the happy man, *success, fortunate*
　　　Or can such wealth their master bring to woe?
　　　Can honours force their honours them to ban?[121]
　　　Can all this good so grieve us thus, what no?
　　　Yes, yes, alas, it proveth often so,
　　　Of ages past examples never ground,[122] *establish*
　　　Of these our days too many may be found.

　　　　Be therefore all these goodly gifts to blame,
　　　Because they come to wrack that them possess?
　　　No, to be rich it is no manner shame,
840　　Nor honour hurts that[123] helps to redress
　　　The wrongèd folk whom rigour doth oppress, *severity*
　　　Nor aught is evil, whereof the rightful use
　　　Who shall observe may have a just excuse.

　　　　But this abundance, who shall evil abuse, *wickedly*
　　　And quite forget from whence these virtues flow,
　　　The good they have thereby they quite refuse,
　　　And every gift unto a grief shall grow;
　　　Misuse of good thus them shall overthrow,
　　　Even as Midas' pipes, that Marsyas[124] found,
850　　Misused, him harmed with sweetness of the sound.

　　　　This Marsyas was a boisterous country man,
　　　The pleasant pipes of Pallas once he found,
　　　The which to blow as soon as he began,
　　　Even of themselves did give so sweet a sound,
　　　That better thought he not above the ground,
　　　Wherein he straight did take so great a pride,
　　　As though his mouth did all this music guide.

---

[119] 822] An echo of Narcissus's words 'inopem me copia fecit', 'abundance makes me poor' (*Met.*, III. 466).

[120] 825–29] A little confusingly, the poet goes on to put forward a series of 'straw man' assertions which he will refute in the next stanza.

[121] 832] 'Can honours force those who possess them to curse ("ban") honours?'

[122] 835–36] 'The examples of the past never in fact provide the foundations of actions, of which we have too many instances in the present.'

[123] Nor honour hurts that] 'Nor is honour harmful as long as it . . .'

[124] Marsyas] Marsyas is said to have picked up the flute or *aulos* which Pallas Athena had discarded. Apollo flayed him after Marsyas challenged him to a music contest (*Met.*, VI. 382–400).

    Through which, the muses with their harmony
    He thought could not so sweet a sound prepare,
860 And eke Apollo, god of melody,
    He made descend down from his shining chair,
    Also with him presuming to compare,
    Full well content to lose his life if he
    Made not his pipes more sweetly to agree.

    Then music's god who, seeing all his pride,
    Him first did far excel in cunning play,
    And then to make him by his covenant bide,
    He made the skin of all his body flay,
    An evil reward for this, his vain assay,
870 Unhappy gift that gives no better gain,
    Nay, foolish man, that guides it to thy pain.

    So that hereby I gather every gift,
    Misused, may harm the honours of the same,
    And though to some, that nature's bounty left
    A grace whereof another shall be lame,
    This goodly gift is not a whit to blame,
    Although their honours through the same shall quail,
    The rightful use that lack of such a vail.   *gift*

    For if so be that Marsyas had known
880 That of himself not all his cunning came,   *skill*
    He neither would have striven to have blown,
    Nor yet presumed to venture for the game,
    With him that was the author[125] of the same;
    If he had known how well to use this gain,
    He it might well have kept, and not been flayn.

    But who can know, that will disdain to learn,
    And who can learn, that recks not to be taught?
    So well to use his wealth, who can discern,
    That this disdain, this venom great, hath caught?
890 This same made Marsyas, that he never raught[126]
    To know of whom his melody did rise —
    This made Narcissus Echo eke despise.

    And, to conclude, this causèd wit forsake
    Advice, whose lack did lose him all his gain,
    For look, even as Narcissus by the lake
    His beauty lost by beauty's sore disdain,
    And that his profit purchased all his pain,
    So wit, that hath disdain, shall so presume,
    That through his wit, his wit shall clean consume.   *decay*

---

[125] author] Apollo was the god of music.
[126] 'raught'] This means 'reached after' but is usually followed by an object rather than an infinitive, and it is possible that 'sought' was intended.

900	Wherefore this vice, that every virtue mars,
That private weal converts to private[127] woe,
That each degree their rightful duty bars,[128]
Who readeth this tale, I wish, so well might know,
That in their hearts no seed thereof might grow
Whereof each wight devoid,[129] by good advice,
May rightly use their gifts of greatest price.

Thus have you heard the simple sense
That I have gathered by my simple wit,
Of Ovid's tale, whose wise and hid pretence,
910	Though as I should perhaps I have not hit, *represented exactly*
Yet as I could, and as I thought it fit,
I have declarèd what I can conceive,
Full glad to learn what wiser folk perceive.

And now, to keep my covenant, and proceed
Of others' judgements to declare the fecte,[130]
Of this same tale Ficinus[131] writes indeed
A wise opinion, not to be neglect
Of such as seem to be of reason's sect,
The which I would not skip among the rest,
920	Lest his invention some may think the best.

A rash man's mind, that hath no skill, sayth he,
By this Narcissus very well is meant,
His proper shape, that hath no power to see,
That is the proper office which is sent[132]
Unto the mind, by no mean can convent[133]
To see and mark, as each man ought of right,
And to perform according to their might.

But as Narcissus only did desire
His shadow in the water to embrace,
930	So this same mind doth nothing else require
Of brittle beauty but to mark the case
That in the body hath the biding place,

---

[127] private] Here, though not at the beginning of the line, the spelling is 'prevate'. There is perhaps an intended shift in meaning from 'private', in the sense of exclusive, to 'private' in the now obsolete sense, 'deprived'.

[128] 902] That hinders people from all stations of life from doing their duty.

[129] devoid] free of disdain

[130] fecte] apparently a variant of 'feck', value

[131] Ficinus] Marsilio Ficino (1433–99), the humanist philosopher and Neoplatonist. The relevant account of Narcissus can be found in the seventeenth chapter of the sixth book of Ficino's commentary on Plato's *Symposium*. See *Marsilio Ficino's Commentary on Plato's 'Symposium': The Text and a Translation, with an Introduction*, ed. and trans. by Sears Reynolds Jayne, University of Missouri Studies 19.1 (Columbia: University of Missouri Press, 1944).

[132] 921–24] Ficino thought that Narcissus represented a mind which was attracted to the superficial, physical beauty of the body rather than to its own beauty.

[133] convent] The verb 'convent' ('assemble', 'summon') doesn't seem to fit the context. Perhaps 'consent' or 'convert' (meaning 'turn' or 'direct') is intended. However here, as elsewhere, a more pervasive lack of clarity in the stanza makes it difficult to make a firm emendation.

Which only is the shadow of the mind,
As it might know in case it were not blind.

    Thus mind, thus nought desiring but his shade,
That is the beauty in the carcase frail,
Not being able to discern the trade   *path*
The which it ought of right for to assail,   *venture on*
Hereby forsaketh quite the one avail,   *completely, aid*
940   And loseth both his proper shape herein,
And eke his shadow hath no power to win.

    For every mind becomes the body's man,   *servant*
In so loving it, itself doth quite despise;[134]
The body's use, and yet it no way can
Enjoy and have, according to the guise   *practice*
And order due that nature doth devise,
But thus doth both the body's use mistake,
And of itself the office true forsake.

    The office of the mind is to have power
950   Upon the body, and to order well
The body's office eke in every hour;
It is of the mind to learn the perfect skill,
The vain desires that rise, him[135] by to kill,
Whereby the mind doth keep his perfect strength,
And eke the body vanquish low at length.

    Now where the mind is drownèd with desire
Of such delights as to the body long,   *pertain*
The body then must needs consume with fire,
Of raging lusts about the same that throng,
960   So that the mind is cause of both their wrong,
To put itself out of the proper place,
And bring the body to so evil a case.

    For thus the mind, that ought of right to be
The teacher of the body to do well,
Doth make the same to every evil agree,
Procuring that it should of right expel,   *endeavouring to obtain*
Whereby in both a moving blind doth dwell,   *desire*
Even as within Narcissus did remain,
That thought his shadow to be such a gain.

970   And as Narcissus never could attain
His shadow, which he wishèd for so fast,
And that his love did lead him to his pain,
Even so this mind, that reason's bounds hath passed,

---

[134] 943] Ficino makes the paradoxical point that Narcissus in a sense does not love himself enough, in that he represents the mind which neglects itself to worship its body.

[135] him] 'hem' (them) is perhaps intended. Thus the mind should learn the skill with (by) which he can kill the desires.

Itself and from the proper place hath cast,[136]
Shall never gain that it doth most desire,
Such is to folly still the following hire. *resulting payment*

    For though it covet much a safe estate
And seek itself to plant in perfect plight,[137]
Yet this desire proceedeth all too late,
980 When will is bent to love vain delight,
Whose rash regard discerns not black from white;
Who would be well, worketh otherwise
Of being well, the surety doth despise.[138]

    And when this mind hath wrought so much amiss,
Thus blindly from his perfect place to fall,
We must needs grant a kind of death it is,
A thing divine and perfect to be thrall
Unto the carcase most corrupt of all,
When this immortal mind shall seek to serve
990 Each mortal thing, his virtue needs must sterve. *starve*

    This is the meaning of Ficinus' sense,
That in this wise, one Plato[139] doth write,
And now, to show the learned men's pretence *purpose*
With Ovid's tale, the readers to delight,
Two there were that somewhat did endite
Of this same fable, which I will declare,
Lest any writer I may seem to spare. *omit*

    The one hereof a sense divine doth make;
No fool he seemeth that Waleys[140] hath to name,
1000 An Englishman, which thus doth undertake,
For soul's behoof, to descant on this same; *advantage*
There be, sayth he, a number much to blame,
That, as Narcissus, lets their beauty quail,
Because they quite misuse their good avail.

    For divers which in beauty much excel,
Either in shape, that is the body's gift,
In knowledge else, which in the mind doth dwell,
Or, to conclude, in riches, which is left
To sundry men by fortune's hiding shift; *mysterious moves*
1010 Before the same,[141] so puffèd up with pride,
That all too base they think with them to bide.

---

[136] 974] The meaning can be clarified by changing the word order here: 'and hath cast itself from the proper place'.
[137] plight] Although plight is now only used negatively, here it means simply 'condition'.
[138] 982–83] These lines might be glossed: 'Those people who wish to be happy, but try to follow a different (and unwise) path to happiness, despise the secure path'. But, as so often, although the gist is clear enough, the finer workings of the syntax are uncertain.
[139] Plato] The relationship between soul and body is discussed in Plato's *Phaedo*.
[140] Waleys] The poet refers to the *Ovidius Moralizatus* (1340) of Thomas Bersuire (Bercorius) which was sometimes wrongly attributed to Thomas Waleys (Wallensis) (fl.1318–49). T. H. follows the Latin text reasonably closely.
[141] before the same] 'when faced with their equals'

What then, to this, what is the due reward?
Forsooth, these darlings, with their great disdain,
Within the well of worldly wealth, regard
This same appearance of their blissful gain,
Which lasteth not but, as the shadow vain,
Doth pass away, even so doth come to go
Each thing we have — the use affirmeth so. *experience*

Now in this well, the appearance of their state
1020 Doth them so please and eke so well content,
That, seeing it, they nothing else await, *give heed to*
They nought can low, they nothing can consent *praise*
To praise or like, but all to this intent,
Themselves full far above the rest advance,
And still to glory of their happy chance.

Thus through this glory of their life too much,[142]
The chiefest life, the life of souls, they lose;[143]
Their blind desire and fond regard is such
Themselves in all this danger for to close, *enclose*
1030 This English writer hereof doth thus suppose;
The other now whom Italy did breed,[144]
As followeth writes, to them that shall yet read.

In Greece there was a passing fair young man,
Whose beauty brought him unto such a pride,
That, through the same, unto such disdain he ran,
As but himself he none could well abide,
But counted other all as vile beside,
Through which his end was wretchedly to die,
Within the woods to starve, and there to lie.

1040 And whereas Ovid doth hereof affirm
That this Narcissus was transformed at last
Into a flower, he only doth confirm
That youth and beauty come and soon be past,
Even as the flower that withereth full fast,
And for because in woods the nymphs do dwell,
His death bewailed of them doth Ovid tell.

Again, where the poet doth avow
That this Narcissus dièd by a lake,
It may well be because he did allow
1050 None fit or worthy to become his make,
But every man despising did forsake,
That[145] some of hatred and of malice fell, *cruel*
For his disdain did drown him in a well.

---

[142] 1026] 'Thus through this excessive worship of their (mortal, bodily) life'
[143] the life of souls, they lose] This translates the Latin 'animae vita perdunt', demonstrating that T. H. is following Bersuire's text with care.
[144] 1031] This may be a reference to the works of either Niccolò degli Agostini, or his source, Giovanni dei Buonsignori.
[145] That] with the result that

  Thus much this same Italian writer here
Doth find as true, his writings do profess,
So it may well be all that wrote appear[146]   *either*
Of this same fable, other more or less,
That still disdain doth cause the greater distress
Of every good that nature's bounty gives,
1060 To each estate upon the earth that lives.

  Wherefore who hath no sparkle of this vice
Are like to kindle in themselves no flame
Of any evil, but still by good advice
Shall so themselves, and all their doings, frame
As shall at all deserve no manner blame;
Who wants this vice thereby shall chiefly stay   *prevent*
To every evil the very ready way.

  Thus have you heard what hath been thought
By sundry folk of this same Ovid's tale,
1070 Whereby I prove that all herein have sought
To show that Ovid wrote for good avail,
Declaring how they likest are to quail,
That greatest store of any good receive,
The rightful use hereof and least perceive.

  To much possess, so that it is no praise,
But things possessèd rightfully to use,
For each possession by and by decays,
And such as by possessing shall abuse
All they possess, with shame, shall soon refuse,
1080 Wherefore the most are worthy to possess
Whose spotless deeds the richest use express.

  And thus my simple travail I commend
Unto everyone, praying you to take
The same in worth, and when more years shall send
More wit, and eke more knowledge shall awake,
Such labours like I mean not to forsake,
As knoweth God who keep us alway,
Save and defend us from all decay.

Quod. TH.

FINIS.

Imprinted at London by Thomas Hackett, and are to be sold at his shop in Canon Street over against the three cranes.

---

[146] appear] This word is perhaps derived from the French *apparier*, to agree.

THOMAS HEDLEY

THE JUDGEMENT OF MIDAS

being

OF SUCH AS ON FANTESYE DECREE & DISCUSS (*c.* 1552)

THOMAS HEDLEY
THE JUDGEMENT OF MIDAS (*c.* 1552)

[*Metamorphoses*, XI. 157–78]

Sprengius, *Metamorphoses Ovidii* (1563), p. 135ʳ

Little is known of Thomas Hedley. A work called *The Banishment of Cupid*, translated from the Italian by Hedley, was printed by Thomas Marsh in 1567.[1] However, no copies seem to have survived of this text. The Midas broadside, untitled in both early editions, was published towards the end of Edward VI's reign, in 1552. It is an intervention in a 'flyting', or exchange of invective, which took place between Thomas Churchyard and Thomas Camel in 1551 to 1552.[2]

'The Judgement of Midas' is loosely based on Book XI of the *Metamorphoses*. Midas, a Phrygian king, is best known for his ability to turn everything he touched to gold. According to Ovid, this cursed gift filled him with disgust at the idea of wealth and made him turn to the woods and fields, and to the worship of Pan. This is the prelude to the tale adapted here by Thomas Hedley. Although Hedley cuts the role of Tmolus from his translation,[3] other aspects of the story, namely Apollo's anger and Midas's chagrin, are expanded. The tale's conclusion, in which Ovid explains how Midas's barber whispers the secret into a hole in the ground, and is betrayed by the whispering wheat which grows there, is omitted. However Hedley's concluding reference to Midas and his ears being buried underground perhaps recalls the tale's original ending.

Although there has been some critical discussion of Hedley's short poem in the context of Tudor political controversy, 'The Judgement of Midas' has received very little attention as an

---

[1] J. Payne Collier, *Extracts from the Registers of the Stationers' Catalogues from 1557 to 1587* (London: The Shakespeare Society, 1853), p. 155.
[2] For a fuller account of the flyting, see introduction, pp. 8–9.
[3] See introduction, p. 9.

example of Tudor Ovidianism. One of the few critics to have engaged with the poem within a mythical rather than a political context is James Orchard Halliwell-Phillipps, who reproduces the text of the poem and suggests that it might have influenced the representation of Bottom with his ass's head. He links Hedley's phrase 'fair long ears' with Titania's reference to Bottom's 'fair large ears', and also suggests that Bottom's rustic enthusiasm for music takes on an additional humorous significance if we associate him with Midas.[4]

The entire flyting, including 'The Judgement of Midas', was reprinted in 1560. The text printed here is based on the first edition, rather than this later edition, as errors crept into the reprinting and there is no evidence of any further input by the poet himself. The poem has not since been reprinted.

EDITIONS

Thomas Hedley, trans., *Of such as on fantesye decree & discuss: on other me[n]s works, lo Ouids tale thus* [Judgement of Midas] (London: Hary Sutton, [1552?]), STC 18969.5.

Thomas Churchyard (et al.), *The Contention bettwyxte Churchyeard and Camell, vpon Dauid Dycers Dreame sett out in suche order, that it is bothe wyttye and profytable for all degryes* (London: Owen Rogers for Mychell Loblee, 1560), STC 5225.

FURTHER READING

Chris Boswell, 'The Culture and Rhetoric of the Answer Poem: 1485–1626' (unpublished doctoral thesis, University of Exeter, 2004).

Carole Rose Livingston, *British Broadside Ballads of the Sixteenth Century* (New York: Garland, 1991).

Scott Lucas, 'Diggun Davie and Davy Dicar: Edmund Spenser, Thomas Churchyard and the Poetics of Public Protest', *Spenser Studies*, 16 (2002), 151–65.

Cathy Shrank, 'Trollers and Dreamers: Defining the Citizen-Subject in Sixteenth-Century Cheap Print', *Yearbook of English Studies*, 32 (2008), 102–18.

THE JUDGEMENT OF MIDAS

Of such as on fantasy decree and discuss
On other men's works, lo Ovid's tale thus.

Rude Pan would needs one day, in company,	*Rustic*
Compare to mend Apollo's melody,	*Allege, improve*
And took his homely pipe and 'gan to blow;	
The gentle god, that saw his rudeness[5] so,	
(Although himself knew how for to excel)	
Contented stood, to hear his cunning well.	*skill*
Pan played, and playèd boisterously,	*roughly*

---

[4] James Orchard Halliwell-Phillipps, *An Introduction to Shakespeare's 'Midsummer Night's Dream'* (London: William Pickering, 1841), p. 19.
[5] rudeness] either rusticity and ignorance or bad manners

      Apollo played, but much melodiously,
      And such a tune, with such music, gave,
10   As well became his knowledge for to have.
      Midas stood by to judge and to decree
      Which of them both should best in music be,
      And as he heard Pan play and use his song   *perform*
      He thought it such as he had likèd long,
      And wonted was to hear of others oft.
      Apollo's harp and song went very soft,
      And sweet and strange, as none might sweeter be,
      But yet, thought Midas, this music likes not me,
      And therefore, straight, full loud he cried, and said:
20   'Pan, to mine ears, of both hath better played.'
      Quoth then Apollo: 'Since thus thou deemest Pan
      Me to excel, that god of cunning am,
      And so dost judge of things thou can'st no skill,[6]
      Midas, henceforth lo thus to thee I will: *give order*
      Thou shalt have ears to show and tell, iwis,   *truly*
      Both what thy skill and what thy reason is,
      Which on thy head shall stand and witness be
      How thou hast judged this rural god and me;
      Nay, be content, for I have it said.'
30   A full sad man stood Midas then, dismayed,
      And as he felt to try if it so was,
      He found he had two ears, as hath an ass,
      Newly grown out where as his own ears stood.
      Sore changèd then his colour and his mood,
      But yet forthy, having no word to say,   *for this reason*
      He shook his ears, and sadly went his way.
      I know no more, but this I wot and know,
      That though the Phrygian king be buried low,
      And both his ears eke with him hidden be,
40   And so far worn[7] that no man shall them see,
      Since such there are that live at this day yet,
      Which have his skill, his judgement, and his wit,
      And take upon them both to judge and know,
      To them I wish even thus, and to no more,
      That as they have his judgement and his years,
      Even so I would they had his fair long ears.

T. Hedley

Domine salvum fac regem
Et da pacem in diebus nostris.[8]

Imprinted at London by Hary Sutton, dwelling in Paul's churchyard.

---

[6] can'st no skill] The phrase 'can skill' (have discrimination or knowledge) was a common construction in the period (*OED* n 5.a).

[7] worn] 'worne' may be a misprint for 'downe'

[8] *Domine salvum fac regem | Et da pacem in diebus nostris*] 'Lord, keep the king safe, and give peace in our days'. This prayer for the safety of the king reflects the political circumstances surrounding the publication of 'Midas'.

ARTHUR GOLDING

SALMACIS AND HERMAPHRODITUS

from

THE FIRST FOUR BOOKS OF P. OVIDIUS NASO'S WORK,

ENTITLED METAMORPHOSIS

(1565)

ARTHUR GOLDING

SALMACIS AND HERMAPHRODITUS

from

THE FIRST FOUR BOOKS OF P. OVIDIUS NASO'S WORK, ENTITLED METAMORPHOSIS (1565)

[*Metamorphoses*, IV. 285–388]

Lodovico Dolce, *Le trasformationi* (1553), p. 92

Arthur Golding's *Metamorphosis*, as well as being the first complete translation of Ovid's poem into English, is one of the most significant translations, of any text, in the Tudor period, and a key influence on Shakespeare's (and thus our) reception of Ovid. Golding (1535/6–1606) was born into a prosperous merchant family. He matriculated as a fellow commoner at Jesus College Cambridge in 1552. His early translations, all from Latin, included the first full English translation of Caesar's *De Bello Gallico*. In 1565 he published the first four books of Ovid's *Metamorphoses*; the full translation appeared in 1567. Many of his other translations were of religious works, including Calvin's *Commentaries on the Psalms* (1571) and Augustine Marlorat's *Catholic Exposition upon the Revelation of Saint John* (1574), an attack on the Papacy.

Golding's Ovid may speak with an English accent, but his *Metamorphosis* follows Ovid's text reasonably closely, and, although a moralizing commentary is included, it is confined to the comparatively brief preface and epistle. However, like T. H., he instructs his readers to search for deeper meanings in the poem, and includes on the title page an admonitory couplet:

With skill, heed and judgement, this work must be read,
For else to the reader it stands in small stead.

As Madeleine Forey notes, the vocabulary and atmosphere of the poem are subtly Christianized,[1] and Golding is drawn to the idea that Ovid may have had some access to the Bible:

---

[1] *Ovid's 'Metamorphoses'*, trans. by Arthur Golding, ed. by Madeleine Forey (London: Penguin, 2002), pp. xvi–xvii.

What man is he but would suppose the author of this book
The first foundation of his work from Moses' writings took?

It has been established that Golding was using an edition of the poem which included Regius's commentary, elements of which he sometimes incorporated into the body of his translation.[2]

The episode included here is narrated by Alcithoë, one of the Minyades, or daughters of Minyas, women who refuse to join in the worship of Bacchus, and instead stay at home spinning, weaving and telling tales of doomed love and metamorphosis. The tale, which derives from Book IV of the *Metamorphoses*, focuses on a beautiful young man, the son of Hermes and Aphrodite. Salmacis, an idle nymph, is smitten with love for Hermaphroditus and jumps into a pool after him, hoping to cement their union. He views her advances with horror and struggles to escape. She prays to the gods that they may never be parted and has her wish granted when they fuse together to form a single androgynous figure. Hermaphroditus then begs the gods to grant his own prayer that the pool may have the same emasculating effect on all who bathe in it. In his prefatory epistle to the Earl of Leicester Golding offers the following moralization of the tale:

> Hermaphrodite and Salmacis declare that idleness
> Is chiefest nurse and cherisher of all voluptuousness,
> And that voluptuous life breeds sin; which, linking all together,
> Make men to be effeminate, unwieldy, weak and lither.[3]

Immediately after Alcithoë has finished telling the tale of Salmacis and Hermaphroditus, the last of the series, she and her sisters are transformed into bats as a punishment for their neglect of Bacchus. The best known of the Minyades' stories is that of Pyramus and Thisbe, but Salmacis and Hermaphroditus was also a popular tale, the subject of separate treatments by Thomas Peend (1565) and Francis Beaumont (1602). This extract is based on the 1565 edition of the first four books of the *Metamorphoses*. There are few noteworthy differences between the two texts, and the 1565 version has been selected because this early edition exerted an influence on Thomas Peend's own treatment of the tale.

Golding's contemporaries recognized the significance of his achievement. Thomas Peend claimed to have given up his own attempt to translate the entire poem when faced with Golding's version, and many Elizabethan commentators praised the translation, including Francis Meres and George Puttenham.[4] Its influence can be traced in the works of many writers, including Spenser and Marlowe, as well as Shakespeare. Although it was later overshadowed by Sandys's translation (1626) and by the multi-authored translation edited by Samuel Garth (1717), Golding's Ovid has been studied with renewed interest in more recent years, partly for its own sake — Ezra Pound even called it 'the most beautiful book in the language'[5] — and partly on account of its importance for an understanding of Shakespeare's use of Ovid.

EDITIONS[6]

The fyrst fower bookes of P. Ovidius Nasos worke, intitled Metamorphosis, trans. by Arthur Golding (London: Willyam Seres, 1565), STC 18955.

---

[2] *Ibid.*, pp. xxii–xxiii.
[3] *Ibid.*, p. 8. 'Lither' means wicked.
[4] *Ibid.*, p. xviii.
[5] Ezra Pound, *An ABC of Reading* (New York: New Directions, 1960), p. 127.
[6] This is only a selective list. Further editions of Golding's *Metamorphosis* were published in 1575, 1584, 1587, 1593, 1603 and 1612.

The xv bookes of P. Ovidius Naso, entytuled Metamorphosis, trans. by Arthur Golding (London: Willyam Seres, 1567), STC 18956.

Shakespeare's Ovid: Being Arthur Golding's Translation of the 'Metamorphoses', ed. by W. H. D. Rouse (London: De La More Press, 1904).

Ovid's 'Metamorphoses': The Arthur Golding Translation, 1567, ed. by John Frederick Nims (New York: Macmillan, 1965).

The xv books entytuled Metamorphosis by P. Ovidius Naso (Amsterdam: Theatrum Orbis Terrarum; Norwood, NJ: W. J. Johnson, 1977).

Ovid's 'Metamorphoses', trans. by Arthur Golding, ed. by Madeleine Forey (London: Penguin, 2002).

FURTHER READING

Madeleine Forey, '"Bless thee, Bottom, bless thee! Thou art translated!": Ovid, Golding and *A Midsummer Night's Dream*', *Modern Language Review*, 93 (1998), 321–29.

Raphael Lyne, *Ovid's Changing Worlds: English Metamorphoses, 1567–1632* (Oxford: Oxford University Press, 2001).

A. B. Taylor, 'Lively, Dynamic, but Hardly a Thing of "Rhythmic Beauty": Arthur Golding's Fourteeners', *Connotations*, 2 (1992), 205–22.

—, 'Melting Earth and Leaping Bulls: Shakespeare's Ovid and Arthur Golding', *Connotations*, 4 (1994–95), 192–206.

—, 'Spenser and Arthur Golding', *Notes and Queries*, 32 (1985), 18–21.

SALMACIS AND HERMAPHRODITUS

Learn why the fountain Salmacis defamèd is of yore,
Why with his waters over-strong it weakeneth men so sore,[7]   *its*
That whoso bathes him there comes thence a perfect man no more.   *complete*
The operation of this well is known to every wight,   *person*
But few can tell the cause thereof, the which I will recite.
    The water-nymphs did nurse a son of Mercury's in Ide,[8]
    Begot on Venus, in whose face such beauty did abide,
As well therein his father both and mother might be known,
Of whom he also took his name. As soon as he was grown
10 To fifteen years of age, he left the country where he dwelt,
And Ida that had fostered him. The pleasure that he felt
To travel countries, and to see strange rivers with the state
Of foreign lands, all painfulness of travel did abate.
He travelled through the land of Lycie[9] to Carie[10] that doth bound

---

[7] 2] The line creates an effect of paradox although the water's power, rather than its physical strength, is signified.
[8] Ide] Mount Ida, the highest mountain in Crete
[9] Lycie] Lycia is a region of Anatolia, in modern Turkey.
[10] Carie] Caria is a region of Western Anatolia.

Next unto[11] Lycia. There he saw a pool which to the ground
Was crystal clear. No fenny sedge, no barren reek, no reed, *sedge*
Nor rush with pricking point was there, nor other moorish weed. *marshy*
The water was so pure and sheer a man might well have seen *clear*
And numbered all the gravel stones that in the bottom been.
20   The utmost borders from the brim environed were with clowres, *grassy ground*
Beclad with herbs ay fresh and green and pleasant smiling flowers. *always*
A nymph did haunt this goodly pool, but such a nymph as neither
To hunt, to run, nor yet to shoot, had any kind of pleasure.
Of all the water-fairies she alonely was unknown *only*
To swift Diana. As the bruit of fame abroad hath blown, *trumpeting*
Her sisters oftentimes would say, 'Take lightsome dart or bow, *enlivening*
And in some painful exercise thine idle time bestow.'
But never could they her persuade to run, to shoot, or hunt,
Or any other exercise, as Phoebe's knights[12] are wont.
30   Sometime her fair well-formèd limbs she batheth in her spring,
Sometime she down her golden hair with boxen comb doth bring,
And at the water as a glass she taketh counsel ay
How everything becometh her. Erewhile[13] in fine array,
On soft sweet herbs, or soft green leaves, herself she nicely[14] lays,
Erewhile again, a-gathering flowers, from place to place she strays,
And, as it chanced, the selfsame time she was a-sorting gays,[15]
To make a posy, when she first the youngman[16] did espy,
And in beholding him desired to have his company.
But though she thought she stood on thorns[17] until she went to him,
40   Yet went she not before she had bedecked her neat and trim,
And pried and peered upon her clothes that nothing sat awry,
And framed her countenance as might seem most am'rous to the eye,
   Which done she thus began: 'O child, most worthy for to be
   Esteemed and taken for a god, if (as thou seem'st to me)
   Thou be a god, to Cupid's name thy beauty doth agree.
Or if thou be a mortal wight, right happy folk are they
By whom thou cam'st into this world, right happy is, I say,
Thy mother and thy sister too (if any be), good hap
That woman had that was thy nurse and gave thy mouth her pap.
50   But far above all other, far more blessed than these is she,
Whom thou vouchsafest for thy wife and bedfellow for to be.
Now if thou have already one, let me by stealth obtain
That which shall pleasure both of us. Or if thou do remain
A maiden, free from wedlock bond, let me then be thy spouse, *virgin*

---

[11] bound next unto] adjoin

[12] Phoebe's knights] Unusually these 'knights' are female. Compare Sandys's description of Callisto as 'a squire of Phoebe's' (l. 16).

[13] Erewhile] The *OED* only gives the meaning 'A while before, some time ago, formerly'. However here 'erewhile' seems to mean 'sometimes'.

[14] nicely] 'Indolently' is perhaps signified (*OED* 2) although 'daintily, elegantly' (*OED* 3) is another possible reading.

[15] gays] bright, decorative objects. Compare 'nosegay'.

[16] youngman] Sometimes, as here, 'youngman' was printed as a single word at this time.

[17] she stood on thorns] Compare Gale's impatient Pyramus and Thisbe who 'sit on briars' (l. 145). This is one of a handful of small adjustments with which Golding enhances the comic aspect of Salmacis's character — another is the alliterative doublet 'pried and peered'.

	And let us in the bridely bed ourselves together rouse.'	*bridal, arouse*
	This said, the nymph did hold her peace, and therewithal the boy	
	Waxed red; he wist not what love was, and sure it was a joy	*knew*
	To see it, how exceeding well his blushing him became.	
	For in his face the colour fresh appearèd like the same	
60	That is in apples which do hang upon the sunny side,	
	Or ivory shadowed with a red, or such as is espied	
	Of white and scarlet colours mixed appearing in the moon,	
	When folk in vain with sounding brass would ease unto her done.¹⁸	*do*
	When at the last the nymph desired most instantly but this,	
	As to his sister brotherly to give her there a kiss,	
	And therewithal was clasping him about the ivory neck,	
	'Leave off', quoth he, 'or I am gone and leave thee at a beck,¹⁹	
	With all thy tricks.' Then Salmacis began to be afraid,	
	And 'to your pleasure leave I free this place, my friend', she said.	
70	With that she turns her back as though she would have gone her way,	
	But evermore she looketh back, and, closely as she may,	
	She hides her in a bushy queach, where kneeling on her knee,	*thicket*
	She always hath her eye on him. He, as a child, and free,	*without restraint*
	And thinking not that any wight had watchèd what he did,	
	Roams up and down the pleasant mead, and, by and by, amid	
	The flattering waves he dips his feet, no more but first the sole,	*caressing*
	And to the ankles afterward both feet he plungeth whole,	
	And for to make the matter short, he took so great delight	
	In coolness of the pleasant spring, that straight he strippèd quite	
80	His garments from his tender skin. When Salmacis beheld	
	His naked beauty, such strong pangs so ardently her held,	
	That utterly she was astraught. And even as Phoebus' beams,	*distracted*
	Against a mirror pure and clear, rebound with broken gleams,	
	Even so her eyes did sparkle fire. Scarce could she tarriance make,	*delay*
	Scarce could she any time delay her pleasure for to take,	
	She would have run, and in her arms embracèd him straight way;	
	She was so far beside herself, that scarcely could she stay.	
	He, clapping with his hollow hands against his naked sides,	
	Into the water, lithe and bain with arms displayèd, glides,	*supple, spread out*
90	And, rowing with his hands and legs, swims in the water clear,	
	Through which his body fair and white doth glistringly appear.	
	As if a man an ivory image, or a lily white,	
	Should overlay, or close²⁰ with glass that were most pure and bright.	
	'The prize is won', cried Salmacis aloud, 'he is mine own',	
	And therewithal in all post-haste²¹ she, having lightly thrown	
	Her garments off, flew to the pool and cast her thereinto,	
	And caught him fast between her arms, for aught that he could do.	
	Yea, maugre all his wrestling and his struggling to and fro,	*despite*
	She held him still, and kissèd him a hundred times and mo,	*more*
100	And willed he, nilled he,²² with her hands she touched his naked breast,	

---

¹⁸ 63] A reference to the Roman practice of trying to reverse an eclipse of the moon by beating cymbals.

¹⁹ beck] nod, gesture. The phrase 'at a beck' seems here to have a meaning similar to 'in a trice'.

²⁰ close] enclose, or perhaps set (*OED* 3b)

²¹ post-haste] with the speed of one travelling post, a dispatch rider

²² nilled he] did not will. These opposed verbs were frequently paired. Compare the derived expression 'willy-nilly'.

And now on this side, now on that, for all he did resist,
And strive to wrest him from her gripes, she clung unto him fast,
And wound about him like a snake which, snatchèd up in haste,
And being by the prince of birds borne lightly up aloft,
Doth writhe herself about his neck and griping talons oft,
And cast her tail about his wings displayèd in the wind;
Or like as ivy runs on trees about the utter rind, — *outer*
Or as the crabfish,[23] having caught his en'my in the seas,
Doth clasp him in on every side with all his crooked clees. — *claws*

110   But Atlas' nephew[24] still persists, and utterly denies
    The nymph to have her hopèd sport; she urges him likewise,
And pressing him with all her weight, fast cleaving to him still:
'Strive, struggle, wrest and writhe', she said, 'thou froward boy, thy fill; — *obstinate*
Do what thou can'st, thou shalt not scape. Ye gods of Heaven, agree — *grant*
That this same wilful boy and I may never parted be.'
The gods were pliant to her boon. The bodies of them twain
Were mixed and joinèd both in one. To both them did remain
One countenance, like as if a man should in one bark behold
Two twigs both growing into one, and still together hold.

120 Even so, when through her hugging and her grasping of the t'other,
The members of them mingled were, and fastened both together,
They were not any longer two, but, as it were, a toy — *novelty*
Of double shape. Ye could not say it was a perfect boy,
Nor perfect wench; it seemèd both and none of both to been.
Now when Hermaphroditus saw how in the water sheen,
To which he entered in a man, his limbs were weakened so,
That out fro thence but half a man he was compelled to go, — *from*
He lifteth up his hands and said, but not with manly reer: — *shout*
'O noble father Mercury, and Venus, mother dear,

130 This one petition grant your son, which both your names doth bear,
That whoso comes within this well may so be weakened there,
That of a man, but half a man he may fro thence retire.'
Both parents, movèd with the chance, did stablish this desire — *mishap, support*
The which their double-shapèd son had made, and thereupon
Infected with an unknown strength the sacred spring anon.

---

[23] crabfish] Golding here 'Englishes' Ovid's 'polypus', sea-polyp.
[24] Atlas' nephew] In fact Narcissus's maternal grandmother, Dione, was Atlas's daughter.

THOMAS PEEND

THE PLEASANT FABLE OF HERMAPHRODITUS
AND SALMACIS (1565)

THOMAS PEEND

THE PLEASANT FABLE OF HERMAPHRODITUS AND SALMACIS (1565)

[*Metamorphoses*, IV. 288–388]

Sprengius, *Metamorphoses Ovidii* (1563), p. 51ʳ

Thomas Peend (fl. 1565–66), also known as de la Pend, was a barrister who published just two works, a translation of one of Bandello's tales and *The Pleasant Fable of Hermaphroditus and Salmacis*. This early Elizabethan adaptation of Ovid is brisk and lively, and can be seen as a transitional point between T. H.'s 'Narcissus', which seems to be the product of an earlier period than its publication date (1560) would suggest, and the far more elegant and accomplished epyllia of the later Elizabethan era. Sophie Chiari says that Peend, 'while developing a new, erotic and fairly exuberant literary style, sticks to the past, halfway between tradition and innovation'.[1] Formally the text is also split into two: the first half is a comparatively free translation, with several additions and elaborations, and this is followed by a long, wide-ranging moralization.

The poet's choice of myth anticipates later Elizabethan Ovidianism. Many Elizabethan adapters of Ovid turned to titillating and transgressive stories, with the figure of the predatory female pursuing the reluctant youth being particularly popular. Shakespeare's *Venus and Adonis* offers a similar pairing, and the story of Salmacis is frequently noted as an influence. The idea of the hermaphrodite, like all non-standard sexual possibilities, intrigued other Elizabethans: a hermaphrodite is introduced in Book III of Spenser's *Faerie Queene* and the period's many cross-dressing heroines also tap into this interest in androgyny.

The seventeenth-century antiquary Anthony Wood includes a brief account of Peend in his *Athenae Oxonienses*, yet offers no details of his college affiliation. He worked as a barrister, and wrote the dedicatory epistle to *Hermaphroditus and Salmacis* from 'a chamber over against

---

[1] Sophie Chiari, ed., *Renaissance Tales of Desire: Hermaphroditus and Salmacis, Ceyx and Alcione, Theseus and Ariadne* (Cambridge: Cambridge Scholars Publishing, 2009), p. 18.

Sergeant's Inn in Chancery Lane'. In this epistle Peend describes how he had been working on a complete translation of Ovid's poem, before discovering that another poet, clearly Arthur Golding, had beaten him to it. His claim to have embarked on a full-scale translation has been viewed with some scepticism. A. B. Taylor convincingly argues that his *Hermaphroditus and Salmacis* seems to have been influenced by Golding.[2] Both, for example, add a detail not present in Ovid, a comparison between the predatory nymph and a crab grasping its prey in its claws. The close parallels cast doubt on Peend's assertion that it was written independently, without any knowledge of the rival work. However, Raphael Lyne is more inclined to believe that Peend's assertion has at least some basis in fact, noting that 'it may be possible to infer some degree of attachment to the claimed project from the way he freights his poem with allusions to other myths from the *Metamorphoses*'.[3] Whether or not he had really translated a considerable portion of the *Metamorphoses*, Peend only managed to publish one other work, 'The Most Notable History of John Lord Mandosse' (1565) from Matteo Bandello's *Novelle*; his familiarity with this popular work is in evidence in *Hermaphroditus and Salmacis*. Many scholars and critics have acknowledged *Hermaphroditus and Salmacis* as an interesting moment in literary history, an early forerunner of the epyllion. But few have paid much attention to the poem, or rated it very highly. C. S. Lewis's judgement is particularly withering. Comparing Peend with T. H., he remarks, 'he too adds a moral, and he too is very, very bad.'[4] R. W. Maslen, noting similarities between the protagonists of both myths, suggests that Peend may have read T. H.'s poem. The structure of Peend's poem follows that adopted by T. H.: a translation followed by a lengthy moralizing commentary. Peend translates Ovid reasonably closely, with the main changes to the text coming in the form of additional discussions and observations. The comparisons with other beautiful youths, the contrast with Cupid, and the reflections on the boy's loss of identity are all new, for example. These embellishments are more conservative than those adopted by the later writers of epyllia. Peend's additions are presented as authorial observations which don't substantially alter the central narrative, whereas poets such as Marlowe and Beaumont would freely add completely new episodes.

The poem is written in fairly jogtrot fourteeners — although it slips into octosyllabic rhyming couplets towards the end of the moralization — and Lewis's evaluation is no more than a little harsh. Readers are divided in their assessment of the poem's tone. Michael Pincombe, for example, contrasts Peend's interpretation of the Hermaphroditus myth as an allegory of enslavement with Jonathan Bate's emphasis on polymorphous liberation. Ruth Gilbert asserts that the poem reveals misogynistic anxiety about the loss of masculinity.[5] Raphael Lyne finds more ambivalence in Peend: 'the tone is curious, since although it shows its misogynistic colours, warning men to beware, it does not over-indulge in anti-female rhetoric'.[6] R. W. Maslen goes a little further. He describes Peend as 'self-consciously witty',[7] and also identifies a possible humorous undermining of the poem's apparently stern warnings against the wiles of wanton women.

Peend's poem was never reprinted, although extracts were included in *The British Bibliographer* (1812),[8] and it is perhaps unlikely that it exerted a great influence on his later Elizabethan successors.[9] Taylor claims to see evidence of a debt to Peend in Marlowe's *Hero and Leander*, but the parallels he adduces are not fully convincing.[10]

---

[2] A. B. Taylor, 'Thomas Peend and Arthur Golding', *Notes and Queries*, 16 (1969), 19–20 (p. 19).
[3] Lyne, *Ovid's Changing Worlds*, pp. 39–40.
[4] C. S. Lewis, *English Literature in the Sixteenth Century Excluding Drama* (Oxford: Clarendon Press, 1954), p. 250.
[5] Ruth Gilbert, *Early Modern Hermaphrodites: Sex and Other Stories* (Basingstoke: Palgrave, 2002), pp. 60–61.
[6] Lyne, *Ovid's Changing Worlds*, p. 39.
[7] Maslen, 'Myths Exploited', p. 23.
[8] Sir Egerton Brydges and Joseph Haslewood, *The British Bibliographer*, 4 vols (London, 1812), II, pp. 344–49.
[9] Though see p. 8 for an account of its possible influence on Francis Beaumont.
[10] A. B. Taylor, 'A Note on Christopher Marlowe's *Hero and Leander*', *Notes and Queries*, 16 (1969), 20–21.

EDITIONS

Thomas Peend, *The Pleasant fable of Hermaphroditus and Salmacis* [. . .] *with a morall in English Verse* (London: Thomas Col[well], 1565), STC 18971.

Sophie Chiari, ed., *Renaissance Tales of Desire: Hermaphroditus and Salmacis, Theseus and Ariadne, Ceyx and Alcione* (Cambridge: Cambridge Scholars Publishing, 2009).

FURTHER READING

Jim Ellis, 'Imagining Heterosexuality in the Epyllia', in *Ovid and the Renaissance Body*, ed. by Goran B. Stanivukovic (Toronto: University of Toronto Press, 2001), pp. 38–57.

Roger Ellis and Liz Oakley-Brown, eds, *Translation and Nation: Towards a Cultural Poetics of Englishness* (Bristol: Multilingual Matters, 2001).

C. S. Lewis, *English Literature in the Sixteenth Century Excluding Drama* (Oxford: Clarendon Press, 1954).

Jenny Mann, 'How to Look at a Hermaphrodite in Early Modern England', *Studies in English Literature*, 46 (2006), 67–91.

Michael Pincombe, 'The Ovidian Hermaphrodite: Moralisations by Peend and Spenser', in *Ovid and the Renaissance Body*, ed. by Goran B. Stanivukovic (Toronto: University of Toronto Press, 2001), pp. 155–70.

J. H. Runsdorf, 'Transforming Ovid in the 1560s: Thomas Peend's *Pleasant Fable*', *American Notes and Queries*, 5 (1992), 124–27.

Lauren Silberman, 'The Hermaphrodite and the Metamorphosis of Spenserian Allegory', *English Literary Renaissance*, 17 (1987), 207–23.

A. B. Taylor, 'Thomas Peend and Arthur Golding', *Notes and Queries*, 16 (1969), 19–20.

——, 'A Note on Christopher Marlowe's *Hero and Leander*', *Notes and Queries*, 16 (1969), 20–21.

THE PLEASANT FABLE OF HERMAPHRODITUS AND SALMACIS

To M. Nicholas Sentleger Esquire[11]

When I had employed some time in translating Ovid's *Metamorphoses*, and had achieved my purpose in part thereof, intending to have travailed further, I understood that another had prevented[12] me. And so, after that I had received copies thereof from the printer, I was resolved to stay my labour, and to reserve that to the use and behoof[13] of my private friend, which I intended to have made common to every man. Howbeit because I know myself on divers causes alleged[14] to your worship, being no less learned yourself than affectioned[15] to every commendable faculty, having nothing more fit at this time, I thought it good to gratify you with some

---

[11] Nicholas St Leger was a Member of Parliament and a staunch Protestant.
[12] prevented] anticipated
[13] behoof] benefit
[14] alleged] This seems to be a verb derived from 'allegiance' although no instances are cited in the *OED*.
[15] affectioned] well disposed

part thereof, and that not altogether under the note and figure according to the text.[16] Applying also a moral to the fable. And because it hath pleased you upon your good will, rather than for the worthiness hereof, to accept and commend my copy in writing,[17] I am now therefore bold to publish it in print under the patronage of your name. The rather to amend the volume of this other history.[18] And thus neither my first labours shall altogether sink, nor I shall seem to abuse the writer or reader of those four books of the *Metamorphoses*, which be so learnedly translated already. Thus yours, for his small power assured, wisheth you Galen's[19] health, the good fortune which Polycrates[20] enjoyed for the most part of his life, and Nestor's[21] years.

T. Peend.

From my chamber over against Sergeant's Inn in Chancery Lane. 1564.

Dame Venus once, by Mercury compressed,[22] a child did bear,	
For beauty far excelling all that erst before him were.	*earlier*
This noble child by name was called Hermaphroditus so,	
Of both his parents' names it is derivèd, as ye know.	
His shape it did so far exceed[23] the graces of all other,	
That then the countenance of the child might well deserve his mother.	
His portraiture, divine it was, so perfect in each point,	*appearance*
His noble limbs so fair to sight, so set in every joint	
That he might seem Dame Nature's work as far for to excel,	
10 As do the gods the shape of men, as ancient stories tell.	
As to his face, it was so fair, and bright with beauty's shine,	*lustre*
That it excelled the glistering beams in Phoebus' face divine.	
A pattern plain to mend her mould Dame Nature there might see;	*evident*
Thereby appeared how marvellous the works of God they be.	
The Phrygian boy, by th'eagle caught on Jove t'attend and wait,	*Ganymede*
Liriope's son, Narcissus fair, nymph Echo her[24] dainty bait,	
Not Attis[25] fine, which was some time accepted well with Jove,	
Nor yet the boy in incest got,[26] which Venus so did love,	
All these were not to be compared with young Hermaphrodite.	
20 Nor Cupid sure, his brother blind,[27] if poets truly write,	
Might not with him in shape compare, but yet to fortune he	
Was subject more than this, as we by th'end may plainly see;	

---

[16] In other words, this is an adaptation rather than a close translation.
[17] copy in writing] manuscript
[18] He is perhaps saying that he wants to offer a complementary supplement to Golding's translation.
[19] Galen's] The famous physician, a Roman of Greek origin who lived in the second century CE. His influence continued well into the Renaissance.
[20] Polycrates] The sixth-century BCE tyrant of Samos was famously fortunate. He is said to have thrown away a valuable jewel as an apotropaic device to avoid a reversal of fortune. However the jewel was later discovered in a fish and returned to him.
[21] Nestor] The mythical Greek king, who was one of the Argonauts and later fought in the Trojan War, is a byword for old age and wisdom.
[22] Compressed] to embrace sexually, generally without any connotations of force
[23] 5–19] The enthusiastic account of Hermaphroditus's beauty is much expanded.
[24] Nymph Echo her] Echo's. The possessive pronoun 'her' here follows the noun to signify a genitive.
[25] Attis] the consort of Cybele. He is said to have been sent mad by Cybele, and castrated himself, as a punishment for seeking another woman in marriage.
[26] 18] Adonis, the child of Myrrha by her father Cinyras
[27] his brother blind] Blind Cupid, as a son of Venus, was Hermaphroditus's half-brother.

For Cupid he doth yet now live, a stubborn, witless boy,
But Hermaphrodite death at last had power for to destroy,
Howbeit by doleful doom, he lost himself before he died;[28]
Such was his lot. Yet seems it strange, one from himself to slide;
Some would not think that any man might change his nature so,
That from himself, by destiny, he might depart or go.
Howbeit the stranger that it seemed, the rather did I choose
30   To write of him whose lot it was by ill luck himself to lose.
Among a thousand stories which are worthy to be scanned
In golden verse by skilful pen I took this same in hand,
To show my ready will to you, till greater power in me,
As correspondent to my mind, likewise it may agree.
Wherefore the whilst I shall desire your mastership[29] to take   *meanwhile*
This same in worth[30] of worthier work, and full account to make,
That want of will is not in me, though power thereto do not agree.
But now this son of Mercury's in Ida mount was fed,
And fostered; there full fifteen years his life also he led,
40   And then, desirous for to know the state of countries strange,
All Lycia[31] land, by travel great, to Caria[32] he did range.
Whereas upon a time, what with his travail[33] that was great,
And eke the weather being hot, he, wearied then with heat,
And ready for to rest himself, by chance he did espy
A well, with water fair and clear as crystal to the eye,
Which neither bush at any time, nor weed it overgrew,
Much like unto the well it was, whereto Actaeon[34] drew,
When that Diana and her nymphs, all naked in the same,
He saw, by chance, as he did seek his lately coursèd game.   *pursued*
50   About that spring an idle nymph, fair Salmacis,[35] did use,   *frequent*
Which even as soon as with her eyes the young man fair she views,
Straight set on fire; the smouldering heat doth strike unto her heart,
And thorough piercèd by the dint of cruel Cupid's dart,
She straight desires with him to join, her lust for to fulfil;
She trims herself, and goes forthwith for to declare her will;   *smartens*
To whom when that she came, straight way, with comely grace she gan to say:
'O worthy child,[36] whose shape doth show, as it doth seem to me,
That surely thou some god, and not a earthly wight should be.
Right happy are thy parents sure, and eke the nurse in lap,
60   Which hath thee laid oft times, and given thy lovely lips the pap.
But happiest of them both, I say, a blessèd one is she,

---

[28] 25–30] This section on identity may echo the tale of Narcissus.
[29] Your mastership] a respectful form of address, commonly used in petitions at this period
[30] in worth] at its proper value
[31] Lycia] a region of Anatolia, in modern Turkey
[32] Caria] a region of western Anatolia
[33] travail] 'travayle' in the original. Either 'travel' or 'travail' might be intended.
[34] Actaeon] The allusion to Actaeon's story reflects Peend's readiness to draw implicit and explicit parallels with other tales from the *Metamorphoses*.
[35] Fair Salmacis] Although he embellishes Ovid's account of Hermaphroditus's beauty, Peend omits Ovid's more extended and alluring portrait of Salmacis (*Met.*, IV. 302–16). This focus on the beauty of the youth, rather than the woman, anticipates Marlowe's *Hero and Leander* and Shakespeare's *Venus and Adonis*.
[36] child] youth of gentle birth

Which as thy wife within one bed might join herself with thee.
My dear, vouchsafe to hear my suit, grant my request, I pray,
That if you be not married yet then, then grant this I say,
That I may rest my happy limbs in blessèd bed with thee,
So I with Juno for to change my state would not agree.
If thou be married, let me steal one turn, my heart, my joy.'
She said, and therewith held her peace. But lo, the shamefast boy
Was dashed, and out of countenance clean. He blushed as red as blood,   *put to shame*
70   He wist not then what love did mean; it would have done one good   *knew*
To see how well the blushing shame the amazèd boy as it became.
Such was his lively countenance, such was his comely hue,
Whom when the nymph had long beheld, not able to subdue
Her heat, affection and desire, not able to sustain
The force of those so fervent flames, she doth attempt again
By other means to try the boy; each practice doth she prove.
But nought at all could move his heart, being rude, as yet, to love;   *unskilled*
She seeketh to embrace his neck, and asketh for a kiss,
But then the boy, resisting her, was movèd much with this,
80   And said, 'Leave off these wanton tricks, no longer trouble me,[37]
Else will I soon be gone, and leave the place and all with thee.'
Then Salmacis, afraid, did make as thence she would be gone,
But in a bush hard by the same, she hid herself anon.
The boy thought now that all was safe, from shame as yet now free,
Does off his clothes, and thinketh sure that none the same doth see,   *takes off*
And like a wanton kid he skips, and in the mead doth run.
Then in the well, to bathe his feet, he so at first begun,
But thus at last the water clear, it doth delight him so,
He gives his body to the streams, and wadeth to and fro,
90   And further forth with softly[38] foot he doth begin to go.
At last with arms outstretchèd he his body clean doth dip;
By swimming, through the silvery streams, his ivory corpse doth slip.   *living body*
The nymph this while, beholding him, no longer then could stay,
But off her mantle being thrown, she would leap in straight way.
The boy amid the waves doth swim, as white as any snow;
No swan could seem more white than he, that ever any saw.
The nymph her heart doth pant with joy, she scant abides to stay,   *scarcely*
Until her garments all were off. She plyeth so her prey,   *attacks repeatedly*
Even as the eager mastiff dog,[39] whom scant his keeper stays,
100   But at the baited bear he strives, for to be gone always.
Even as the hawk doth bate[40] when that she sees the partridge sprung,
So Salmacis, to her it seems each time it is too long,
That lets her from the prey. But lo, as merry as a pie,   *magpie*
The boy doth frisk and play, he thinks that none may him espy.
But as the hare within her form, when she doth fear no ill,
The hound is on her suddenly, then pressed the fool to kill,   *hurried*
So Salmacis unto her prey, into the water goes,

---

[37] 80] Compare Golding, *Metamorphosis*, III. 413–14.
[38] softly] soft, gentle. The word was fairly commonly used in this adjectival sense in the period.
[39] 98–106] Peend anglicizes Ovid's animal similes.
[40] bate] beat the wings impatiently

As though that then for all the world her lust she would not lose;
Not to persuade him now she means, as she did erst before,
110 But now she's pressed her lust to serve, or else to die therefore; *driven*
She is to folly so full inclined, that nothing then might change her mind.
But lo the boy, as soon as he did there the nymph espy,
Even as the little roach, with fins outreachèd, fast doth fly *extended*
The ravening pike which after him in greater haste doth hie,
So up and down the spring they fleet, the one himself to save,
The nymph her joy by spoil doth seek of th'other for to have. *rapine*
The flightful[41] boy, like as the hare, for life the hound doth fly,
The nymph always, even as the hound, when he doth come so nigh,
That even his nose may touch her heels, he girdeth forth amain,[42]
120 With gaping mouth, being always like[43] his prey for to obtain.
The nymph did drive him up so near, that even of force at last
He is compelled for to resist, and strive for him as fast,
Her rage by strength for to suppress, she forceth on him so,
That, wearied nigh, the tender boy he wots not what to do. *knows*
To strive he is compelled, or else to yield against his will
Unto his foe, which forceth so, her lust for to fulfil.
And yet some women say that they[44] be innocents, god wot;
This nicey[45] nymph doth now display whether it be true or not;
In goodness simple[46] sure they be, else subtle enough I warrant ye.
130 So nice and fine before that time this weakling nymph did seem,
That force and might to break an egg in her ye would scantly deem.
And yet by force she keepeth now the young man at a bay,
As in a corner doth a dog keep up the striving gray. *badger*
And then at last, espying well advantage fit thereto,
She catcheth him about the neck, as loath to let him go.
Even as the ivy winds about the tree, so doth she clasp
The body of the striving boy, which trembled like the asp. *aspen*
Even as the crab, in cruel claws when he hath caught his foe,
With grip doth gird him, so as though he should not scape him fro, *encircle*
140 Even so the nymph, though Venus' son do as he may resist,
In words protesting plain how that she shall not have her list, *pleasure*
Yet hoping well, with pressing weight, she cleaveth to him so,
That though he strive and writhe, she swears he shall not from her go.
'Wherefore, thou froward boy', she says, now struggle on thy fill,
But now by force I will obtain that shall content my will;[47]
Thou shalt not scape me sure, go to with stubborn striving still.'

---

[41] flightful] The *OED* offers three distinct meanings: fugitive, transitory; producing flight, cowardly; well-adapted for flight. The word is used again at line 278. Although the *OED* does not offer this precise definition, 'fleeing' would seem to be the best gloss for both Peend's uses of 'flightful'.

[42] 119] 'He braces himself to go forwards at full speed'

[43] like] apparently on the point of

[44] 127–33] The reflections on women's behaviour and Salmacis's misleading appearance are Peend's own.

[45] nicey] nice. This word has several distinct shades of meaning. Peend might wish to signify 'wanton' (*OED* A 2a) or perhaps, given the tone of the lines, he uses the word ironically to mean 'fastidious' (A 4b). 'Nice' seems to be used in this latter sense a few lines later, at line 130.

[46] simple] Perhaps playing on two different senses of the word simple, *OED* 1 'guileless' and *OED* 7a 'small, slight'.

[47] 143–45] Compare Golding, *Metamorphosis*, IV. 458–59.

With pressèd lips perforce[48] to him an hundred kisses she
Doth give, whereby it may appear she liked his company.
This said. Unto the heavens on high she lifteth up her eyes,
150 And sayth, 'O gods that see all things, and sit above the skies,
Grant that this wilful boy may never part from me,
But let us still in one remain.' The gods they did agree
To her request. And Venus then, being movèd with their moan,
She did vouchsafe to join their bodies both in one.
One countenance did set forth a thing full strange to see,
A man and woman both, with one corpse to agree,
And yet the same no perfect man, nor woman for to be.
But now, when that Hermaphrodite did see in water plain,
He entered like a man therein, and should come forth again
160 But half a man, himself he lost, his fortune it was so.
Wherefore he lifted up his hands, and prayed his parents to,
That who so ever entreth here, his lot likewise may be,
That he to man and woman both, in shape may so agree.
Their parents heard the plaint the which their double-shapèd son
Had made, and so with virtue strange the spring was spread anon,
Thus both in wish they did agree, and now contented well they be.
Now, Ovid here might seem to some a trifling tale to tell,
But yet it shows a worthy sense, if it be markèd well.
The poets use in pleasant toys great wisdom for to show;
170 A subtle sense this tale doth bear albeit perceived of few.
By Venus' son, here understand such youths as yet be green,
And from the spot of filthy lust the striplings that be clean,
Which yet have not enthralled themselves unto affection vile,
Nor know the poison strong, the subtle bait, which lovers doth beguile,
Even such as newly have cast off a boy, and entered in
A young man's age; such one as doth to know himself begin,
Of age well able for to rule himself without a guide,
Such one as first into the world beginneth for to slide,
To learn and see the trades of men, to choose the good from ill,
180 By young Hermaphrodite, such one here understand we will.
By Caria, signify the world, where all temptations be,
Whereas the good and ill always together we may see.
By Salmacis, intend each vice, that moveth one to ill,   *signify*
And by the spring, the pleasant sport that doth content the will.[49]
So that when any young man first, without a guide or stay,
Doth enter in the world so wide, unskilful of the way,
Not knowing yet the wily bait, nor the temptations vile,
Whereby the subtle sort oft-times, the silly do beguile,   *simple*
He blindly runneth on each where, and doubting of none ill,
190 Because himself he meaneth none, he thinks that no man will
(do otherwise.)

---

[48] perforce] by force. But there is some ambiguity as perforce can also mean 'by necessity, unavoidably', and, taken out of context, this might read like a description of a girl having attentions forced on her by a man.
[49] will] Pincombe convincingly suggests that 'will' is a *double entendre*, and that the spring represents the female pudendum ('The Ovidian Hermaphrodite', pp. 166–67).

And so, by pleasant shape of vice deceivèd all unware, *unwary*
He drowns himself in filthy sin, taken in the snare.
The more he strives, entangled once, the faster he is in,
Such is the nature of the bait, and sleight of that same gin. *snare*
But after that he is deceived, by practice to his pain,[50]
More wise, always he will beware to come in like again.
Then will he joy to see his wish, on others in like sort,
Which plungèd be in pensive pain, whilst that they seek for sport. *melancholy*

200 A man is said to lose himself, when, reason quite exiled,
Enthralled in slavish woe, he is constrainèd for to yield
To lust and will. Dame Reason's rules, which still should rule our race,
Rejected quite, to affections we give the ground and place,
And like to beasts, esteeming more to serve our sensual lust,
And to adorn the body brave, which shall consume to dust,
More lief than for to deck the mind, which is immortal sure; *desirous*
Such is our beastly nature blind, so is our lust unpure.
So we our chief and greatest good, the treasure of our mind,
Do lose, and so to slavish lust our nature free we bind,
210 And servants, bound unto our will,[51] we work our wretched woe;
So one may lose himself, and be unto himself a foe.
So do we change the happy hope of everlasting joy,
Even for the present pastime, which ourselves doth most annoy. *injure*
We change our nature clean, being made effeminate, *completely*
When we do yield to serve our lust, we lose our former state.
It is the nature of that well, that filthy loathsome lake
Of lust, the strength from lusty[52] men by hidden force to take;
And so it may now plain appear, the poet truth did tell.
As many as hereafter shall once enter in this well
220 Of vice, he shall be weakened so, his nature sure he shall forego.
Thus much hereof, as my rude Muse doth understand the mind
Of Ovid, by this pleasant tale, no further sense I find.
But now the fleeting fancies fond, and eke the shuttle wits, *unsteady*
The mad desires of women now, their rage in foolish fits,
I will display. This nymph, the boy did for his beauty love,
For even the sudden sight of him did her affection move,
And Echo, she Narcissus young, even for his beauty's sake,
Did choose among all other youths, to be her faithful make. *mate*
Medea[53] and Hypsipyle,[54] did love Jason so,
230 Even for his lovely face, that they would from their countries go,
And leave their parents and their friends, to go and be with him,
Which to them both, not long ago, had erst a stranger been. *formerly*

---

[50] 196] Because he has now had actual experience of pain

[51] bound unto our will] trapped by our own lust

[52] lusty] This seems to be an example of the poet playing metamorphic tricks with language. 'Lust', wanton desire, is juxtaposed with 'lusty', in this context presumably meaning 'healthy, vigorous'.

[53] 229–44] Many of the women listed by Peend feature in Ovid's *Heroides*. It seems significant that several of the women are blameless, or sympathetic at least. Medea disobeyed her father and killed her brother in order to help Jason win the Golden Fleece. She then fled with the Argonauts.

[54] Hypsipyle] a queen of Lemnos who had a liaison with Jason when she offered the Argonauts hospitality. She subsequently bore him twins. For Hypsipyle and Medea, see *Heroides*, VI and XII.

Demophon,⁵⁵ by his seemly shape, did like fair Phyllis' eyes,   *please*
And Dido,⁵⁶ she Aeneas brave therefore did love likewise,
And in like sort did end her life, when that she might no more
Enjoy her joyful lust as she was wont some time before.
It seemèd death, what so did them divorce their lovers fro.⁵⁷
Fair Helen,⁵⁸ Menelaus' wife, to Paris fine also
Did yield, with him to Phrygian town, a stranger, for to go.   *Trojan*
240   To Paris' arms herself she took, and Menelaus old forsook.
The lusty girl began to loathe such sage pastime as he
Could make; she rather chose with Paris young to be.
The learned Sappho⁵⁹ did some time to comely Phaon sue
For grace. And Byblis,⁶⁰ she her brother did pursue,
For beauty that in him did shine; she followed him therefore
So long, till that her fainting limbs could carry her no more.
King Nisus' daughter dear also, fair Scylla,⁶¹ was beguiled,
By Minos' yellow shining hair,⁶² which, as her foe in field,
Against the walls of Megaris,⁶³ did bear his seemly shield.
250   And yet King Minos' wife was of another mind;
In Taurus' black ill-facèd sire,⁶⁴ more pleasure she did find;
The captain's rousy scuff,⁶⁵ black poll, to her so fair did seem,
That she her husband's golden hair did not so much esteem.
The Emperor Otho's daughter dear, Adelasie,⁶⁶ did so
Regard the lively Aleran, that she with him did go
To countries strange, content by hazard of her life,
Against the will of all her friends, for to become his wife.
With prince-like life, for him alone, an empire she would lose;   *spirit*
With him to lead a simple life, much rather she did choose.
260   All pleasures in the world, in him alone she then did take,

---

⁵⁵ Demophon] Demophon, King of Athens, married Phyllis, daughter of King Lycurgus of Thrace. In some accounts of the myth she killed herself after he failed to return to her.

⁵⁶ Dido] According to Virgil's *Aeneid*, Dido, Queen of Carthage, committed suicide after she was abandoned by Aeneas.

⁵⁷ 237] 'Whatever parted them from their lovers seemed as terrible as death to these women'

⁵⁸ Helen] Helen's love for Paris is the subject of one of the sets of paired letters in the *Heroides*, XVI and XVII.

⁵⁹ Sappho] According to some accounts Sappho committed suicide after being rejected by Phaon, a ferryman. *Heroides*, XV, which is of doubtful authorship, is a letter from Sappho to Phaon.

⁶⁰ Byblis] Her story can be found in *Met.*, IX. She writes an impassioned letter to her brother, revealing her incestuous love for him.

⁶¹ Scylla] Nisus's daughter Scylla became infatuated with Minos, her father's enemy, and she cut off Nisus's purple lock of hair which guaranteed his city's safety (*Met.*, VIII).

⁶² yellow shining hair] The emphasis on Minos's hair may have been triggered by the importance of Nisus's hair in the story.

⁶³ Megaris] Megara, a city in Attica

⁶⁴ Taurus] As Peend sets out in the glossary, this name denotes the Minotaur's father rather than the Minotaur himself. So it is possible that Peend's 'syre' is a misprint for 'lyre', complexion, appearance. Peend's rationalization of the myth is linked to accounts such as that of Palaephatus. Little is known of this writer but he probably lived in the fourth century BCE. In *On Incredible Things* he too asserts that the bull was simply a man named Taurus, although he claims he was good looking whereas Peend describes him as 'ill-faced'.

⁶⁵ rousy scuff] The phrase 'rousy skuffe' is obscure and may be a misprint. Possibly it should be glossed 'filthy neck'. 'Rossy' is a rare word meaning filthy from 'ross', rubbish, and scuff or skuffe may mean the nape of the neck (scruff). Alternatively 'scurf', scaly skin, may be intended, and rousy might be a misprint for 'lousy'.

⁶⁶ Adelasie] This story is included in the *Novelle* of Matteo Bandello (c. 1480–1562). Neither Bandello nor Peend seem to disapprove of Adelasie's love for Aleran, and the lovers are eventually reunited with Otho.

All friends, for him alone also, she gladly did forsake.
With him for need right well she was contented coals to make,⁶⁷   *out of necessity*
To couch in cottage low, on simple food to fare,
For all the world, excepted him, she took no kind of care.
He was her bliss, her joy was he, and nothing else esteemèd she.
And Hero⁶⁸ fair unto her fere Leander fair did take,   *mate*
And Thisbe she did kill herself for comely Pirame's⁶⁹ sake.
Orestes'⁷⁰ lively looks did much Hermione delight;
King Tancred's⁷¹ daughter, Gismond, did love Guistard's beauty bright;
270   The nymphs did Hyacinthus,⁷² for his seemly shape, desire;
His lovely cheer full soon did set their youthly hearts on fire.   *youthful*
And Juliet Romeus young for beauty did embrace,⁷³
Yet did his manhood well agree unto his worthy grace;
So seemly shape did love procure, and Venus' birds came to the lure.
And Aphrodite, dame so coy, did love Adonis⁷⁴ so,
That she with him, always, contented was to go;
In slender hand, the craggy bow she did vouchsafe to bear,   *rough*
And run a-hunting after him, to kill the flightful⁷⁵ deer.
The stubborn boy, blind Cupid here, with shaft did strike his mother dear.
280   Sith beauty's grace, as pleasant bait, these ladies did deceive,   *since*
What did Adonis' mother⁷⁶ in her father old perceive,
Why she should seek by incest vile her mother's bed for to defile?
What flinging fit did force her so? What mad desire doth move   *turbulent*
Her thus? Why should she seek an old and cankered lad to love?
And why did Phaedra⁷⁷ sue unto her boistous son-in-law,   *unpolished*
Hippolyte blunt, being rude to love,⁷⁸ unto her lust to draw?
Why did his fierce and frowning face, his hard complexion, seem
To her a fair and manlike hue, what made her so to deem?
Sith beauty's goodly grace, sometime so well it likèd her,
290   That she above her country, did young Theseus⁷⁹ prefer.

---

⁶⁷ 262] They work as charcoal burners.
⁶⁸ Hero] Leander was drowned while swimming across the Hellespont to visit Hero. The doomed love of Hero and Leander is the subject of letters XVIII and XIX of Ovid's *Heroides*.
⁶⁹ Pirame's] Pyramus's. Their well-known story is told in *Met.*, IV.
⁷⁰ Orestes] The son of Agamemnon married Hermione, daughter of Helen and Menelaus. *Heroides*, VIII is addressed by Hermione to Orestes; she begs to be saved from marriage to Pyrrhus.
⁷¹ Tancred's] The story of Tancred, who slew his daughter's lover, and sent her his heart in a golden cup is the first story to be told on the fourth day in Boccaccio's *Decameron*.
⁷² Hyacinthus] The story of Hyacinthus, accidentally killed by his lover Apollo, is told in *Met.*, X. It is possible that Peend confused him with Hylas, the young Argonaut, who was dragged down into the water by nymphs, smitten with his beauty. The story is told in Apollonius of Rhodes' *Argonautica*.
⁷³ 272] This story was also included in Bandello's *Novelle*.
⁷⁴ Adonis] *Met.*, X.
⁷⁵ Flightful] See note to l. 117.
⁷⁶ Adonis' mother] Myrrha, who lusted after her father Cinyras (*Met.*, X)
⁷⁷ Phaedra] Phaedra's fateful passion for Hippolytus, son of her husband Theseus, is the subject of plays by Euripides and Seneca.
⁷⁸ rude to love] Hermaphroditus was also described as 'rude [. . .] to love' (l. 77).
⁷⁹ Young Theseus] The myth's timescale is not fully consistent. Phaedra is generally presented, within the context of the Hippolytus story, as the young wife of a middle-aged Theseus, father of a grown-up son. However, the Theseus who is aided by Phaedra's sister Ariadne, and who is sometimes depicted as sailing off with Phaedra as well, is generally depicted as a young man.

Her sister Ariadne[80] aye his shape esteemèd so,
That she her brother did betray, and fled her parents fro.
Such be the fond and frantic fits which in the blinded brain
Of wanton women, oftentimes, with swingeing[81] sway doth reign.
And Venus[82] eke, which likèd so Adonis' lovely grace,
That she from him would not abide in any place;
In warlike Mars, that bloody knight,
Sometime also she did delight.
Sith she for comely beauty then,
300   These lusty youths did love,
What odd conceit did move her so,
To serve that grisly sire,
The coppersmith deformed,
Whom neither Nature with good grace
Nor learning had adorned,
But even a rude and boistous carl,   *churl*
Whose colour in his face,
A Croydon-sanguine[83] right did seem,
This is a doubtful case;
310   That she which erst did seek so much
For beauty's goodly grace,
To love Adonis fair alone,
Should seek sometime to embrace
Sir Vulcan, with his drowsy[84] poll,
A smith which did on stithy roll,   *anvil, sway*
I dare not sure dissolve this doubt,
I fear to judge on this.
To have to do with gods above,
How dangerous it is;
320   Tiresias[85] old, which was sometime
A judge of Juno's game,
In jesting strife, for telling truth,
The judge did bear the blame.
He lost his sight, for judging right,
Oh judge unwise, thou knowest the price,
Of telling truth, more was the ruth;
Tiresias, thou prophet old,   *pity*

---

[80] Ariadne] Minos's daughter helped Theseus escape from the labyrinth and destroy the Minotatur (*Met.*, VIII). Letter X of the *Heroides* is Ariadne's letter to Theseus, supposedly written after being abandoned by him on Naxos.
[81] swingeing] *1565* 'swinging', but this is probably a variant spelling of 'swingeing', either in the sense of 'scourging' or simply 'great', rather than swinging, swaying.
[82] Venus] The story of how Vulcan trapped Venus, his wife, and her lover Mars in a net is told in Book VIII of the *Odyssey*.
[83] Croydon-sanguine] The *OED* quotes Robert Nares's definition of this obscure expression, 'supposed to be a kind of sallow colour'.
[84] drowsy] This is spelled 'drousie', which is probably a variant of drowsy. However 'drossy', 'impure' might be intended, given the emphasis on disgust in this section, and reflecting the fact his hair is blackened by soot. His limp causes him to sway or stagger as he works (cf *Amores*, II. 17. 19–20).
[85] Tiresias] The seer metamorphosed from a man into a woman and then back again, and was punished by Juno for deciding in Jove's favour in a debate over whether the man or woman derived most pleasure from sex. He confirmed that the woman did. Juno struck him blind, but Jove gave him the gift of prophecy in compensation (*Met.*, III).

Which had'st the grace for to unfold
The secrets hid of things to come,
330 Thou, Juno she did make thee blind,
Yet Jove to thee was not unkind.
He did restore, as good therefore,[86]
Thy lack of sight, thy knowledge doth
Right well acquit. That is the troth,   *cancel a debt*
For by the same, unto the skies,
Thy worthy name, it did arise.
Howbeit I am not so bold
With judgement this for to unfold.[87]
The goddess grave I more regard,
340 Than hope to have of Jove's reward.
For doubt of blame, I dare not say
Or show the same, which erst alway
I thought.[88] For sure, if I may choose,
Dame Venus' love I will not lose,
Sith men bare blame for telling troth,
To show the same I would be loath.
Wherefore now I will cease to write,
And you hardly, by judgement right,   *boldly*
As one exempt from Venus' might,
350 May be more bold, this to unfold.
And so to you I leave it now,
That this most weighty doubt,
At further leisure, when you list,
Yourself may find it out.

T. D. Peend.

That the unlearned might the better understand these, I have compendiously noted the histories and names not familiar to our English phrase.[89]

Venus: wife to Vulcan, feigned of the poets to be the goddess of love, and by another name is called Aphrodite.

Mercury: the son of Jupiter and Maia, one of the daughters of Atlas, whom the poets called god of eloquence, and is called Hermes, otherwise the messenger of Jupiter.

Phoebus, Apollo: and is taken for the sun.

Narcissus: son of Liriope, a child of passing beauty, which did so much delight in his own shape, as the poets feigned, that he died for love of his own shadow and was turned into a flower.

---

[86] as good therefore] Jove compensates, makes amends for, Tiresias's blindness with an equal good.
[87] He seems now to return to his earlier concern about the reasons why women and goddesses are attracted to unattractive or unsuitable men.
[88] 341–43] He hints that he has a theory to explain women's attraction to inappropriate men but doesn't dare reveal it because telling the truth might lead to divine displeasure.
[89] Peend's prose is rather awkward; he frequently presents clauses as sentences. Where possible, without losing clarity, punctuation has been adjusted to avoid this.

Phrygian: one of the land of Phrygia.

Cupid: son of Bacchus[90] and Venus, and is feigned of the poets to be the god of love, and is called blind, because lust blindeth judgements of men.

Echo: a nymph which loved Narcissus. And the sound that cometh from the valleys and hollow places and doth sound again six or seven words, in some places, by reason of the reverberation of the air, as some say.

Jove: son of Saturn and Ops, King of Crete, and was feigned chief of the gods.

Juno: sister and wife of Jove or Jupiter.

Medea: daughter of Oeta,[91] king of Colchis, which loved Jason. Who, when he had sworn never to forsake her, she did help him to kill the serpent and win the golden fleece. And so when she did privily go away with Jason, she killed her young brother Absyrtus, and did pluck him in pieces, to stay her father which pursued after her. And when she had lived many years in Greece, with Jason, and had children by him, at last Jason forsook her and married Glauce, daughter of King Creon. Medea, so refused, slew the sons which she had by Jason, and setting his palace on fire, she burned Glauce and her father therein.

Hypsipyle: daughter of Thoas, king of Lemnus, which loved Jason exceedingly, and bore him two children at a burden.[92]

Jason: son of Aeson, whom Pelias his uncle, being king of Thessaly, did send with many other valiant gentlemen to fetch the golden fleece. Which, the adventures thereof achieved, by the help of Medea, he won, and brought it away.

Demophon: son of Theseus and Phaedra. Which, returning from the battle of Troy, was by tempest brought into Thracia, where Phyllis, daughter of Lycurgus, then queen, received him, and after married him, which from thence went to Athens, promising her to return shortly. Which when he performed not, Phyllis, not able to sustain the raging fits of so fervent love, hung herself on an almond tree, and so the poets feigned that she was turned into an almond tree.

Dido: daughter of Belus, king of Tyre, and wife of Sychaeus, whom when Pygmalion the king, and brother to Dido, had slain for his riches, Dido sailed into Africa with his treasure, and there built the famous city of Carthage. And afterward in love with Aeneas; when he had departed from her, to seek the land of Italy, according to Cassandra her prophecy,[93] she broke her neck for sorrow, falling into the fire etc. Or according to Virgil slew herself with Aeneas his sword.

Aeneas: a noble man of Troy, son of Anchises and Venus, which escaping with his father, wife and other his countrymen, after great travail and many chances, arrived in Italy, where after

---

[90] Bacchus] Several different gods are sometimes described as the father of Eros or Cupid, with Mercury and Mars being most commonly named, but Bacchus does not seem to be a widely recognized candidate.
[91] Oeta] Aeëtes
[92] burden] birth. The children were twins.
[93] Cassandra her prophecy] Her prophecy that the Trojans would find a new home in Italy is recalled by Anchises in *Aeneid*, III. 183–87.

great battle he slew King Turnus and married Lavinia, daughter to King Latinus, and so became king of Italy.

Helena: begotten of Jupiter, in the likeness of a swan, on Leda, wife of Tyndareus, king of Laconia. And was for her passing beauty twice stolen, first by Theseus, being but a girl, and the second time being wife to Menelaus, by Paris. For whom the Grecians warred ten years' space with the Trojans, and so Troy being burned, received her again.

Paris: son of Priam, king of Troy, by his wife Hecuba, with whom when she was great with child, she dreamed that she had brought forth a firebrand which should burn Troy, wherefore the king, afraid, commanded that the child should be killed as soon as he was born. His mother Hecuba, moved with motherly pity, did privily send him to a shepherd to be brought up. And when he waxed a young man, Juno, Pallas and Venus, goddesses striving in beauty for a golden apple whereon was written 'be it given to the fairest', they were sent by Jupiter to the judgement of Paris. To whom when Juno had promised rule and kingdom, Pallas wisdom, and Venus pleasure, and the fairest woman in the world, he gave the apple to Venus. And so after came in favour with his father, and sailing to Sparta, he brought fair Helen away with him, and so the battle of Troy began.

Sappho: a woman of the isle Lesbos, learned in poetry, being forsaken of a young man called Phaon, whom she loved, she cast herself from the hill Leucates into the sea, and so perished by love of him.

Phaon: when he had carried Venus over a ferry,[94] she gave him to be the fairest and best shaped man alive.

Byblis: daughter of Miletus, which inflamed with detestable love of her brother Caunus, when he forsook his country to avoid that mischief, she followed him till she died for faintness.

Scylla: daughter of Nisus, King of Megaris, which for the love of Minos, then besieging the city of Megaris, she brought to him a purple hair which she cut off from her father's head. And that hair being on his head, he could not be overcome, and by like destiny, with the hair he lost his kingdom. And Minos despised her for her mischievous deed, and tying her with a cord to the end of his ship he hung her in the water.

Minos: begotten by Jupiter in the likeness of a white bull on the fair Europa,[95] daughter to Agenor, king of Phoenicia, and for his justice is feigned of the poets to be a judge in Hell.

Adonis: a young man of passing beauty whom Cinyras, king of Phoenicia,[96] made drunk by policy of his daughter and a nurse, begat on his own daughter, Myrrha, whom Venus loved.

Hippolytus: son of Theseus, duke of Athens, by Hippolyta. Whom when his stepmother could not win to her lust, she accused him to Theseus as though he would have oppressed her by force. Theseus then, trusting his wife too much, desired his father Aegeus,[97] a god of the sea, that he

---

[94] ferry] Here the place where boats pass over a river, rather than the boat itself.
[95] Europa] The story of Europa's abduction can be found in *Met.*, II.
[96] Phoenicia] Ovid's Cinyras is a descendent of Pygmalion of Cyprus. However the geography of the story is contradictory, as Ovid also implies that it is set in or near Arabia.
[97] Aegeus] It was Poseidon who granted Theseus's request. Peend seems to have been confused by the fact that Theseus is sometimes described as the son of Poseidon, but more usually as the son of Aegeus.

would kill his son. Wherefore when Hippolytus did ride in a chariot by the seaside, Aegeus sent out certain monsters of the sea, called Phoces,[98] wherewith his horses, afraid, broke the chariot and rent him in pieces. But at the request of Diana, goddess of chastity, loving her chaste knight Hippolytus, Aesculapius, the first that invented physic, restored him to life again.

Menelaus: son of Atreus, brother to Agamemnon, and king of the city of Sparta.

Vulcan: son of Jupiter and Juno, which being born ill-favoured and liked[99] not Juno, he was cast into the isle Lemnos, where being nourished with apes[100] he became lame of one foot thereby. And he is feigned to be the god of fire and the smith to make thunderbolts for Jupiter. Which asking to marry Minerva, Jupiter's daughter and goddess of wisdom, he was denied. Wherefore Virgil:

> The gods would not vouchsafe that he
> Should at their table sit,
> And to her bed the goddess she
> Would never him admit.[101]

But afterward this gay squire married to Venus, when he had taken her abed with lusty Mars the god of battle.[102] he had framed such fine chains to bind them that they could not get asunder till he had brought all the gods to laugh at the game.

Pasiphaë: wife of Minos king of Crete which loved a stout captain called Taurus, and conceived by him the cruel and deformed minotaur, whom for his fierceness and ill shape the poets feigned to have been half a man and half a bull, and therefore was enclosed in a labyrinth, made by the cunning Daedalus, and there fed with flesh of men.

Hero: a maiden of singular beauty, of the city Sestos in Hellespont.

Leander: a young gentleman of the city Abydos, which a great river did divide from Sestos, where he was wont to swim by night to his lover Hero, and so at last was drowned.

Pyramus: a young gentleman of Babylon which loved Thisbe.

Thisbe: a maid of singular beauty, which when she loved Pyramus exceedingly, and they were kept asunder by their parents, yet one night they escaped out, and had agreed before to have met under a tree without the town. Thisbe, coming thither first, seeing a lion, did flee into the wood; her rail[103] being fallen off, the lion rent it in pieces. Pyramus, coming after, finding the cloth rent, thought that Thisbe had been devoured of some beast, and so slew himself. Which when Thisbe returning again did see, she killed herself with the same sword.

---

[98] Phoces] seals
[99] liked] pleased
[100] apes] This is perhaps a confusion caused by the fact that the god was helped by a people of Lemnos called the Sintians. Peend may have misread this word as *simianus*, ape. Vulcan is usually described as having either been born lame, a factor behind Juno's disgust, or else as having been lamed by the fall.
[101] This would seem to be Peend's own translation of Virgil, *Eclogues*, IV. 62–63.
[102] It is implied that Vulcan only marries Venus after he has captured her with Mars, although in fact she was unfaithful to Vulcan after their marriage.
[103] rail] cloak

Orestes: son of King Agamemnon, which slew his mother Clytemnestra because that she, for love of Aegisthus, had slain his father. And he married Hermione, and after being mad, his most faithful friend Pylades keeping him, he came into the country of Tauris, where according to the custom he should have been slain and sacrificed, but being known of his sister Iphigenia, he slew the king Thoas, and escaped with his sister, and after had his wits perfect again.[104]

Hermione: daughter of Menelaus, and that Helen, so renowned for her beauty, which being a girl was married to Orestes. And when King Pyrrhus, son of the valiant Achilles, had married her afterward, Hermione by letters required him humbly to claim his right and deliver her. And so Orestes slew Pyrrhus and received Hermione again.

Hyacinthus: a young man, of passing beauty.

Mars: god of war, and son of Jupiter and Juno.

Theseus: son of Aegeus, king of Athens, and of Aethra, daughter to Pittheus, king of the City Troezen. A puissant knight, which did many great feats and adventures, as Hercules did. Being but a young man he fought with Hercules against the Amazons, warful[105] women. He slew Creon, king of Thebes, which suffered not men slain in war to be buried.[106] He slew Minotaurus, and delivered his country from the tribute of fourteen noble children, every nine years, sent to Crete to be slain, for that the citizens of Athens had slain Androgeus, son of Minos king of Crete. He slew a monstrous bull which had spoiled the country Attica. He slew Geryon and Procrustes, robbers. And afterward with his faithful friend Pirithous he went to Hell to fetch Proserpina, whom Pluto had stolen from her mother Ceres, goddess of corn, and queen of Sicily. But Pirithous being slain by the three headed hound Cerberus, porter of Hell, Theseus was kept in prison there till he was delivered by mighty Hercules.

Ariadne: daughter to Minos, king of Crete, which by a bottom[107] of thread taught Theseus to come out of the labyrinth after he had killed her brother Minotaurus. She forsook her country and followed him, whom he left in the isle of Naxos. So Bacchus the god of wine took her to wife, and Venus gave her a crown whereon Bacchus set nine stars and fired it in the sky. And so the star is called the Gnossian crown.

Phaedra: daughter of King Minos and Pasiphaë, with her sister Ariadne did fly her country with Theseus, and became his wife after he had forsaken Ariadne.

Adelasie: daughter and only child of the Emperor Otho the third. So exceedingly she was enamoured of the most valiant Aleran, son of a duke of Saxony, that she procured him privily to convey her away, which by the help of an old lady her nurse, he brought to pass. And afterward being robbed of such money as they had provided, they lived long in a wood and made coals for their living, and bore him seven sons there, and afterward by the valiant feats of her eldest son they were known to the emperor, and so had his favour again, and enjoyed the empire after him.

---

[104] These episodes are the subject of Euripides' *Iphigenia in Tauris*.
[105] warful] bellicose
[106] Cf. Sophocles, *Oedipus at Colonus*.
[107] bottom] skein or ball

Juliet: a noble maiden of the city Verona in Italy, which loved Romeus, eldest son of the Lord Montesche,[108] and being privily married together, he at last poisoned himself for love of her. She, for sorrow of his death, slew herself in the same tomb with his dagger.

Tiresias: an old prophet of the city Thebes in Boetia, a country in Attica, and is now called Vandalia.

Diana: daughter of Jupiter and Latona, and sister of Apollo, and is called goddess of hunting and chastity, and is the moon also.

Nymphs: were maidens which followed Diana and, worshipping her, did live solitary in woods, by rivers' sides, and other pleasant places to avoid company, and chiefly used hunting to subdue the tediousness of time.

Actaeon: son of Aristaeus by Autonoë, daughter of Cadmus, builder of the city Thebes, which after he had been a-hunting came by chance to a secret well or spring where he saw Diana naked, washing of herself. Whereat she, taking displeasure, turned him into a hart, and so, as he would have returned home, he was rent in pieces of his own hounds.

> Ovid Epist.
>
> Actaeon once, unwitting, did
> Dian naked see,
> Wherefore unto his hounds she made
> Him then a prey to be.[109]

All which was feigned for that he had spent his substance, and undone himself by hunting and keeping of hounds.[110]

Gismond: only daughter of Tancred, king of Salerne, which loved a servant of her father's, and being taken in adultery together in a cave in the ground, the king caused her lover Guistard to be hanged therefore, and sent his heart unto her, which embracing it, laid it on her breast against her own heart, and drank a cup of poison immediately, whereof dying, she desired that they might be buried together.

FINIS.

---

[108] Montesche] This is how the name is spelled in William Painter's *Palace of Pleasure*. Bandello has 'Montecchio'.
[109] This seems to be Peend's own translation of Ovid's *Tristia*, II. 105–06.
[110] This euhemerizing moralization can be traced back to Palaephatus and was also offered by Golding in the preface to his translation of the *Metamorphoses* (1565).

WILLIAM BARKSTED
MYRRHA, THE MOTHER OF ADONIS (1607)

WILLIAM BARKSTED

MYRRHA, THE MOTHER OF ADONIS (1607)

[*Metamorphoses*, X. 287–528]

Lodovico Dolce, *Le trasformationi* (1553), p. 216

William Barksted[1] was an actor, and at one point was a member of the Children of the King's Revels who acted at the Whitefriars in 1607 and 1608.[2] By 1609 he was working with the Children of the Queen's Revels and took part in the first production of Ben Jonson's *Epicoene*.[3] Later he joined an adult company, The Lady Elizabeth's Men. Even taking into account the fact that young men in their twenties, as well as boys, acted in the children's companies, it is clear that Barksted's *Myrrha* is a very youthful work. Another narrative poem, *Hiren, or the Faire Greek* appeared in 1611, but, as the poet describes this as 'the bashful utterance of a maiden muse', its composition may predate *Myrrha*. It is thought that William Barksted, together with Lewis Machin, had a hand in the writing of *The Insatiate Countess* (first published in 1613 and frequently attributed to John Marston).

Myrrha, The Mother of Adonis is clearly conceived as a prequel to Shakespeare's *Venus and Adonis*, and follows Shakespeare's emphasis on Adonis's indifference. In the final stanza Barksted pays homage to Shakespeare's poem, deprecating his own achievement. The poem reflects the now established conventions of the epyllion,[4] and Barksted (in the manner of Marlowe) confidently weaves new elements, including several etiological digressions, into the story, although parts of *Myrrha* follow Ovid fairly faithfully. The two most striking innovations are the encounters with Cupid and with Poplar, a satyr. Whereas Ovid's Orpheus narrates Myrrha's tale, Barksted makes Myrrha one of his admiring auditors. Cupid has also come to listen to his music and is smitten with desire for the beautiful and innocent girl. Barksted

---

[1] He is also sometimes referred to as Barkstead, Barksteed or Baxter.
[2] The title page of *Hiren* describes him as one of the 'Servants of His Majesty's Revels'.
[3] Ben Jonson, *The Workes of Benjamin Jonson* (London: William Stansby, 1616), p. 600.
[4] See introduction, p. 6.

inspires sympathy for Myrrha by showing her spirited resistance to Cupid's advances, and by strongly hinting that her passion for her father, Cinyras, was maliciously inspired by Cupid's parting kiss.

The poem is usually cited in the context of its relationship with *Venus and Adonis*, and has attracted comparatively little critical attention, although Swinburne describes Barksted as 'a narrative poet of real merit' and Douglas Bush allows that *Myrrha* is 'not without gleams of poetry'.[5] Like H. A., Barksted is perhaps more interesting as an inventive and imaginative reader of Ovid (and other poets) than as an artist. The scansion is sometimes awkward and the reader is too often aware of the poet casting around for a rhyme. But the scene in which Myrrha stages an imaginary debate with her father, imitating his voice, is memorable, as is the character of Poplar, whose relationship with the conflicted narrating voice is discussed further in the introduction.[6]

Only one edition was published. It is conspicuously badly printed and Grosart notes that 'typographical and punctuation errors not only obscure the meaning but again and again make places absolutely unintelligible'.[7] We have suggested several emendations, some following Grosart, which are identified in the notes. Unambiguous typographical errors have been silently corrected. The poem was originally published with additional eclogues by Lewis Machin. These have not been included in this edition, although the commendatory verses by Machin and others have been retained. The poem was reprinted by Grosart in 1876, and a facsimile was included in Paul W. Miller's *Seven Minor Epics* (1967).

EDITIONS

William Barksted, *Mirrha the Mother of Adonis: or, Lust's Prodegies. Whereunto are added certain eclogues by L. M.*[8] (London: John Bache, 1607), STC 575:10.

—, *The Poems of William Barksted*, ed. by Rev. Alexander. B. Grosart ([Manchester]: [C. E. Simms], 1876).

Paul W. Miller, *Seven Minor Epics of the English Renaissance, 1596–24* (Gainesville, FL: Scholars' Facsimiles & Reprints, 1967).

FURTHER READING

Sarah Carter, *Ovidian Myth and Sexual Deviance in Early Modern English Literature* (London: Palgrave Macmillan, 2011).

Jim Ellis, *Sexuality and Citizenship: Metamorphosis in Elizabethan Erotic Verse* (Toronto: University of Toronto Press, 2003).

Noam Flinker, 'Cinyras, Myrrha, and Adonis: Father-Daughter Incest from Ovid to Milton', *Milton Studies*, 14 (1982), 59–74.

M. A. Palmatier, 'A Suggested New Source in Ovid's *Metamorphoses* for Shakespeare's *Venus and Adonis*', *Huntington Library Quarterly*, 24 (1961), 164–69.

---

[5] Algernon Charles Swinburne, *The Age of Shakespeare* (London: Chatto & Windus, 1908), p. 133. Douglas Bush, *Mythology and the Renaissance Tradition in English Poetry* (New York: Norton, 1963), p. 188.
[6] See introduction, pp. 9–10.
[7] *The Poems of William Barksted*, ed. by Rev. Alexander. B. Grosart ([Manchester]: [C. E. Simms], 1876), p. x.
[8] L. M.] These additional eclogues, by Lewis Machin, are not included here.

MYRRHA, THE MOTHER OF ADONIS

Horace

Nanciscetur enim pretium, nomenque poetae.⁹

London. Printed by E. A. for John Bache, and are to be sold at his shop in the Pope's Head Palace, near the Royal Exchange. 1607.

To his beloved, the author

Praise, wheresoe'er't be found, if it be due,
Shall no vain colour need to set it forth;
Why should I idly then extol the worth,
Which here, dear friend, I find belongs to you?
And if I erred, full well the learnèd knew
How wide amiss my mark I taken had,
Since they distinguish can the good from bad,
And through the varnish well discern the hue.
Be glad therefore, this makes for you, and know,   *operates in favour of*
When wiser readers here shall fix their sight,
For virtue's sake, they will do virtue right,
So shalt thou not, friend, unrewarded go.
Then boldly on, good fortune to thy muse,
Should all condemn, thou can'st as well excuse.

I. W.

To his loving friend and kinsman, W. B.

Thamis¹⁰ ne'er heard a song equal to this,
Although the swan¹¹ that owed this present quill   *owned*
Sung to that echo her own epitaph,
As proud to die and render up her wing
To Venus' swan, who doth more pleasing sing.
Produce thy work, and tell the powerful tale
Of naked Cupid and his mother's will.
Myself I do confine from Helicon,¹²   *banish*
As loath to see the other Muses nine,
So immodestly eye shoot,¹³ and gaze upon
Their new born envy, this tenth Muse of thine,
Which in myself I do in thee admire,

---

⁹ Nanciscetur enim pretium, nomenque poetae] *1607* 'nansicetur'. 'For he will win the honour and name of a poet' (Horace, *Ars Poetica*, I. 299).
¹⁰ Thamis] Thames, derived from the Latin 'Tamesis'
¹¹ swan] The poet apparently figures himself and Barksted as two swans, and admits his own inferiority. He perhaps has the seventh stanza of Barksted's poem in his mind.
¹² Helicon] Mount Helicon in Boeotia was sacred to the Muses.
¹³ eye shoot] To shoot one's eyes means to gaze eagerly.

As Aesop's satyr[14] the refulgent fire,
Which may me burn, I mean with amorous flame,
In reading, as the kissing that did him.
And happy Myrrha that he rips thy shame,   *lays bare*
Since he so quaintly doth express thy sin;
   Many would write, but see men's works so rare,
   That of their own they instantly despair.

Robert Glover[15]

To his esteemed friend, W. B.

Not for our friendship, or for hope of gain,
Doth my pen run so swiftly in thy praise;
Court-servile flattery I do disdain,
Envy, like treason, still itself betrays;
This work detraction's sting doth disinherit,
He that gives thee all praise gives but thy merit.

Lewes Machin[16]

To his respected friend, W. B.

Poet, nor art thou without due desert, styled by that name;
Though folly smile, and envy frown, to hear the same;
Yet those who read thy work with due respect,
Will place thee with the worthiest of that sect.
Then let not ignorance nor envy move thee,
Thou hast done well, they do not that reprove thee.
Yet some (true worth ne'er wants an opposite) will carpers be;
Grieve not at this, not virtue's self can scape their obloquy,
But give the reins unto these baser spirits,
Whose judgements cannot parallel thy merits;
Such fools, to seem judicious, take in hand
To censure what they do not understand.
Yet cannot they detract, or wrong thy worth, maugre their spite,   *despite*
For thou dost chant incestuous Myrrha forth with such delight,
And with such golden phrase gild'st o'er her crime,
That what's most diabolical seems divine,
And who so but begins the same to read,

---

[14] This story is not told by Aesop. However, Sir Edward Dyer (1543–1607) wrote a poem about a satyr who attempted to kiss the fire brought to earth by Prometheus.
[15] Glover] Nothing seems to be known of Robert Glover. However, it is possible he was the son of a herald, also called Robert Glover, who was said to have had a son of the same name.
[16] Machin] Lewis Machin (*fl.* 1607–13) was a dramatist who collaborated on *The Dumb Knight* (1608) with Gervase Markham, and may also have collaborated on *The Insatiate Countess*, the Quarto of which was printed in 1613. Barksted's and Machin's revision of the original text by John Marston may have occurred anytime between 1608 and the date of publication.

Each powerful line attracts him to proceed.
Then since he best deserves the palm to wear, who wins the same,
Do thou alone enjoy those sweets which bear thy Myrrha's name,
And ever wear, in memory of her, an anadem[17] of odoriferous myrrh,
And let Apollo think it no dispraise to wear thy myrrh, and join it with his bays.

William Bagnall[18]

MYRRHA, THE MOTHER OF ADONIS

I sing the ruin of a beauteous maid,
    White as my paper, or love's fairest dove.
Shine bright Apollo, Muse be not afraid,
    Although thou chantest of unnatural love;
Great is my quill to bring forth such a birth
As shall abash the virgins of our earth.
    Smoke golden censors upon Paphos'[19] shrine,
    Drink deep, Lenaeus,[20] to this work of mine.[21]

Cupid to Thracia went to hear a song
10   Of Orpheus, to whom even tigers came,
And left their savage nature, if there long
    They did with his sweet melody remain;
Wolves lost their preys, and by signs prayed him sing,
Beasts left the lion, and chose him as their king;
    Cecropian[22] apes did on his music wait,
    Yet of them all, not one could imitate.

('Tis said, when Orpheus died, he did descend
    To the infernal, so the Furies boast,   *underworld*
Where now they give him leave his eyes to bend,
20   Without all fear, on her whom he once lost
By a regardant[23] look, but 'tis not so;
Jove not reserved such music for below,
    But placèd him amongst celestial stars,
    To keep the scorpion, lion, bear from jars.   *discords*

---

[17] anadem] garland
[18] Bagnall] A. K. McIlwraith suggests that Bagnall should be identified with the W.B. who wrote commendatory verses for Massinger's *The Duke of Milan* (1623) and *The Bondsman* (1624) ('"W.B." and Massinger', *Review of English Studies*, 4 (1928), 326–27). Bagnall wrote a prefatory poem which is included in a selection of metrical versions of the psalms by members of the Inns of Court. This manuscript (Oxford, Bodleian Library, MS Rawlinson poetry [or poet.] 61) was transcribed by Robert Crane in the 1620s.
[19] Paphos] a city in Cyprus, associated with Venus, the Roman equivalent of the Greek Aphrodite
[20] Lenaeus] an appellation of Dionysus (Bacchus), god of wine, meaning 'the loosener'
[21] 1–8] The indentation in *1607* is irregular. This pattern, used in the opening pages, has been retained here throughout.
[22] Cecropian] Cecrops I, a mythical king of Athens, was supposed to have been half man, half fish. Perhaps Barksted is alluding to the fact that apes seem half human.
[23] Regardant] In heraldry, 'regardant' is used to denote an animal looking backwards over its shoulder.

    For ever since the fall of Phaëthon
        That then displacèd them, they were at strife
    For their degrees, till his alluring tone,
        Who, though in death, hath the office of his life,
    Though more divinely, and where he attracts
30   More glorious bodies to admire his acts,
        Fair[24] stranger shape of creature and of beast,
        With his concordant tunes, placed them in rest.)

    The ditty was (and Cupid lent an ear)
        Upon the death of his Eurydice,
    Which still he sung, as if his former fear
        Of losing her was now, or else would be.
    The echo beat the noise up to the spheres,
    And to his passionate song gods bent their ears;
        It was a sign he was new come from hell,
40   Their tunes so sad, he imitates so well.

    Such passion it did strike upon the earth,
        That Daphne's root groaned for Apollo's wrong;
    Hermaphrodite wept showers, and wished his birth
        Had never been, or that he more had clung
    To Salmacis, and Clytie grieved in vain
    Leucothoë's wrong, the occasion of her bane.[25]
        'My wilful eye', this should the burden be,
        'Hath robbed me of twice slain Eurydice.'

    Cycnus,[26] still proud, though he confuted be   *confounded*
50   For Phaëthon's loss, would needs afresh complain,
    Thinking therewith to sing as sweet as he,
        But pitiless he sung, and died in vain.
    Echo was pleased with voice-resounding brim,   *bank*
    As proud to lose her shape to answer him.
        Hither resorted more than well could hear,
        But on, my Muse, and speak what chancèd there.

    Amongst the rest of Vesta-vowèd[27] girls,
        Came Myrrha, whose thoughts no guile then knew,
    Like a bright diamond circlèd[28] with pearls,
60   Whose radiant eye dealt lustre to the hue
    Of all the dames, whose face, so far above,
    Though the rest beauteous all, unwounded made Love love,[29]

---

[24] Fair] Grosart suggests 'far'.

[25] 41–46] Orpheus's song first causes two reluctant objects of pursuit, Daphne and Hermaphroditus, to reproach themselves, and then affects a nymph, Clytie, who is filled with guilt because her jealousy caused her to betray Leucothoë, beloved of Apollo, to her father (*Met.*, III. 234–55).

[26] Cycnus] a kinsman of Phaëthon, metamorphosed into a swan (*Met.*, II. 367–80)

[27] Vesta-vowèd] Vesta was the Roman goddess of the hearth. Her priestesses, the Vestal Virgins, tended her sacred fire in Rome. The reference to a Roman deity is anachronistic.

[28] diamond circlèd] Grosart suggests that diamond is disyllabic here, and circlèd trisyllabic.

[29] Love love] In a reversal of the normal pattern it is Cupid ('Love') who is smitten in this encounter, while Myrrha remains unwounded by his arrows. The length of the line underlines the significance of the moment.

For never since Psyche was made a star
Did he see nature excel art so far.

He changed his shape, his wings he oft hath torn,
    And like a hunter to this nymph he came,
With gold-tipped javelin and a bugle horn,
    Such as they bear to make the lion tame;
First he did kiss her hand, which then did melt
70   With love's impression, Cupid the like felt;
    Struck dumb, he stood in an unwonted guise,
    Such magic[30] beauty carries in her eyes.

At length quoth he, 'Should I not say I love,
    I should both Cupid and his mother wrong;
By thee, fair maid,[31] a power far above,
    My heart is the true index of my tongue,
And by my naked words you may discover,
I am not traded like a common lover.   *practised*
    Rare objects rare amazements breed, 'tis true,
80   And their effects are tried in me by you.

My barren brain can bless me with no store
    Of able epithets, so what praise I give   *suitable*
Makes not you richer though it makes me poor,
    Therefore in vain against the stream I strive;
Th'o'er curious painter, meaning to excel,
Oft mars the work the which before was well,
    And he shall dazzled be, and tired soon,
    That levelleth his shafts to hit the moon.'

With this, she turned her blushing head aside,
90   And veiled her face with lawn, not half so white,
That even the blending roses were espied,   *her cheeks*
    Despite the clouds that hid them in despite;[32]
She threw her thin breath through the lawn, and said: *directed*
'Leave, gentle youth, do not thus snare a maid,
    I came to Orpheus' song, good then[33] forbear,
    It is his tune, not yours, can charm mine ear.'

'Let Orpheus learn', quoth he, 'of thee to sing,[34]
    Bid him charm men, Myrrha, as thou can'st do;
Let him tame man, that is the lion's king,
100   And lay him prostrate at his feet below,
As thou can'st do; nor Orpheus nor the spheres

---

[30] magic] Probably a noun here rather than an adjective, although it is possible that 'carries' is being used intransitively.
[31] By thee, fair maid] He swears by Myrrha, rather than by himself or his mother Venus.
[32] 92] In this example of *epanadiplosis*, when the same word begins and ends a line, the word 'despite' is used in two different senses.
[33] good then] 'good then' seems to be used here with a meaning similar to the phrase 'good now', which the *OED* defines as 'an interjectional expression denoting acquiescence, entreaty, expostulation, or surprise'.
[34] 97] an ironic reminder that Orpheus does narrate Myrrha's story (*Met.*, X)

Have tones like thee, to ravish mortal ears;
    Yea, were this Thracian harper judge to tell,
As thee[35] he'd swear he sung not half so well.

Nor dying swans, nor Phoebus when he loves,
    Equals thy voice, though he in music courts;   *woos*
And as the god[36] whose voice the firm earth moves,
    Making the terrors of the great his sports,
Whose first word struck into the Chaos light,[37]
110   So if that contrary thou take delight,
    At thy word, darkness would o'ercloud the air,[38]
And the fairest day give place to thee, more fair.

Fame hath resigned her lasting trump[39] to thee,
    As to the worthier; then thy fame display —
Tell Venus thou art fairer far than she,
    For thine own worth becomes thee best to say;
Time will stand still, the sun in motion stay,[40]
Sirens be mute to hear thee speak of Myrrha,
    Thy voice, if heard in the low shades should be,
120   Would a third time fetch back Eurydice.

Give ear, eternal wonder, to a swain,
    'Twas writ in stars that I should see that face,
And seeing love, and in that love be slain,
    If beauty pity not my wretched case.
Fortune and love, the stars and powers divine,
Have all betrayed me to those eyes of thine.
    O prove not then more crueller than they,
    Love's shafts[41] and fate's wheels, who hath power to stay.'

'Stay there', quoth she, 'give back those powers their own,
130   Or not impose their powerful force on me;
Have I the least word or the least glance thrown,
    To make you attribute what's destiny
Unto my beauty? If love and fate you wound,
Throw vows to them, their altars are soon found,
    Would'st thou have me pity before they do?
    Love's blind,[42] and fortune's deaf, so I am too.

---

[35] As thee] The phrase seems to have been awkwardly moved to the beginning of the line for the sake of the rhyme.

[36] And as the god] Barksted goes on to lose sight of the way the sentence opens here.

[37] 107–09] No god or Titan in Greek mythology is clearly identified as the world's creator. Ovid expresses uncertainty as to whether some god, or simply nature, brought an end to Chaos (*Met.*, I. 21). Barksted's description, with its emphasis on the divine word, seems more influenced by a Judaeo-Christian view of creation.

[38] 111] Cupid's elaborate compliment is also probably an ironic reference to the eclipse which marks Myrrha's fall at *Met.*, X. 448–50.

[39] trump] sound of the trumpet, indicating triumph or renown

[40] stay] cease moving. The reference to upheaval in the heavens, particularly when coupled with an invitation to hubris, is foreboding as well as flattering.

[41] Love's shafts] It is ironic that Cupid should deplore the effects of his own arrows.

[42] Love's blind] another ironic reminder of the identity of Myrrha's admirer

I know not love, sure 'tis a subtle thing,
  I, by these blushes that thy charms have raised,
T'allay more[43] quiet, tell love's little king,
140   I serve a mistress he himself hath praised,
Though he envy, a rare and sacred flower,
Whom he had will to wrong, but never power.'
    Now Cupid hangs the head, and melts in shame,
    For she did utter Vesta's holy name.

And as you see a woman teeming young,   *pregnant with*
  Bearing the growing burden of her womb,
Missing the dainty she hath looked for long,
  Falls straight in passionate sickness, pale and dumb,
For seeing she hath lost it, will not tell
150   For what she in this forcèd passion fell.   *unnatural*
    So when his hopes were lost, he would not say
    What was the cause, but this to her did lay.   *expound*

'Virgin, beware that fire within thy breast,
  To Vesta dedicate, do not expire,
As she must wary be that is the best
  To keep it, it is known no lasting fire;
The fuel, cold fruitless virginity,
Which, if zeal blow not violent, will soon die;
    This strict's a virgin's life, and who but knows,
160   That love and chastity were ever foes.

And if e'er love assail those virgins' forts,
  Those ivory bulwarks that defend your heart,
Though he be king of sports, he never sports,
  When as he wounds, but plays the tyrant's part,
And so much more he will triumph o'er thee,
By how much thou contents[44] his deity;
    I know you to be chaste, but yet fair maid,
    If e'er you love, you'll find what I have said.'

'Sir', quoth she, 'when I love, you shall be mine,
170   But know the time when you shall claim me yours:
When as the fire's extinct at Vesta's shrine,
  And Venus leaves to haunt the Paphian[45] bowers,   *ceases*
When men are perfect friends, tigers at peace,
Discord in heaven and powers divine do cease,
    When fortune sleeps, and the north star doth move,
    When turtles leave to mourn their mates, I'll love.'

---

[43] T'allay more] perhaps used here to mean 'alloy, dilute'. 'More' might be a misprint for 'my'.

[44] By how much thou contents] It is possible that Cupid is saying that the more beautiful and lovable someone is, the more she will suffer from love. 'Content' is here used as a transitive verb meaning to please or gratify (OED v1 b); Myrrha of course 'contents' Cupid and is made to suffer greatly. But one might also speculate whether 'content' is a misprint for 'contemns', or 'contests'. It would seem more logical that Cupid, at this point, should warn Myrrha that those who scorn love are most likely to become its victims.

[45] Paphian] The adjective is derived from Paphos, the city in Cyprus sacred to Venus.

E'er this was ended, Orpheus' song was done,
    And all the virgins fell into their ranks;
Each took their leave of him, so did the sun,
180   Who now was posting to the western banks,
And the wild beasts, whom he had made more tame,
Seemed to depart with reverence at his name;
    Each one gave place to Myrrha, as their duty,
    She being preferred in state, first as in beauty.

Now Cupid of her his last leave doth take,
    So have I seen a soul and body part;
He begs a chaste kiss for her mother's[46] sake,
    And vows she shall be sovereign of his heart,
But whether he dissembling did it, or 'twas fate,
190   (As extremest love turns to the direst hate,
    Being repulsed) but this kiss did inspire
    Her breast with an infernal and unnamed desire.[47]

Night, like a mask, was entered heaven's great hall,   *masquer*
    With thousand torches ushering the way;[48]
The compliments of parting were done all,
    And homewards Orpheus chanteth many a lay;
Venus had sent her coach, drawn by a dove,
For little Cupid, the great god of love,
    And this hath sprung; as men have sayen of yore,   *made to fly up*
200   For Myrrha's sake, he vowed to love no more.

Black as my ink[49] now must my verse commence —
    You blushing girls, and parents silver-gray,
As far as Thrace from us, so far from hence
    Go, that you may not hear me say
A daughter did with an adulterous head,
And heavy lust, press down her father's bed;
    Such songs as these more fit the Tartar's[50] ears,
    Had Orpheus sung it,[51] beasts had poured out tears.

Unhallowed lust, for love lies drowned in poison,
210   In what black ornament shall I attire thee,
Since I must write of thy so sad confusion?
    Shall I say Cupid with his brand did fire thee,
Accuse the Fates, or thee shall I accuse?
Myrrha weeps yet, only say this, my Muse:
    Wise destiny, true love, and mortal thought
    Would ne'er confirm this; this the Furies brought.   *sanction*

---

[46] her mother's] There seems no reason for Cupid to invoke Myrrha's mother at this point. It seems likely that 'his' is intended as Venus is an emblem of love.
[47] 192] The unexpected Alexandrine reflects the chaotic and unnatural nature of her passion.
[48] 193–94] The same description of night appears in the final speech of *The Insatiate Countess*.
[49] Black as my ink] This comparison echoes the earlier description of Myrrha as 'white as my paper'.
[50] Tartar's] Tartars were proverbially savage and warlike.
[51] Had Orpheus sung it] In Ovid Orpheus *is* the narrator.

She loves her father, daughter ne'er loved so,
    For as her mother loved, so loved she him,
Thirsting in fire those softer sweets to know,
220   Amidst whose waves Venus in pride doth swim;
So young she was yet, that her father kissed her,
Which she so duly looks for, he ne'er missed her,
    Yet could he have conceived, as he did after,   *understood*
    Those kisses relish much unlike a daughter.

Give to her gold of Ophir,[52] Indian shells,
    Clothe her with Tyrian purple,[53] skin of beast,
Perfume her ways with choice Arabian smells,
    Present her with the phoenix in her nest,
Delight her ear with song of poets rare,[54]
230 All these with Cinyras might nought compare.
    'The comfort of the mind being tane away,
    Nectar not pleaseth, nor ambrosia.'

The feast of Bacchus at this present time
    Was by the giddy Maenades intended;   *directed*
There Myrrha danced, and Orpheus sung in rhyme,
    Crowned with green thyrses;[55] now, the triumphs ended,
With praise to Bacchus all depart with spright[56]
Unto their feasts, feasts that devour the night,
    For lo, the stars in travel in the sky,
240   Brought forth their brightness to each waking eye.

High midnight came, and she to bedward hies,
    Pretending rest, to beguile nature's rest;
Anon the gloomy gallery she spies,
    Toward her chamber, and the first that blessed
Her care-filled eyes, her father's picture was,
Armed but the face, although it dumb, alas;   *except for*
    She asked and if he called; seeing no reply,   *whether*
    She answered for her father, and said 'aye'.

'Daughter', quoth she, 'why art thou thus alone?
250   Let doves so mourn girl, that hath lost their mates;
Thine is to come, then prithee, cease thy moan,
    Care should not dwell with great and high estates;
Let her that needs, and is not fair at all,
Repine at fortune; love shall be thy thrall,
    Winged as he is, and armèd; thou shalt see,
    I have the power to give, and give him thee.'[57]

---

[52] Ophir] a region mentioned in the Bible and associated with great wealth. Its location and identity are uncertain.

[53] Tyrian purple] a prized purple dye made from molluscs, particularly associated with Tyre

[54] 225–29] Barksted perhaps has the story of Pygmalion, Myrrha's ancestor, in mind at this point. The sculptor courted the statue with shells, Tyrian cloths, birds and jewellery (*Met.*, X. 260-69).

[55] thyrses] Thyrsi are staffs crowned with ivy, but Barksted seems to use the word to signify a garland.

[56] with spright] 'In a sprightly manner' seems the intended meaning, although 'spright' usually means 'spirit'.

[57] 254–56] It is ironic, given the poem's opening episode, that Cinyras promises that Cupid shall be her servant. The unintentional ambiguity of his final promise, to give her love, is a nice touch, particularly as it has been deliberately planted in 'his' words by Myrrha.

>'Father', quoth she, and spoke with smaller voice, *softer*
>   'Nature hath made me yours, yours I must be;
> You choose my choice, for in you lies my choice.'
> 260   Hereat she starts, as what not fears the guilty,
> Thinking the shadow knew her double sense,
> And blushing, in strange fear departeth thence,
>   Blaming herself for uttering her black fault,
>   To him who armèd stood 'gainst her assault.
>
> Anon she spies many a youthful lord,
>   In several tables, each in several guise, *paintings, distinctive*
> Whose pictures they had sent with one accord,
>   To show their manly features to her eyes,
> Whose dumbed, persuasive images were placed,
> 270   To see if any in her looks were graced;[58]
>   But here in vain their fair assays do prove,
>   For had they spake they could not win her love.
>
> Over her mother's shape a veil she drew,
>   And weeping said, 'May I ne'er see thee more;
> Poor abused image, dost not turn thy hue,
>   To see so foul an object thee before?
> Did'st thou but know what's sprung from out thy womb,
> Thy shape could speak whilst thou thyself stood dumb;
>   Art would claim nature in thy heavy woes,
> 280   Thy shape have limbs, thy limbs be stiff as those.'[59]
>
> Anon she leapt on it with ardent heat,[60]
>   And full of tears, yet falls upon her back,
> Wishing, even in that grief, the lustful feat
>   Were now performed — women oft longings lack;[61]
> Down sunk she, down, and with so deep impress,
> That had Hermaphroditus been there, he might guess
>   Salmacis were again his prostitute, *devotee*
>   Or one more fair than to deny her suit.[62]
>
> A strange conceit had now possessed her brain,
> 290   Nigh equal to her lust, thought innocent; *guileless*
> She gave up to desire, and leaps amain
>   From the bruised bed, with bloody framed intent
> To hang herself; O me, most woeful theme.

---

[58] if any in her looks were graced] if any are favoured by her glance
[59] 280] Myrrha seems to suggest that if her mother knew her secret she would be transfixed while her painting would come to life.
[60] There is perhaps a missing stanza here, returning us to the portrait of Cinyras.
[61] lack] The sense here doesn't seem fully clear. It is printed '(woemen oft longings lack' with no closing bracket. Lack may be a misprint for 'slack' (slake).
[62] Or one more fair than to deny her suit] *1607* 'or one more farre, then to denie her suite'. But Barksted is probably suggesting that she is like a second Salmacis, but one so beautiful that Hermaphroditus would have responded to her advances.

She now espied an high and sturdy beam —
   Many have lived to an unpitied death,
Who might have died sometimes with famèd breath.[63]   *at an earlier time*

Yet doth she think what terror death would be,
   And on her heart imprints his character;[64]   *distinctive mark*
Fain would she die, yet first would pleasèd be
300   With damnèd lust, which death could not deter:
'O sin', says she, 'thou must be nature's slave;
In spite of fate, go to a pleasing grave.
   When I have sinned, send, Jove, a thunder stroke,
   And spare thy chosen tree, the harmless oak.'

She thinks again, and sees nor time nor place
   To quench the thirstiness of her parched blood;
Time still ran on with an averted face,[65]
   And nothing but her passions did her good;
This thought confounds her, and she is resolved
310   In death's bleak azure arms to be involved.
   Fates, you are women, save your modesties;
   She'll kill herself, you need but close her eyes.

And like as when some sudden ecstasy,
   Seizeth the nature of a sickly man,
When he's discerned to swoon, straight by and by
   Folk to[66] his help confusedly have ran,
And seeking with their art to fetch him back,
Too many throng, that he the air doth lack;
   So Myrrha's thoughts confusedly did stound her,   *stun*
320   Some adding comfort, whilst the rest confound her.[67]

Like to a fountain's head, so showed her head,[68]
   From whence, since passion first took hold of her,
Two springs did run thorough each flower-filled mead,
   And at her lips stayed, where she Cinyr   *Cinyras*
Would so have done; her face with tears ran o'er,
Like Hebe's[69] nectar showed, spilt on heaven's floor.
   Or as the blooms in May the dew drops bears,
   So Myrrha's cheeks look, sprinkled with her tears.

---

[63] 295–96] Barksted suggests that many might have enjoyed a good reputation if they had only died earlier. Yet again, he seems to articulate a classical rather than a Christian attitude towards suicide.

[64] 298] 'Character' is generally used to signify some physical mark or symbol, and 'imprints' thus also has a literal force.

[65] 307] The common idiom, time running, shades into anthropomorphism at the end of the line.

[66] to] *1607* 'by'

[67] 313–18] Malone suggests that Barksted was influenced by a similar image in *Measure for Measure*, II. 4. 24. Angelo compares his rushing blood to 'foolish throngs' which try to assist a fainting man but only hinder his breathing. See *The Plays and Poems of William Shakespeare in Sixteen Volumes*, ed. by Edmond Malone (Dublin: John Exshaw, 1794), I, p. 290.

[68] head] The half-punning repetition of 'head' may be compared with Ovid's observation that Myrrha's *medulla* (which means both pith and marrow) remained the same after her metamorphosis (*Met.*, X. 492).

[69] Hebe's] Hebe was the cupbearer of the gods.

Her hair, that with such diligence was used
330   To be combed up, and did like clouds appear,
Where many spangles, star-like, were infused,
    To attend the lustre of so bright a hair,
Whose beams, like bright Arachne's[70] web composed,
Taught Pallas a new envy, now unlosed,   *unloosed*
    Hiding her face, yet making it seem rarer,
    As blazing comet's train makes the star fairer.

Despair, that teacheth holy ones to die,
    When as affliction ministers her part,
Had breathing now in Myrrha, and well nigh,
340   Like Venus, made her grasp a flaming heart;[71]
Cupid was born at Etna, a hot sprite,
Whose violence takes edge off from delight,
    For men deep loving oft themselves so waste,
    That proffered dainties they want power to taste.

Sprengius, *Metamorphoses Ovidii* (1563), p. 125ʳ

Digress no farther, lest thou prove obscene,
    But tell by this how Nurse had broke the door,
And trembling both through age and fear,
    Forgot the natural sense she had before,
Yet with her outcries, from the shades of death
350   Called Myrrha's spright, who with unwilling breath   *spirit*
    Re-enters flesh, scorning to give it grace
    With wonted beauty that adorned her face.

---

[70] Arachne's] *Met.*, VI. 1–145. Arachne and Barksted's Myrrha, in different ways, are both victims of divine resentment.
[71] flaming heart] In the first sonnet of Dante's *Vita Nuova* the lady is forced by Cupid to eat a burning heart.

She took the halter,[72] and held up her chin,
    Chafing her temples with a violent heat,
Making her soul return with torments in,
    As it went out, being come unto retreat;
Nurse heaved her trembling body on the bed,
Where, sinking as in grave, she seemèd dead;
    Chaste had my verse been, blessed Myrrha's hap,
    If here my pen could write thy epitaph.

When having gotten ope her heavy eyes,
    Life mocking death, with a fresh crimson hue,
She thus bespake: 'if there be sorceries,
    Philtres, enchantments, any fury new,
That can inspire with irreligious fire
The breast of mortal, that untamed desire
    Possesseth me, and all my body's merit
    Shows like a fair house, haunted with a spirit.

The four and twenty winds are not so fierce
    As what doth blow the fuel in my breast,
Not the soft oil Apollo did disperse
    On Phaëthon's brow,[73] to keep his sun-beamed crest
From face of heavenly fires, could aught prevail
'Gainst raging brands which my poor heart assail;
    Scorched with material flames, we soon do die,
    And, to purge sins, we embrace purgatory.[74]

But this a heat that nor in life or death
    Can render any humour but despair,
Nor can it with the short cut of my breath
    Take hence my shame, that shall survive mine heir,
Nor can the act, after 'tis done, content,
But brings with it eternal punishment,
    Lesseneth the pleasure of the world to come,
    Gives the judge leave,[75] and strikes the guilty dumb.'

The jealous nurse did apprehend her strait,[76]   *solicitous*
    Yet would extract the quintessence of all:
'And therefore child', quoth she, 'use no deceit,
    But tell me freely whence these tears do fall.
I am thy nurse, and from my agèd breast,
Thou had'st thy second being; tell the rest,
    I do conjure thee, by these silver hairs,
    Which are grown white the sooner in thy cares.

---

[72] halter] a rope with a noose
[73] Phaëthon's brow] *Met.*, II. 122–24.
[74] 375–76] A real fire will quickly kill someone, bringing relief from suffering, and the fires of purgatory may be embraced as they purge away one's sin.
[75] Gives the judge leave] This seems to mean 'gives the judge the authority or excuse to be severe'.
[76] strait] It is unclear whether the nurse understands her plight, 'strait', or understands her immediately, 'straight'.

> If any orpèd witch of Thessaly[77] *furious*
>   Have power upon thee, gentle girl, relate;
> Or if thou have profaned some deity,
>   We shall some mystic fires propagate,
> To atone with them; or if with barbarous hand,
> Devoid of thy first chastity thou stand,
>   Unfold to me; griefs uttered find redress,
> 400   Fires undiscerned burn the more pitiless.
>
> Or if the son of beauty shoot at thee
>   His fiery shafts,[78] O tell me, and the rather
> Because thy confidence shall answered be,
>   With this my child — I'll hide it from thy father.'
> As doth a dying man hold fast what so he grasps,
> So she her fervent arms 'bout her nurse clasps,
>   And nuzzles once more 'twixt those dugs her face,
>   Whilst o'er those islands flow salt tears apace.
>
> That word of 'father' was, like Perseus' shield,[79]
> 410   To make the poor maid stone; now Nurse doth threat,
> Unless she will in gentle manner yield,
>   She would tomorrow show how, in a heat,
> She would have made away her desperate life,
> And she must tell the man that forced that strife
>   Within her breast. Through fear she[80] thus did frame,
>   And made her tongue the trumpet of her shame.
>
> Her voice half stopped with sighs, O fatal voice,
>   Pronounced these words, yet did the accents fail:
> 'How blessèd is my mother in her choice,
> 420   How fully she with nature did prevail.'
> This said, her blushing face sinks in her shroud,[81]
> Like Cynthia muffled in an envious cloud,
>   When lo, the dying taper in his tomb,[82]
>   Gave darkness to itself and to the room.
>
> Now had she time to wail, and well she might,
>   Guilty of sorrow; there might you have seen,
> As glow-worms add a tincture to the night,
>   Glimmering in pallid fire upon some green,
> Mixed with the dew, so did her eyes appear,
> 430   Each golden glance joined with a dewy tear;

---

[77] Thessaly] Thessaly, in Greece, was particularly associated with witches. One example is Erichtho, who appears in Lucan's *Pharsalia*, VI. 507–69.
[78] His fiery shafts] an ironic reference to Cupid
[79] Perseus' shield] It was the Gorgon Medusa, rather than Perseus's polished shield, which turned people to stone. The shield protected him from the Gorgon, allowing him to look at her reflection while he fought her.
[80] she] i.e. Myrrha
[81] shroud] This could mean simply a garment, but the additional meaning, 'winding-sheet', may also be present.
[82] tomb] presumably a reference to the lantern or sconce

Oft shut her eyes, like stars that portend ill,
With bloody deluge they their orbs did fill.

The nurse, amated with the latter words,   *dismayed*
   Whose agèd hairs stood up like silver wire,
Knew speech was vain, where will the scope affords,[83]
   And whispering softly, says, 'child, thy desire
I'll put into thy arms, sleep seize thy head,
'Tis now night's noon, all but the stars seem dead;
   Our vanities, like fireworks, will ascend,
440   Until they break, uncertain where to end.'

Never did mortal with a vicious thought
   Wish to bring vice's embryon to a form,   *embryo*
But still the prince of darkness to them brought   *invariably*
   Occasion's forelock,[84] which they off have torn;
Sin like a cedar shadows all our good,
While virtue's bounded like a narrow flood;
   As see now, how the occasion of misfortune,
   Myrrha's much abusèd mother did importune.[85]

Now came the time of Ceres' sacred rite,
450   And mysteries, when all wives young and old,
Clothèd in veils, all of transparent white,
   Kneel to her, and to the Attic[86] priest unfold
The firstlings of the field, wreathed gilded corn,
Chaplets of dill, plucked in a blushing morn,
   And many such; nor may they husbands see
   In nine days, till they end their mystery.

Now Nurse was double diligent, watching her time,
   And told old Cinyras a lovely maid
Sighed for him, and still with cups of wine,
460   Betwixt each word his palate she assayed.
Heated with wines, he had the nurse repair,
And bring to him the maid that was so fair.
   Bacchus and Venus, wine and frolic lust,
   Are sworn to blood, and keep together must.

Myrrha no sooner heard this glad reply,
   But as a poor bird, long time in a snare,
Ready for famine and her woe to die,
   Whom an unskilful fowler, unaware,

---

[83] where will the scope affords] where desire, 'will', has the power to attain its end
[84] Occasion's forelock] The idea of seizing the personified figure of Occasion by the forelock was proverbial. In Alciato's book of emblems, the *Emblematum liber* (1531), it is explained that the back of the head is bald because, once an opportunity is let slip, it cannot be retrieved.
[85] 447–48] Virtue's natural disadvantage against vice is reflected in the fact that Myrrha's mother unwittingly enabled her own betrayal.
[86] Attic] pertaining to Attica, or Athens

	Hath given freedom, to her food doth haste —
470	So Myrrha thought each hour an age was past
	In her strict torment, but being 'scaped away,
	Her woes forgot, she thinks upon her prey.[87]

And as she did ascend those stairs to lust,
   In the midway she heard her father speak,
And ne'er lay partridge closer to the dust,
   At sound o' the falcon's bell, than she, too weak
To encounter or resist; and fears are such,
In love, by love, that they increase love much.[88]
   Love, like to monarchs, hath his state high reared,
480   Who[89] ever will be loved where they are feared.

To a hundred several passions she doth yield,
   And as we see in autumn of the year,
Some gallant oak stand ready to be felled,
   Upon whose ribs a hundred wounds appear,
Forced by the brawny arms of hinds unlithe,[90]   *servants*
Who works a passage to the weeping pith,[91]
   Uncertain, though wind-shaken, where to fall,
   So stood her mind, doubtful of rest at all.

Nurse opes the door and brings her to the bed,
490   The darkness of the night abated shame
And leaves her, that must leave her maidenhead,
   To the begetter of his own defame;
With faltering hams,[92] having got 'twixt the sheets,
In fearful lust this Prodegiae[93] meets;
   He begs a kiss, then blushed she as he spake it,
   Yet he must give it, she wants power to take it.

Now trembling lay she by her father's side,
   Like silly dove within the eagle's gripe,
Nor does she use soft shrieks as doth a bride,
500   I mean a maid,[94] when as the fruit so ripe
Of maidenhead is forcèd from their womb —

---

[87] her prey] Myrrha was first compared to a captive bird but is herself a predator.

[88] In love, by love, that they increase love much] Fears which beset one in the context of love, 'in love', and which are caused by that love, 'by love', work to increase love.

[89] Who] i.e. the monarchs

[90] unlithe] Perhaps a misprint for 'unnethe', 'with difficulty'. The word 'unlithe' is not listed in the *OED*.

[91] 485–86] The subject of 'works' must be either 'arms' or 'hinds', even though the verb does not agree with these plural nouns. The reference to 'weeping pith' is not derived from Ovid, and clearly anticipates Myrrha's own metamorphosis into myrrh.

[92] faltering hams] 'Ham' here means the back of the knee or thigh. This slightly strange phrase is apparently borrowed from Golding: 'with that her faltering hams did quake' (*Met.*, X. 526).

[93] Prodegiae] The word is capitalized and italicized in *1607*. It seems that Barksted wants to include both Myrrha and Cinyras within it, as an unnatural hybrid.

[94] I mean a maid] Perhaps the poet is playing on the similarity between the word 'bride' and some spellings of 'bird,' such as 'brid' or 'bridde'.

Her father's arms to her was as a tomb;
   She, dead[95] in pleasure, durst not show her voice,
Lest Cinyras should know this fair foul choice.

But when that Cupid once had whetted her,
   She twines her lily stalks about his neck;
So clings young ivy 'bout the aged oak there,
   Venus doth smile,[96] but frowning Juno[97] checks.   *takes offence*
Their stolen delight no nuptial tapers shone,[98]   *caused to shine*
510 No virgin belt untied,[99] but all undone;
   The Athenian god[100] kindled no hallowed fires,
Dark was the night, suiting to their desires.

The morrow came, toiled with wakes and lust   *exhausted*
   She leaves her father; when as the rising sun,
Covering the eastern pines and mountain dust,
   Spied Myrrha from her couch of sin to run,
Then blushed he first, and backward would ha fled,
And ever since in's rising he's still red;[101]
   Ne'er turquoise[102] was at sick blood more estranged,
520 Than Myrrha, when her chastity was changed.

Oft would she lean against her father's knee,
   And tie his garter in a true love's knot,
And then undo't again, as to show she
   Were undone, yet he conceived it not,
And, woman-like, that keep not secrets long,
She showed her love in dumb shows without tongue;
   Her lust she knew, yet hardly it concealed,
Like fairy's treasure, vanished if revealed.

A third night came, darker than shores below,
530 When Cinyras, father of fearful lust,
Willing to see the soul that did bestow
   So many pleasures on him (Jove is just)
Did reach a taper, whose confusive light   *confusing*
Struck like a blasting at that horrid sight;
   The light fell from him, loathing his defame,
Things senseless oft are moved when men not shame.

---

[95] dead] Her moral death and her sexual pleasure are both implied, given the frequent use of 'die' at this period to signify orgasm.
[96] Venus doth smile] *1607* 'Venus smile'. Grosart suggests that 'doth' should be added.
[97] Juno] the goddess who presided over marriage
[98] 508–09] The syntax of this section isn't fully clear. In *1607* 'checks' is followed by a full stop. If this reflects the poet's intentions then 'shone', in the next line, must be used transitively, to mean 'illuminated'. But it is possible that the full stop is incorrect, and that 'stolen delight' is the object of 'checks' rather than 'shone'.
[99] untied] A Roman bride had her belt tied in a special knot which the groom had to untie.
[100] Athenian god] Hymenaios, or Hymen, was sometimes identified as a beautiful Athenian youth.
[101] 517–18] This etiology seems to be Barksted's innovation.
[102] turquoise] The turquoise was meant to brighten or fade depending on the health of its wearer.

>At length, with bloody eye fixèd on her,
>   Out of an ivory scabbard hanging by,
>He drew a monumental scimitar,
>   Thinking with death that both their shames should die. 540
>But night, that oft befriended her,[103] with sin
>In her black womb too, did her freedom win,
>   For through the dark she slipped, and left her sire
>   To mourn his fate, not execute his ire.
>
>Sped with her lust, and flying thence apace,
>   In fears and trembling — fear doth give us eyes —
>For safety, to the gods she lifts her face,
>   And her clasped hands, to what she now not sees.
>Jove's brow was dark, Boötes[104] had amain
>Driven his oxen to the lower plain, 550
>   Phoebe fled heaven; her[105] face no tincture bears,
>   Because she saw a deed worthy her tears.
>
>The morning came, where yet the fatal print
>   Of Myrrha lay upon the pillow. Cinyr[106] he,
>Clogged with distress, a father's curse did hint,
>   Upon that place of foul inchastity.
>The sight of what we loathe breeds loathing more,
>And virtue once renounced engenders store;[107]   *plenty*
>   Leave we him toused in care, for worldly we   *tossed*
>   Love to leave great men in their misery. 560
>
>Seven winters' nights she fled before the moon,
>   Who knew the unchaste act she had enforced;
>Through Araby, in fear, she posteth soon
>   To odorous Panchaia, whose confines divorced   *separated*
>Her father's lands; here grew all choicest fumes
>That to Jove's temples often men presumes,[108]
>   And on his altars them accumulate,
>   And how they first sprung, hear hereof the fate.
>
>Hebe now banished from th'etherian bowl,   *heavenly*
>   Upon a feast day 'mongst the gods above, 570
>Where 'twas made lawful, all without control

---

[103] Befriended her] In *1607* the comma is placed after 'sin', at the end of the line, rather than after 'her'. But the words 'in her black womb too' don't seem to make full sense in isolation.

[104] Boötes] The Greek name (pronounced 'boo-OH-teez') of the constellation signifies 'ox-driver'.

[105] her] i.e. Phoebe's. The etiology explaining the moon's colour matches that to account for the redness of the setting sun.

[106] Cinyr] *1607* 'Cynix'. 'Cinyr' is used elsewhere as an abbreviated form of the name, and it seems likely that this was the poet's intention here.

[107] 557–58] The meaning here isn't fully clear. Does 'virtue once renounced' also engender store of 'loathing'? A more expected point might be that 'virtue once renounced' engenders greater sin, through indifference or despair. But that doesn't seem to fit this context.

[108] presumes] Here 'presumes' seems to imply 'offers presumptuously', although the word choice was probably driven by the need for a rhyme.

Might freely drink, it chanced the queen of love,
Whether she longed or envied Hebe's star,
(Women are envious where they long for nectar)
    Forced her to skink[109] so much, the juice ran o'er,
    So that Jove's drink washed the defiled floor.

With this he stormed, that's priests from altars fly,   *so that his*
   Straight banished Hebe, and the world did think
To a second Chaos they should turnèd be;
580   The clouds for fear wept out th'immortal drink,
And on Panchaia there this nectar fell,
Made rich th'adjacent lands with odorous smell,
    And such rare spices to the shores are given,
    As Jove would think no nectar were in heaven.

There was a satyr,[110] rough and barbarous,
   Pleasing his palate at a trembling spring,
Under a beech with boughs frondiferous,
   Thought he had seen a nymph, or rarer thing
Than flesh and blood, for in the calmèd stream
590 He saw her eyes, like stars, whose rays did gleam
    'Bove Phoebus far, and so amazèd stood,
    As if she had been goddess of that flood.

And as you see a man that hath been long
   Possessèd with a fury of the shades,
After some prayers, and many a sacred song,
   With blessèd signs, the evil spirit vades,   *vanishes*
So fell his rudeness from him, and her shine
Made all his earthy parts pure and divine.
    O potent love, great is thy power befall'n,
600   That makes the wise mad, and the mad man calm.

Thus he begins: 'Fairer than Venus far,[111]
   If Venus be, or if she be 'tis thee;
Lovely as lilies, brighter than the star
   That is to earth the morning's Mercury;[112]
Softer than roses, sweeter breathed than they,
Blushed 'bove Aurora, better clothed than May,
    Lipped like a cherry, but of rarer taste,
    Divine as Diana, and as fully chaste.[113]

---

[109] skink] pour out, or fill a vessel with, alcoholic drink
[110] There was a satyr] Barksted returns rather abruptly to the story of Myrrha.
[111] 601] Venus addresses Myrrha's son, Adonis, as 'thrice fairer than myself' in Shakespeare's poem (*Venus and Adonis*, l. 7).
[112] morning's Mercury] The planet Venus is sometimes referred to as the Morning Star.
[113] 601–08] There are many comparable examples in classical literature of men addressing elaborate admiring speeches to beautiful strangers. Parallels include: the meeting of Odysseus with Nausicaa (*Odyssey*, VI. 110ff); Aeneas's encounter with his mother Venus in disguise (*Aeneid*, I. 314ff); and Polyphemus's address to Galatea (*Met.*, XIII. 789ff).

	Pardon my rude tongue, if I chance to err,	
610	As Hermes' self might err, being the god	
	Of eloquence, for your bright eye doth bear	
	All earthly blessings in a fair abode.	
	Excuse me if I trip, I mean your weal,	*falter, well-being*
	Error's no error where 'tis done with zeal;	
	Love, like material fires is made to flame,	
	When 'tis suppressed, with fanning fires first came.'	
	With this the maid, so took,[114] hung down her head,	
	Wondering that such a shape had such a tongue,	
	Able to steal her love, had she not fled,	
620	And from his ardent gripes her body wrung,	
	Flying like Phoebe after stricken deer,[115]	
	And as he followed, she fled more, for fear;	
	Zephyr came forth to dally with her hair,	
	While the poor satyr cried, 'Stay, maid so fair'.	
	But he on sudden, like a subtle snake	
	Rolled in a heap, shoots forth himself at length,	
	And to his vigorous arms greedy doth take	
	His yielding prey, won with his words not strength.	
	To be a woman is by nature given,	
630	But to be constant is a star, which heaven	
	Hath sealed on their sex' forehead, as a sign	
	That constancy in women is divine.	
	Thou[116] did'st deceive me, Myrrha, when I said	
	Thou flew'st for fear; thou gav'st me cause to fear,	
	And I might justly have this 'gainst thee laid —	
	Thou wentest wide[117] by paths that were so near;	
	Who begin ill, most often end in ill,	
	And she that doth her first pure youth so spill,	
	In lawless lust, though made a wife to one,	
640	Remains like wax for each impression.	
	But see the goodness of the deities,	
	Who still with grace prevents our ill presage;[118]	
	This grove was hallowed to no Hyadres,	*Hydras*
	But chaste Diana, who, with violent rage,	
	Descending from her tower of crystalline,	
	To keep the place still sacred and divine,	

---

[114] took] More than one meaning of 'take' might fit in here. 'Caught', 'overtaken' or 'charmed' are all possibilities.
[115] 621] The comparison between Myrrha and Phoebe is unusual as Myrrha might seem to have more in common with Phoebe's prey than with the hunter herself. We see this confusion between prey and predator elsewhere in the poem.
[116] Thou] The poet now seems to address Myrrha directly.
[117] Thou wentest wide] *1614* 'Thou wentst t'avide'. The reference to going astray near familiar paths alludes to incest as figuratively staying too close to home.
[118] presage] omen, seems yet another example of a slightly imprecise word, chosen for the sake of the rhyme.

Against her rites, brought with her thereupon — *in anticipation of*
　White poplar[119] from the banks of Acheron.[120]

　Then, with a charm that did her face eclipse,
650　　And made her crescent quake, the juice she powers — *pours*
　Upon the satyr's face and profane lips,
　　Which quickly over all his body showers.
　Her borrowed power of art being finishèd,
　Derived from Phoebus as her light, she said
　　Nine times the holy rhyme, which spoke, will clear
　　All profane matter, and this spoke she there.

　'Sleep, Poplar, sleep', that was the satyr's name,
　　Who had been long a king within these woods,
　'Since thou my sacred grove 'gan to profane,
660　　A sleep seize on thee, still as Stygian floods;
　By Styx, I vow, the partial destinies,
　Did they conspire, should ne'er unclasp thine eyes.'
　　Having thus said, the satyr vanished so,
　　As men's prospect, that from a mirror go. — *image*

　'I think', quoth she, 'accursèd is this place,
　　For here the man for whom I sorrow now,
　Heedless Actaeon[121] with immodest face,
　　Saw all our naked and did overview, — *nakedness, survey*
　As men rich jewels do, thinking there lies
670　Yet some rich virtue hidden from their eyes;
　　And even there', quoth she, and then did point,
　　'Revenged, I saw his hounds tear joint from joint.

　But since', says she, 'thou as a king did'st reign,
　　And art a trophy too of Dian's power;
　Thus much the goddess of the floods doth deign,
　　To change thy shape into a vertic flower.' — *vertical*
　Then thrice three words, thrice striking charmèd wand,[122]
　The ground did cranny, and there, out of hand, — *open in chinks, immediately*
　　Appeared green Poplar, younger than before,
680　　Which bowed the head, and Dian did adore.

　The pale-faced Myrrha sat like guilty spright
　　'Fore the infernal judge, yet did not see
　Diana great, for dull are mortals' sight,
　　And all invisible is chastity,[123]
　But heard a voice as she was vanishing,

---

[119] White poplar] Leuce, a nymph carried off by Hades, was turned by him into white poplar after her death. Acheron is associated with the tree.
[120] Acheron] one of the rivers in Hades
[121] Actaeon] See *Met.*, III. 155–252.
[122] wand] *1614* 'wood'
[123] all invisible is chastity] This assertion is problematic in the light of Actaeon's story.

Saying, 'Defiled maid, dost wonder at this thing?
   O Myrrha, ere my crescent's beauty change,
   Thou shalt be turned into a shape as strange.'

With this the verdant new-sprung poplar plant,
690   Moved with the wind, seemed to bow down the head,[124]
As cheering Myrrha, who did comfort want,   *consoling*
   Being amazed at what Diana said.
Having recovered sense, she flies the place,
For fear of Phoebe's coming to the chase;
   To Saba land she hies, where, all afraid,
   My muse shall sing the downfall of the maid.

Then first hung down Poplar his heavy brain,
   For Myrrha's loss, whose love brought him that [rue],[125]
And for he once in woods a king did reign,
700   A crown he still wears, richly wrought with blue,
And yellow eke, as figures both of love,
Which Venus dropped down[126] him from above.
   Bacchus doth love him, for in feasts of wine,
   He wears a poplar garland mixed with vine.

The leaden god of sleep on his juice feed,
   The virtues of him sundry do declare;
His sudden taste a heaviness doth breed,
   And drowns in rest senses oppressed with care;
In places far remote he loves to grow,
710   And eke by rivers that run thick and slow,
   Where drowsily this woodish demigod,   *sylvan*
   With every gale of wind his head doth nod.

Now to proceed: after a small repose,
   That the accursèd seed 'gan swell her womb,
When her dry brain no more tears could expose,
   She, waiting for a sad and heavy doom
(For often men offending still do fear,
Though Jove be far off, yet his judgement's near)
   Down would she sit, and so unfold her moan,
720   That Echo sighed hers, and forgot her own.[127]

Distressèd 'twixt the tediousness of life
   And trembling fear of death, she thus began:
'For when we cease to be, the crimes are rife,   *strong*
   Which youth committed, and before us then;
For agèd memory doth clasped contain,

---

[124] seemed to bow down the head] Perhaps Barksted was influenced here by Ovid's account of the metamorphosed Daphne, who seems to nod her 'head' in assent after Apollo has claimed her as his tree (*Met.*, I. 566–67).
[125] rue] A word is clearly missing from the end of this line in *1607*, almost certainly, as Grosart suggests, 'rue'.
[126] dropped down] 'On' has perhaps been omitted here.
[127] 720] This is of course the normal function of Echo rather than a special exception.

Those shapes of sin, which hot blood held as vain;
   O cursèd fates!', quoth she, 'that brought to pass
   This prodigy 'twixt me and Cinyras.

O leave to leap for joy, thou pretty child,
730   To hear of Cinyras, or I'll leave rather
To speak of him, whose bed I have defiled,
   And made him prove thy grandsire and thy father.
Was I predestined to select no other,
But fated for the sister and the mother
   Of thee, my babe? Heaven here hath been sinister,
   The child shall call his grandsire,[128] son his mother sister.

Oft do two roses grow out from one stem,
   And one of them is full blown 'fore the other;
So fares it now with thee, my virgin gem,
740   Whom nature would call son, but shame says brother.
Shall I not blush when thou art ripe, to gather
The circumstances of who was thy father?
   Yes, sure I shall, yet shame forgets all shame,
   I'll charge thy father of a heavenly name.   *accuse*

But O, I fear me lest some prodigy,
   The heavens agree that I to light should bring,
To fright e'en the iron age, that chastity
   Might take example by my suffering,
That I a monster-mother should be made;
750   If so, O over equal gods, let Myrrha fade   *just*
   Into some shape, worthy your high device,   *noble plan*
   Pity to me would make Jove seem unwise.

Alter, O gods, death that is due to birth,
   Nor let the dead repine that I should see
Elysium's blessed shades, nor the men of earth
   Annoyed be with my impurity;
Let them enjoy the fields and learned songs
Of high-browed[129] Orpheus, let the unfleshed throngs
   That have deserved this, and much more, be glad;
760   My stars, my double life, and fate, are sad.

You wearied race of Danaans,[130] unblessed girls,
   In vain leave off your unwombed[131] tubs to fill,

---

[128] The child shall call his grandsire] 'Father' needs to be inserted here to complete the sense.

[129] high-browed] The *OED* lists no occurrences of either meaning of the word 'high-browed' — possessing a lofty forehead, intellectual — before the nineteenth century.

[130] Danaans] All fifty daughters of Danaus, betrothed to the sons of their father's brother Aegyptus, with the exception of Hypermnestra, killed their husbands on their wedding night. They are usually referred to as the Danaides. In one tradition, their punishment is the endless task of filling a bottomless or perforated bathtub, or using leaking jugs to do so, the unremitting toil referred to by Ovid in *Metamorphoses*, IV. 462–63, where he calls them the Belides, after their grandfather Belus. In *Heroides*, XIV (Hypermnestra to Lyncaeus), Ovid exploits the other tradition, where the surviving Lyncaeus avenges the murder of his brothers by slaying all of Hypermnestra's sisters.

[131] unwombed] This word is not listed in the *OED*. It is probably meant to invoke both the sieve-like nature of the Danaides' jugs, and the sisters' rejection of marriage.

And with your tears, that stained the Indian pearls,
   Weep out o'er Myrrha, and ere night you will,
At my sad story, o'erbrim with your tears
Your whirlpool vessels, which so many years
   Returned no interest; if you well deplore,   *lament*
   You'll drown in tears, or labour so no more.

Conclude my fate, quick, you eternal council,
770   Or else I fear the ne'er-returnèd dead,
Clad in the fearful shapes of night and hell,
   Will rise before the general day[132] be spread,
And hurry me in flesh to Acheron,
To taste Hell's torture both in soul and bone;
   Then blast me, thunderer, in righteous ire,
   And I, like Semele,[133] will meet thy fire.'

The gods to her last wish was tractable,[134]
   Her tongue portcullised twice was as she spake;   *closed securely*
Air was her voice, and Myrrha now not able
780   To thank the gods; her joints in sunder brake,
Leaves were her locks, of golden hair bereaved,
Her arms long boughs; deem and be not deceived,   *discern*
   Tree 'gan she to be, yet 'twixt her thing so staid,[135]
   You could not say she was or tree or maid.

First grew her hair up like the summer corn,
   Or as a blazing star whose streams rise upward,
And being changed, fell leaves, that up were borne
   By the rude winds, yet had you but have heard,
You'd swear a sigh for Myrrha's transmigration
790 Had been decreed by all the windy nation,
   And every autumn since, a thing most rare,
   The falling leaves resemble Myrrha's hair.

To bark, her ivory skin polished[136] congealed,
   Each blue-ridged current into melting sap,   *vein*
Her nails to blossom fair, and what revealed
   With accents sad, the babe yet in her lap.
Her fingers twigs, her bright eyes turned to gum,
Buried in earth, and her own self the tomb;
   Her senses gone, yet this sense did she win,
800   To aye relent the horror of her sin.   *repent*

---

[132] general day] apparently a Christian anachronism. 'General', universal, was often used to describe the day of judgement.

[133] Semele] Semele was destroyed after she asked to see Jove in his full divine glory, when he had promised to grant any request. Whereas Semele did not understand the implications of her request, Myrrha welcomes her anticipated destruction (*Met.*, III. 253–315).

[134] 777] The plural noun does not agree with the singular verb here. Compare note 91.

[135] 783] The line isn't fully clear but seems to invoke the idea of Myrrha briefly being in an intermediate state where she is still partly a woman and yet 'staid', fixed, set, like a tree.

[136] polished] Placing the adjective 'polished' after the noun it qualifies creates an awkward line.

For even as from a guilty man, that's pleading for remorse,   *pity*
    Tears follow tears, as hoping to prevail;
So from this tree, though now a senseless corse,
    Flow precious tears, as seems she doth bewail
In death, with ever living tears, the act foredone.
These pious drops, made densive[137] by the sun,
    Are kept for holy uses, and the myrrh,
    That so distils, doth bear the name of her.

The misbegotten baby swells the tree,
810   And loathing the defiled womb sought vent;
Those pangs that mothers have felt she,
    And solemn sighs had issue, as they'd rent,
And spoil the shape she newly had assumed;
But words within the close bark were inhumed,   *buried*
    Yet wept it out, as it to water would,
    Or seemed it mocked Pactolus' waves of gold.[138]

Till chaste Lucina, whom the poets give
    The midwives' power in producing creatures,
By whose change we last die,[139] and first do live,   *according to whose whim*
820   (Be they not violent each?) she that gives features
Form, or takes away, makes foul or fair;
Descending from her sphere next to our air,
    With arms yspread upon the melting air,
    Brought divine comfort down from heaven with her.

Few words she spake, but every syllable
    Of power to comfort the afflicted ghosts,   *spirits*
Or any other senseless thing make able,
    Do better deeds than those Alcides boasts;   *Hercules*
The tree straight cranes, and springs forth the child,   *bends*
830   Who the first minute, though his countenance smiled,
    Cried out amain; our first prophetic breath
    Shows our first hour, is mother to our death.

The water nymphs then caught him tenderly,
    Who laid him straight on the enamelled banks,
And bathed him with his mother's tears, whereby
    They made him fairer, and in merry pranks   *antics*
The ladies call a convocation there;
Some praise his nose, his lips, his eye, his ear,
    Some his straight fingers, while a sixth doth swear
840   His very breath yet smelleth of the myrrh.

---

[137] densive] This word isn't listed in the *OED* but clearly means dense, solid.
[138] Pactolus' waves of gold] The Pactolus is a river in Turkey. Midas had to wash in the Pactolus to rid himself of the golden touch, and the river was supposed to be rich in gold.
[139] we last die] This is presumably a reference to stillbirths rather than to deaths more generally, as Lucina was only associated with birth.

Another wishes, O, for such a face!
    Nor can I blame her, though she did wish so,
For sure, were I a wench, t'had been my case,
    For nature here made both her joy and woe;[140]
And spite, that but herself commendeth none,
Of force must say, this was a rarer one
    Than either nature did, or e'er shall make,
    Whose life holds up her age, whose death's her wrack.

Eyes like two stars fall'n from their proper spheres,
850   As if they scorned the beaten paths of heaven,
Or envying of beauty of the bears,[141]
    Shown firmer here, and brighter than the seven;[142]
Such was he as was Cupid wont to be
In pictures limned, and that they may agree,   *painted*
    Furnish the babe with wings and quiver light,
    Or from love's god, take wings and quiver quite.

Nought may compare with time in his swift race,
    The babe ere while feels now youth's hot alarms,
And as in years, so beauteous grew his face,
860   That he is fit again for ladies' arms;[143]
Nor Cupid now could wound more dames than he,
That Venus who captives all is not free
    From her own power; she loves Adonis mild,
    That Mars doth storm, and wish he were no child.[144]

Nor Paphos, Amathus[145] nor fishy Cnide,[146]
    Delights she now to haunt, nor Etna now
Burns more than her; she roams the wood so wide
    After her game,[147] that to his game doth bow,[148]   *bend his course*
And will not hear or see; for eyes and ears,
870   If they her hear or see, their use forbears;
    Yet she pursues, and leaves her power uneven   *uncertain*
    On heaven and earth, she loves him more than heaven.

Oft would she say, and bathe those words in tears:
    'O thou fair boy, would God thou lovd'st like me;
But sure thou art not flesh, it well appears,
    Thou wert the stubborn issue of a tree,

---

[140] both her joy and woe] This point is further glossed in the last line of the stanza.

[141] bears] Ursa Major and Ursa Minor

[142] seven] Possibly a reference to the Pleiades or to the Hesperides (sometimes said to be seven, sometimes three). The stars of Ursa Minor have sometimes been identified with the latter group of nymphs.

[143] 860] The first time would have been when he was nursed by women as a baby.

[144] 864] Apparently Mars feels Adonis is too young to treat as a rival. Barksted has perhaps been influenced here by the childish speech and outlook of Shakespeare's Adonis.

[145] Amathus] a city in Cyprus

[146] Cnide] a city in the region of Caria in Greece

[147] After her game] Adonis is her prey, yet he is more interested in the hunt.

[148] to his game doth bow] Several rather different meanings of 'bow' might make sense here. 'Incline' is perhaps intended. Grosart suggests that 'his game' should be emended to 'her game', as though the animals pay homage to Venus.

	So hard thou art.' Then she a sigh would fet,	*fetch*
	And wish that Vulcan had not made his net	
	For boisterous Mars; she'd fainer have been sped[149]	*brought to an end*
880	With this choice flower, clasped in her iron bed.	

Sprengius, *Metamorphoses Ovidii* (1563), p. 49ʳ

She'd ne'er have blushed then, she does make a vow,
   Though all the gods of both worlds had them seen;
She raveth that she ever loved till now,
   That she might worthily ha' been love's queen.[150]
'Well, well', quoth she, 'thou hast revenged the spite
Which from my accursed son's bow did foully light
   On thy fair mother.[151] O immortal boy,
   Though thou be fair, 'tis I that should be coy.'[152]

	But stay, my Muse, in thine own confines keep,	
	And wage not war with so dear loved a neighbour;	*Shakespeare*
890	But, having sung thy day song, rest and sleep,	
	Preserve thy small fame, and his greater favour;	
	His song was worthy merit; Shakespeare, he	
	Sung the fair blossom, thou the withered tree;[153]	
	Laurel is due to him, his art and wit	
	Hath purchased it; Cypress[154] thy brow will fit.	

FINIS.

---

[149] The precise force of 'sped' in this line is uncertain. What Venus seems to be saying is that she would rather Vulcan's net had trapped her in an adulterous embrace with Adonis than with Mars.

[150] 883–84] She seems to regret that Adonis was not her first love, because then she might have been more worthy to be goddess of love.

[151] 885–87] If Venus's words represents Barksted's own sense of the cause of Myrrha's passion, then he is now clarifying what was previously an equivocal account of her encounter with Cupid and contradicting Ovid (*Met.*, X. 311).

[152] 888] Again, Barksted is perhaps thinking of Shakespeare's *Venus and Adonis*, where there is a more extended depiction of the goddess's unrequited love.

[153] 893–94] a reference to the final metamorphoses of both Adonis and Myrrha

[154] Cypress] associated with death and mourning

H. A.
THE SCOURGE OF VENUS (1613)

H. A.

THE SCOURGE OF VENUS (1613)

[*Metamorphoses*, X. 287–528]

Sprengius, *Metamorphoses Ovidii* (1563), p. 126ʳ

The identity of H. A. remains uncertain. A. B. Grosart suggested that he might be 'Austin', a writer singled out for criticism by Thomas Heywood in the epistle to the reader which prefaces *The Brazen Age* (1613).[1] Heywood claimed that this rival passed off as his own 'certain translations of Ovid, as his three books *De Arte Amandi*, and two *De Remedio Amoris* [. . .]. Therefore I would entreat that Austin, for so his name is, to acknowledge his wrong to me in showing them, and his own impudence, and ignorance in challenging them'.[2] Noam Flinker follows Grosart and attributes the poem to Austin.[3] However, there is no conclusive evidence for this identification, and some reason to doubt it. Arthur Melville Clark, for example, points out that *The Scourge of Venus* is clearly based on the *Metamorphoses*, rather than the poems mentioned by Heywood.[4] Matthew Steggle, author of the *ODNB* entry on Henry Austin, puts forward the same argument for not identifying him with the author of the *Scourge*. It has been suggested that the poem might have been written by William Barksted, whose own treatment of the myth is included in this volume, and even that Heywood himself wrote it.[5]

The prefatory remarks on the title-page raise a further confusion surrounding the poem's authorship. These are clearly not written by the poet himself yet they are signed H. A. in the

---

[1] *The Scourge of Venus (1614)*, ed. by Rev. Alexander B. Grosart ([Manchester]: [C. E. Simms], 1876), p. 49.
[2] Thomas Heywood, *The Brazen Age* (London: Nicholas Okes for Samuel Rand, 1613), fol. A2ʳ.
[3] Noam Flinker, 'Cinyras, Myrrha, and Adonis: Father–Daugher Incest from Ovid to Milton', *Milton Studies*, 14 (1980), 59–74.
[4] Arthur Melville Clark, 'Thomas Heywood's *Art of Love* Lost and Found', *The Library*, 4th ser., 3 (1922), 210–22.
[5] Edmund Gosse, *The Jacobean Poets* (London: John Murray, 1894), p. 112; William Carew Hazlitt, *Shakespear* (London: Bernard Quaritch, 1902), p. 61.

1614 edition, and A. H. in the 1620 edition; they remained unsigned in the first edition. It is thus possible, even though the first edition states on the title-page that the poem is 'written by H. A.', that the initials refer only to the text's editor, not to its author. Paul W. Miller argues that the inclusion of these initials was probably a careless printer's error rather than a clue that H. A. is not in fact the poem's author.[6] There seems no easy way of resolving these competing possibilities, and in this edition we have followed the simplest course of ascribing the poem to H. A.

The main source for the poem is Book X of Ovid's *Metamorphoses*. Yet there is an important additional source for some of H. A.'s elaborations to the original, overlooked by other editors and critics, the parallel tale of Byblis's passion for her brother Caunis which Ovid relates in Book IX.[7] H. A. seems to have consulted Golding's translation of Ovid, and these borrowings are particularly apparent in the sections derived from the tale of Byblis.

H. A. seems interested in the characters' psychology; for example, a brief reference in Ovid to the incestuous pair calling each other 'father' and 'daughter' in bed is much expanded, and the poet perhaps thus hints that Cinyras shares Myrrha's passion. He implies that he wouldn't care even if she were his daughter and — although this could certainly be interpreted as a simple strategy to put a bashful girl at her ease and is contradicted by his rage at the discovery of her true identity — there is some interesting equivocation in the long description of his guilt and anguish (another addition by the translator). Is H. A. hinting that Cinyras half suspected who his bedfellow was? Flinker notes that he seems 'unconsciously eager to seduce his daughter',[8] and there is a teasing ambiguity in Cinyras's use of the adjective 'uncertain' here:

She sinned, and knew her father she abused,
I sinned, uncertain who it was I used. (ll. 845–46)

H. A. includes rather more salacious details than Ovid — such as the 'gentle' nurse's lengthy encomium on lusty young men — but also dwells at greater length on the horror of incest and writes from an explicitly Christian perspective. There is some disagreement as to the moral tone of the poem. Payne Collier asserts that it was 'published to take advantage of the grossness of the public appetite' and states that 'it is much to be regretted that the writer employed his talents so ill'.[9] Miller describes H. A. as a 'moral fence straddler', although he does allow the poem 'a certain crude, narrative vitality'.[10] A. B. Grosart is rather more enthusiastic, and picks out several similes and descriptive passages for praise.

The first edition of the poem appeared in 1613, but the second edition, of 1614, has been used as the copy text because it contains two additional stanzas and several minor emendations. Some of these seem to be corrections of errors introduced by the printer, whereas others seem more likely to represent the poet's attempt to improve and clarify his own text. Some of the more significant variants are listed in the textual notes. A third edition, which appeared in 1620, is based on the 1613 text. The poem was not republished until 1876 when Grosart brought out an annotated edition based on the 1614 text (he had no access to the first edition). A facsimile of the first edition was included in Paul Miller's *Seven Minor Epics of the English Renaissance* (1967).

---

[6] Paul W. Miller, *Seven Minor Epics of the English Renaissance, 1596–1624* (Gainesville, FL: Scholars' Facsimiles & Reprints, 1967), p. x.
[7] See introduction pp. 11–12 for a further discussion of this 'portmanteau' effect.
[8] Flinker, 'Cinyras, Myrrha, and Adonis', p. 67.
[9] J. Payne Collier, *The Poetical Decameron, or Ten Conversations on English Poets and Poetry, Particularly of the Reigns of Elizabeth and James I*, 2 vols (Edinburgh: Archibald Constable, 1820), I, pp. 238–39.
[10] Miller, *Seven Minor Epics*, pp. xxv–xxvi.

EDITIONS

H. A., *The scourge of Venus. Or, The wanton Lady. With the rare birth of Adonis* (London: Nicholas Okes, 1613), STC 968.

H. A., *The scourge of Venus. Or, The wanton Lady. With the rare birth of Adonis. The second impression, corrected, and enlarged by H. A.* (London: N[icholas]. O[kes]. for Robert Wilson, 1614), STC 969.

The scourge of Venus (1614), ed. by Rev. Alexander B. Grosart ([Manchester]: [C. E. Simms], 1876).

Paul W. Miller, *Seven Minor Epics of the English Renaissance, 1596–1624* (Gainesville, FL: Scholars' Facsimiles & Reprints, 1967).

FURTHER READING

Arthur Melville Clark, 'Thomas Heywood's *Art of Love* Lost and Found', *The Library*, 4th ser., 3 (1922), 210–22.

J. Payne Collier, *The Poetical Decameron, or Ten Conversations on English Poets and Poetry, Particularly of the Reigns of Elizabeth and James I*, 2 vols (Edinburgh: Archibald Constable, 1820), I.

Noam Flinker, 'Cinyras, Myrrha, and Adonis: Father-Daughter Incest from Ovid to Milton', *Milton Studies*, 14 (1980), 59–74.

THE SCOURGE OF VENUS[11]

To the Reader.

Gentlemen, if your fancy will permit you to favour this book I shall be thankful; if not, I can but repent at the charge of the impression.[12] I mean but little gain to myself, yet much pleasure to you. If it were my own wit and you condemn it I should be ashamed of my public intrusion, but since it was the labour of a man well-deserving, forbear open reprehending for, as I have heard, 'twas done for his pleasure without any intent of an impression. Thus much I excuse him that I know not, and commend that which deserveth well. If I be partial, I pray patience.

Vale.

H. A.

---

[11] *The Scourge of Venus*] The title is somewhat ambiguous. The scourge may be thought of as the instrument of Venus — in other words it may denote the fatal passion felt by Myrrha. Alternatively the word *scourge* may denote a punishment which Venus herself endures, for Myrrha's son Adonis will prove a scourge to Venus when she falls in love with him, as H. A. briefly notes at the end of the poem.

[12] impression] publication

Whilst that the sun was climbing up in haste,
   To view the world with his ambitious eye,
Fair Myrrha, yet, alas, more fair than chaste,
   Did set her thoughts to descant wantonly;   *discourse*
Nay most inhuman, worse than bad, or ill,
   As in the sequel you may read at will.

You that have parents, or that parents be,
   Depart a space, and give not ear at all
To the foul tale that here shall uttered be;
10   Some filthy shame let on all others fall,
If possibly there can be any such,
   From nature to degenerate so much.

Oh then, with Ovid, I am wondrous glad
   That this small world of ours is put so far
From those that such incestuous people had;[13]
   So rest thou still in glory as a star[14]
That scorning thrusts from other nations quite,[15]
   And in thy virtues doth thyself delight.

And now fair Myrrha in her youthly blood   *youthful*
20   Doth on her father dote with fond desire;
Each foul occasion is accounted good,
   That may increase her filthy lustful fire;
And as this shameful matter wanted grace,
   So doubtfully she thus doth plead her case.

'Why should not gods this love of mine permit,
   Or be offended with me for the same?
It doth infringe their sacred laws no whit,
   Adding dishonour, or deserving blame.
I will proceed good reasons for to prove
30   'Tis not unlawful to obtain my love.

In many countries I do certain know
   The parents with their children married be,
Which they do most their godliness to show,
   Because their loves increased thereby they see.
Then shall this luckless plot of ground remain
   Th'occasion that my love I not obtain?

Each wight[16] hath nature set at liberty,
   All things be common for she naught restrains;
Then let the daughter with the father lie,

---

[13] 13–15] Cf. *Met.*, X. 306. The translator speaks alongside his author, and shares his relief.
[14] 16] Cf. *Met.*, XV. 875–76 in which the poet foretells that he will gain immortality beyond the stars.
[15] 17] H. A. appears to be praising Ovid for completely repudiating the sins of other lands.
[16] wight] *1613* 'night'. Here and elsewhere an apparent *1613* error makes some sense within the immediate context but not within the stanza as a whole.

40	Like precedent with all things else remains —	
	The kid, the heifer, and the birds we see,	
	Affect the same of whom they gotten be.	*love*

In happy case then such her creatures are,
    That may do so, and yet do no offence;
They be more happy than is mankind far,
    For they by some malicious base pretence
Have made a curb to hold that still in thrall
    Which nature would have common unto all.

But yet pack hence thou foul, incestuous love!
50   What, wilt upon thy only father dote?
I ought to love him, yet as doth behove,
    Not that the world thereby my shame may note.
O do resolve! The nearness of our kin
    Cuts off all hope thy wishèd suit to win.

Did Cupid then e'er shoot so yet before?
    Can Vulcan forge so foul an arrow now?
Or further, will Dame Venus evermore
    Such cruelty unto her servants show?
No, no, I am deceived, for now I see
60   With poisoned snakes some Fury wounded thee.

How great', said she, 'O Venus may'st thou be,[17]
    How was I ravishèd this present night,
In feeling of your pleasant sports in me?
    I clipped a man in prime of his delight,   *embraced*
What lively pleasures did I there conceive?
    No fault (alas) but they too soon did leave.[18]

Would, Cinyras, thou had'st some other name,
    How fitly might'st thou have a love of me,
How nobly might'st thereby increase thy fame,
70   How quickly should'st a son gain unto thee.
I would enforce dull earthly thoughts, to crave,   *drive away*
    To kiss, and clip, and other pastimes have.

What mean my dreams? Have they effect at all?
    May dreams a future chance to us portend?
"Let then to me such dreams more oft befall;
    "In dreams no present witness can offend:[19]

---

[17] 61] There is an apparent inconsistency in Myrrha's reasoning here, given that she has just attributed her lust to the Furies. Presumably she invokes Venus as the source of passion more generally rather than as the direct instigator of her incestuous infatuation.

[18] 62–66] This account of an erotic dream is derived from the story of Byblis (*Met.*, IX. 481–86). This is one of many such cross-contaminations in the translation. See introduction, pp. 11–12.

[19] 75–76] In *1614* the lines are highlighted using quotation marks in order to identify them as a *sententia*, a proverb or example of conventional wisdom.

> In dreams we may as great a pleasure take
>   As in some sort is found we being awake.
>
> But yet avaunt, pack hence foul filthy fire,[20]   *depart*
>   Wring out some tears to quench this cursèd flame;
> No otherwise than daughter-like require
>   Thy father's love, that blazons out thy shame.   *proclaims*
> Yet put the case he first did seek to me,
>   No doubt I should to his request agree.
>
> Why should it not then stand right so with him,
>   Since of one nature we participate?   *share*
> What if with speech thou shame his love to win?
>   Then may'st thou write: "No time is yet too late."[21]
> What thou dost blush to speak, love bids thee write;
>   Believe me, they read more than we indite.'   *set down*
>
> Resolved on this, with trembling hand she takes
>   The pen and paper, framing for to write;
> Left hand holds wax whilst right the letter makes,
>   Composing what she did in mind indite.   *compose*
> She writes, she doubts, she changeth this for that,
>   She likes, dislikes, and notes she knows not what.
>
> She casts away, and doth begin anew,
>   Yet finds a want in that she framèd last;   *lack*
> She blots, and then again that thing doth view,
>   And now the first more fits than all that's past.[22]
> 'Father', she writes, yet shame did blot it out;
>   Then thus she writes, and casts away all doubt.
>
> 'I know not what, sends to I know not whom,
>   Such health that thou may'st only give to me,
> Which, if I want, my life cannot be long,
>   Even that same health thy lover sends to thee.
> I dare not tell thee who I am for shame,
>   Nor (out alas) once let thee hear my name.   *woe is me*
>
> And if thou ask of me what I desire,
>   Or why so doubtful I do write to thee,
> Would nameless I might tell what I require,
>   Till that my suit were granted unto me;
> Which, if to know thou would'st make further trial,
>   A maiden asketh but a maid's denial.[23]

---

[20] 79] This is a clear echo of Golding's 'Avaunt, foul filthy fire!' (IX. 606).

[21] "No time is yet too late"] This is printed in italics in both *1613* and *1614*, perhaps suggesting that these are words Myrrha might write or else that they are intended as a *sententia*.

[22] 97–100] There are some similarities between the indecisive Myrrha and Shakespeare's Lucrece as well as Byblis. Whereas Byblis writes on a wax tablet, both Lucrece and H. A.'s Myrrha 'blot' their texts: 'What wit sets down is blotted straight with will' (*The Rape of Lucrece*, l. 1299).

[23] 114] She seems to assert that she no longer wants to be a maid.

In token of my wounded heart, I would
    Within these blotted lines there might appear
My colour pale, my body lean and cold,
    My wat'ry eyes, my sighs and heavy cheer;
Then might'st perceive I were in love with thee,
120   And how the flames of love tormenteth me.

I call the gods as witness to the same;
    Poor wretched wench, I strove to fly the dart,
And did my best that outrage for to tame,
    Which Cupid had allotted for my smart;
No wench bore more than did to me betide,
    Which forced me show the cause that I would hide.

Then mercy at thy gentle hands I crave,
    In fearful wise to thee I make my moan,
Thou only may'st thy lover spill or save,
130   No enemy doth sue, but such a one
That is allied most nearly[24] unto thee,
    Yet in a nearer band would linkèd be.

My life is thine and thou did'st give it me,
    Then love thyself, and thou wilt me affect,   *love*
My beauty's much, and is derived from thee,
    Then all thy own be careful to respect.
O stop thy ears, and hear not Myrrha's name,
    And shut thy eyes when thou dost read the same!

My youthful years rash folly doth beseem,[25]
140   The skill of law to agèd folks belong,[26]
And all is lawful that we list, I deem,
    We take no notice of the right or wrong;
If it offend to take thy own in't bed,   *into*
    Let that offence be laid upon my head.

Then set apart the dread of worldly shame,
    And take the gods as precedents herein;
My pregnant wit shall shun all future blame,
    Our pleasure scapes well, hid with name of kin,   *escapes*
And you may clip and kiss and play with me,
150   A daughter's name methinks a cloak will be.

Have mercy now, I have my case expressed,
    Which love enforced my fearful hand to write;
Oh grant thy daughter this her first request,
    That is the occasion of her chief delight;

---

[24] nearly] *1613* 'sweetly'. The *polyptoton* 'nearly [...] nearer' in the revised or corrected text echoes Ovid's 'iunctissima, iunctior' (*Met.*, IX. 549).
[25] 139] Compare Golding's, 'Such youthful years as ours are yet rash folly doth beseem' (IX. 660).
[26] belong] 'Belongs' is required for grammatical sense, but 'belong' has been retained for the sake of the rhyme.

This epitaph deserve thou not I have:
    "The cruel father took the life he gave."

And though my lines are blotted everywhere,
    'Twas with my tears that fell ere it was dry;
And if my letters scribbled do appear,
160   (Whereby you think some other wrote to try
Your mind, because my curious hand is missed)
    A fearful mind doth bring a shaking fist.   *handwriting*

And so these scribbled lines I do commend
    Unto your love, beblurrèd all with tears,
With fervent hope they shall no whit offend,
    The mind is base that still continual fears;
And note you well which is the greater blot,
    To get no child or kill that you have got.'

Thus much this lustful lady writ in vain,
170   And sealed it closely with a precious stone,
A precious stone closed up a filthy stain;
    Her trusty servant forth she calls anon,
And blushing bade him, with a merry cheer,
    He should this letter to her father bear.

This scarcely said, old Cinyras did come,
    And then she cast her letter quite aside;[27]
'Daughter', said he, 'you see the daily throng
    Of suitors that do seek thee for their bride;
Here be their names, my wench, then come and show
180   On which of them thou wilt thyself bestow.'

Now for a space she silent did remain,
    And only gazèd wishly in his face;   *longingly*
She could her tears no longer then restrain,
    But they ran trickling down her cheeks apace;
Her father kisses her and bids her peace,
    And thought it tender-hearted shamefastness.   *modesty*

He dried her cheeks and said, 'My wench, be still,
    Thy years of right a husband now doth claim;
Thou shalt not live a maid by my good will,
190   Nor longer shalt a wanton bed refrain;
Then what, or who, wilt have? Come, tell me now.'
    At length she did reply, 'One like to you.'

He did allow the choice, and praised the same,
    And kissed and clipped her for her loving speech,
Not deeming that it tended to their shame;

---

[27] 175–76] Byblis, by contrast, delivers her letter successfully; it only inspires fury in her brother.

It pleased her well, and wished that he would seech[28]
A further suit, and then made this request:
   'Let me live still with you, let wooers rest.

Your company I most of all affect,
200   Continue but your love, it shall suffice;
These wrangling husbands why should I respect?'
   Her father thus again to her replies:
'Thy godliness' (at which she blushèd red)
   'I like, but thou must taste a bridegroom's bed.

Thou dost not know the pleasure it affords,[29]
   Nor wanton motions that therein abound;   *amorous*
It not consisteth all of pleasant words,
   More gainsome tricks are there still to be found;   *profitable*
A mind so chaste as thine cannot conceive
210   What pleasing sports one shall thereby receive.

It is no dream, nor passion of the mind,
   But a substantial pleasure there doth dwell;
The practic part of dreams therein we find,   *practical*
   Which who so doth omit leads apes in hell;[30]
Why dost thou blush? I know your case, believe,
   Maids must say nay, yet take when men do give.'

And now the sable horses of the night
   Have drawn a mantle o'er the silver sky,
And all the stars do show their borrowed light;
220   Each breathing thing oppressed with sleep doth lie,
Save Philomel, that sings of Tereus' rape,[31]
   And Myrrha plotting some incestuous scape.   *transgression*

No rest at all she took within her bed,
   The flames of Cupid burnt so in her breast,
And many a fancy comes into her head,
   Which overmuch her troubled soul oppressed;
She doubts, she hopes, then fear doth make repair,
   She'll now attempt, then shame doth bring despair.

Look how you see a pleasant field of corn
230   Move here and there by gentle-breathing wind,
Now up and down, as waves in sea are borne,
   So doubtful thoughts had motion in her mind;
Now she'll surcease, and now to him repair,   *desist*
   Instable, like a feather in the air.

---

[28] seech] either 'beseech' or 'seek'. Cf. l. 550.
[29] the pleasure it affords] Cinyras's enthusiastic recommendation of the pleasures of the marriage bed is not derived from Ovid.
[30] lead apes in hell] A proverbial punishment for women who died unmarried
[31] Tereus's rape] See *Met.*, VI. 423–674.

O fie upon this foul incestuous lust,
That very nature greatly doth abhor,
Some plague will fall upon all such, I trust,
If in this world there can be any more.
I hope this little world well freèd is
Of giants and such monstrous beasts as this.

So God preserve it, if it be his will,[32]
And let the Gospel ever flourish here;
Yet I do fear we have some yet as ill —
The pleasing fools do with their folly bear;
In Paradise I see we cannot live,
But we shall find some foul seducing Eve.

My tongue doth stagger to repeat her name,
So foul a blot a Christian cannot brook;
Go seek a glass to see this filthy shame,
Upon God's holy Bible daily look,
And there thou may'st, as in a mirror see,
No Alcoran can yield the like to thee. *Qur'an*

There suck the nectar of His holy word,
And beg thou pardon for thy foul abuse,
For every sore it can a salve afford.
O atheist, learn to make of it good use!
Thou Christian's blot, to leave off further talk,
Whilst thou hast light, endeavour there to walk.

And thou Panchaia, rich in many a thing,
In costus,[33] cinnamon and incense sweet,
That out of trees abundantly doth spring,
Of ammonie,[34] and things for uses meet;
Yet whilst thou yieldest myrrh I weigh thee not,
For thereunto hath Myrrha given a blot.

No measure in her filthy love she found, *moderation*
No ease, no rest, but death doth like her now.
Resolved on this she gets up from the ground,
To stop her breath most desperately doth vow,
And then the noose about her neck she draws,
And said, 'O Cinyras, thou art the only cause.

Farewell, therefore, a thousand times farewell,
Dear Cinyras thou might'st have saved my life,
And think thou, this to me alone befell,
Because I durst not love thee as a wife.
Farewell again. O welcome gentle death!'
And then she went about to stop her breath.

---

[32] 241–58] These lines are of course the translator's own intervention.
[33] costus] a fragrant root, *saussurea lappa*
[34] ammonie] Ammoniacum is the gum derived from *Dorema ammoniacum*.

    A recompense fit for so foul a mind;
    But yet by chance her agèd nurse did lie
    Within a chamber that to hers adjoined,
280 Who overhearing this, to her did hie,
    And seeing her half-murdered so, began
    To shriek and scream, and straight unto her ran.

    Who first did snatch her girdle from her neck,
    And pouring tears upon her plenteously,
    Did hold her in her agèd arms, though weak,
    And kissing her did urge the reason why
    She went about away herself to make,
    Or to her shame so base a course to take.

    Quoth she, 'I pray thee tell the cause to me,
290 Behold these empty dugs, and head all grey,
    These hands that pain have took in rocking thee,
    Let some, or all these, cause thee to bewray   *reveal*
    What cruel means have brought thee in this case.'
    At which the lady turned away her face.

    'O be not coy, sweet! Hide thou nought from me,
    I am thy nurse', she said, 'and have good skill
    In charms, and herbs, and dreams that powerful be;
    Of what thou want'st I'll help thee to thy fill;
    Art thou in love, or witched by any wight?   *bewitched*
300 I'll find thee ease, or else will free thee quite.

    I have been wanton once as well as you,
    Nor[35] yet by age am altogether dull;
    I have been lovesick, as you may be now,
    Of toys and love tricks I was wondrous full;
    How strange so e'er thy case do therefore stand,
    I can and will redress it out of hand.

    Thou art in love, my sweet, I well espy;
    If so, no lack shalt find in me, I swear.'
    The lady in her arms sobbed bitterly,
310 The nurse replied and said, 'Why, do not fear,
    Thy father shall not know of this at all',
    At which she starts and on her bed doth fall.

    And franticly she tumbles on her face,
    And said, 'Get hence, good nurse, I prithee go!
    Constrain me not to show my wicked case.'
    'That case', quoth she, 'I pray thee let me know.'
    'Get hence', she answered, 'or enquire less,
    'Tis wickedness thou would'st have me confess.

---

[35] Nor] *1614* 'Now'

'Tis such a thing, that if I want, I die,   *lack*
320   And being got, is nothing else but shame.'
The nurse hereat did sigh most heavily,
And on her knees besought to know the same,
And holding up her hands as she did kneel,
Said, 'Madam, tell the privy grief you feel.

If you will not discover this to me,
I will acquaint your father out of hand,
How you had hanged yourself, wer't not for me;
But if you tell, your trusty friend I'll stand,
And let your grief of any nature be,
330   It shall go hard, but I'll find remedy.

And if your case be ill, you need not fear,
The heavy load the wickedness doth bring,
I'll teach thee how most easily to bear,
My age hath got experience in each thing.
Tell me what 'tis that doth so nearly touch,
One woman may persuade another much.'

And now the lady raised her heavy head,
Hanging upon her nurse's bosom fast,
As she did rise up from her slothful bed,
340   Being prodigal her crystal tears to waste;
Now she would speak, and now her speech doth stay,   *break off*
Then shame doth cause her turn her face away.

A frantic fury doth possess her now,
And then she draws her garment o'er her face,
And wrings her hands, and to her nurse doth vow
For to acquaint her with her wretched case,
And shedding brinish tears into her breast,   *salty*
Thus much her grief to her at last expressed.

'O happy is my mother's happy state
350   That hath a husband debonair and fair!
Unhappy am I, most unfortunate —'
At which she stopped, as one fall'n in despair;
The nurse soon found synecdoche in this,
And what the whole meant by a part did guess.

Her agèd bones did shake and tremble fast,
Her hoary hair stood staring up on end;
From forth her eyes a heavy look she cast,
And many a sigh her heart distressed did send;
Yet pausing long, not knowing what to say,
360   At last her tongue her mind did thus bewray.   *reveal*

'In this I hope, good lady, you but jest,
To try your nurse's now decaying wit;

So foul a fault is not within your breast,
Then tell me true the occasion of this fit.'
The lady frowned, and stopped her speaking farther,
And said, 'Get hence, is't shame to love one's father?'

'Aye', she replied, 'in such a filthy sort,
It is not love, but lust that you profess;
Necessity with true love cannot sort,
370 Your love contaminates, you must confess.
A daughter's love then to your father show,
Some love good things but with bad love, I know.

Or if your wanton flesh you cannot tame,
Nor cool the burning of your hot desire,
Then take someone that not augments the shame,
And set apart to dote upon your sire.
It is most vile to stand in such a need,
To make the actor baser than the deed.

Besides, his years can yield no such content,
380 That blithesome wanton dames expect to have;   *cheerful*
Herein your bargain you will soon repent,
When you shall find great want of that you crave.
Are you so mad, or will you once believe
Old men content to frolic dames can give?   *merry*

Take this example of me, from the sky:
Behold a shooting star from heaven fall,
Whose glimmering light you scarcely do espy,
But it is gone as nothing were at all;
And so, their sports being scarce begun, doth leave,
390 As in the air concressions[36] we perceive.

Or as the blooms upon the almond tree,
That vanish sooner than the mushrooms come,
Or as the flies, hemera, we do see   *ephemera*
To leave their breath their life being scarce begun;
What, think'st the tree whose root's decayed by time
Can yield like fruit to young ones in their prime?

A rotten stick's more fit to burn than use,
I marvel what from age you do expect;
Let my experience their defect accuse,
400 And teach thee how thy equals to affect;
When they should toy, jocund[37] and sport with thee,
Their gouts, their coughs and cramps will hindrance be.

---

[36] concressions] *OED* cites *The Scourge of Venus* as an example of concression being used as a version of concretion (a coalescence, or clot). It is perhaps a reference to a 'floater' or other visual disturbance.
[37] jocund] This verbal use of 'jocund' is not listed in the *OED*.

    'Tis not their fault, but incident to age,
Which far more imperfections with it brings,
As jealousy, suspicion, fury, rage,
Dislike, disdain, and other suchlike things;
For can the fire, hot in nature, dwell
With water cold, but they at length rebel?

    Even as in summer one may aptly note,
410 The fire and water in one cloud contained,
And neither yet the mastery have got,
Being opposites, their fury's not restrained,
But do contend in strife and deadly war,
Till scolding thunder do pronounce the jar.   *discord*

    Choose from thy wooers some peculiar one,
Whose love may fill the measure of thy hopes,
And blazonize thy wanton sports alone,   *celebrate*
Whose appetite with thy desire copes;
Youth will be frolic in a maiden's bed,   *joyous*
420 Age is unapt and heavy as the lead.

    Youth hath his dalliance and his kind embrace,
Even as the elm's encircled with the vine;
Age loveth rest and quiet in this case,
Saying oaks at such like ivy grips repine;
Youth's pleasing well-tuned years sweet music makes,
When for consort love strings it strains or slakes.   *slacks*

    Yet choose thou one whose tongue's not set on wheels,
Who eats his words before he brings them forth;
That no decorum in his talking feels,
430 Such are but buzzards, blabs of little worth.
And for complexion,[38] herein me believe,   *temperament*
The perfect sanguine sweet content doth give.

    The phlegmatic is, like the water, cold,
The choleric wants sap, like fire dry,
And melancholy, as age, is dull and old,
But in the sanguine moist warm juice doth lie,
Whose beauty feeds the eye with sweet delight —
The rest do rather fear than please the sight.

    What pleasure can a stern grim face afford,
440 A swarthy colour or rough shaggèd hair,
Or raven black? Believe me at a word,
They are to blame that do despise the fair;
They please the eye, provoke dull appetite,
Resemble gods, and do the mind delight.'

---

[38] complexion] Lines 431–36 discuss the four humours or bodily fluids — blood, phlegm, yellow bile and black bile — which were thought to determine, respectively, sanguine, phlegmatic, choleric and melancholic temperaments.

'Cease chatting, gentle nurse', the lady said,
'Or frame thy tale to suit more with the time;
My choice is made, therein I need no aid
Which may be compassed by some help of thine;
It is too late of abstinence to preach,
450   When one is drunk and notes not what you teach.

I seek him not for lust, as you do deem,
For if my mind were only bent thereto,
I could find other men I might esteem,
You know the store of suitors come to woo;
But 'tis some kind of natural instinct,
Or divine flame that cannot be extinct.   *extinguished*

What I do seek I know is wondrous vile,
And have a will for to withstand the same,
Yet can those motions by no means exile,
460   So seeketh lust to bring me unto shame;
Be it worse than nought to have it, flesh doth strive,
Help nurse, else long I cannot live.[39]

Some say, and you can tell the truth likewise,[40]
When women once have felt that they call sport,
And in their womb a timpani[41] doth rise,   *membrane*
For things peculiar they do oft import;[42]   *crave*
And though most odious it do seem to some,
Yet give it them or they are quite undone.

And so my case most desperate stands, you see,
470   I long for this yet know no reason why,
Unless a woman's will a reason be,
We'll have our will although unlawfully;
It is most sweet and wholesome unto me,
Though it seem bad and odious unto thee.

Then wish not to dissuade me in this case,
Nor give me counsel to withdraw my mind;
It likes me well, I weigh not the disgrace,
O teach me then to win him to be kind![43]
Help me, good nurse, in this my cruel state,
480   All other means of comfort comes too late.

---

[39] 462] The final line is hypometrical. It is possible that this is a deliberate reflection of the unnatural and desperate nature of Myrrha's passion, although it is perhaps more likely that a word, perhaps an epithet before 'nurse' (compare 445 and 492), has been omitted.

[40] 463–74] These two stanzas were both added to *1614*.

[41] timpani] tympanum

[42] import] This seems to be a contracted form of *importune*, 'to crave or to beg'. The reference is to pregnancy cravings.

[43] kind] There are tensions between the word's different meanings here. To be *kind*, 'benign', will make Cinyras *unkind*, 'unnatural'.

And since thou needs would'st understand my shame —
Which I did grieve and blush to ope to thee,
And had lear[44] died than told thee of the same —
Now be not slack to lend thy help to me;
Thou forced me for to open my disgrace,
Then lend thy help to salve my wretched case.[45]

You do not know, good nurse, or have forgot,
What 'tis to love and cannot it obtain;
Of youth's kind dalliance age doth take no note,
490 Forgetting it, and think all may abstain;
But "'tis not so", I to those thoughts reply,
Then help me gentle nurse, or else I die.'

'Live still my sweet', quoth she, 'and do possess — '
Yet name of 'father' shame forced her conceal,
And with a staggering speech the word repressed,
And all her help more amply to reveal,
She made a vow, whereby herself she bound,
To do the best that might in her be found.

The feasts of gentle Ceres now began,
500 Which yearly they observed, and held it ill
For thrice three nights to lie with any man;
The wives in white apparellèd were still,
And unto Ceres first fruit of the field,
As garlands made of ears of corn, did yield.

The queen amongst these women did frequent
These rites, and would be absent at no time;
The nurse then, to accomplish her intent,
And finding Cinyras made blithe with wine,
The siren most enchantingly did sing,
510 And thus at last broke silence to the king.

'Renownèd king, but that your constant love
Restrains my tongue and holds my speeches in,
A wanton question I would to thee move.'
'Speak on', quoth he, 'good nurse, thy speech begin,
With Bacchus' feasts do wanton sports agree,
I know thou would'st no ill thing unto me.'

'Then thus', quoth she, 'there is a gallant maid,
Of princely birth and noble high degree,
Who at this time would be right well apaid   *contented*
520 To kiss thy hand — she's so in love with thee;
Such divine beauty in her face doth lurk,
That gods envy at Nature for the work.

---

[44] lear] liefer, rather
[45] to salve my wretched case] Her disgrace, which may mean a physical as well as a moral disfigurement, is here compared to a wound.

Without offence unto your queen and wife,
Unto this lady she is a homely cate, — *dainty*
I love your queen, and honour her as life,
And but admire the other's happy state,
That's made so fair that none can like her be;
Your queen is kind, abuse her not for me.

But if you saw her face, as I have done,
530 And viewed the rest of her proportioned limbs,
You would contemn my mistress' face too soon; — *despise*
Yet love them both, it nought your honour dims,
One as your wife, the next for beauty's sake,
So of them both a beauteous wife do make.

The glory of her hair is wondrous bright,
Upon her brows doth ebb and flow content,
Her eyes in motion do beget delight,
Her cheeks a tincture to Aurora lent,
Her teeth's no pearl, her eyes[46] no rubies are,
540 But flesh and bone, more red and white by far.

No lisping tongue that fondrels[47] count a grace, — *ninnies*
But doth to well-tuned harmony incline;
A neck inferior nought unto the face,
And breasts most apt for to be pressed by thine;
Now if the outer view so glorious prove,
Judge how the hidden parts procure love.' — *urge*

The king, who all this while lent listening ear,
Being wrapped in admiration of her speech, — *wonder*
Began at length more lively to appear,
550 And for to know one thing of her did seech,[48]
Saying, 'Of what years may this lady be?',
'Just of sweet Myrrha's age', replièd she.

He said, 'Then bring her to confer with me,
That I may try if all be true you say.'
'It is most true, as after you shall see,
But', said the nurse, 'you now must let her stay; — *wait*
Perhaps she'll blush, and be too coy by light,
When she will yield more kindly in the night.

Such pretty dames will hardly yield consent, — *not easily*
560 For in their mouths they always carry "nay";
Yet if you give, to take they are content,
And ne'er refuse, what e'er their tongue do say;

---

[46] eyes] presumably a mistake for 'lips'
[47] fondrels] first and only example cited in the *OED*
[48] seech] Grosart thinks 'seech' should be glossed 'beseech'. This is possible, but 'seek' is perhaps the more likely meaning here.

> For so they nature's simple men abuse,
> When what they love they most of all refuse.
>
> If I do fable, put me unto shame,   *talk idly*
> In saying she resembles Myrrha much,
> For 'tis so much, as if it were the same,
> And, when you seek to gain the love of such,
> Let my experience thus much you assure,
> 570 They, falcon-like, stoop to a gainy lure.   *profitable*
>
> And now you may, void of suspected crime,
> Dally with her in your lascivious bed;
> The sacred Ceres feasts are at this time,
> And there your queen is still.' This scarcely said,
> Quoth Cinyras, 'Bring her this night to me',
> Whereto the nurse replied, 'I do agree.'
>
> With hopeful news the nurse returned again,
> And cheered her chick, and bade her not be sad;   *comforted*
> Her wishèd suit she certain should obtain,
> 580 The news whereof made Myrrha wondrous glad;
> Yet as she joyed she was oppressed with fear,
> Such discords of affections in her were.
>
> Away slips time and hasteneth on the night,
> And now the Bear's seen run about the Pole,
> Conducted forward by Boötes bright;
> The other stars about the axe-tree roll,   *axis*
> The southern images[49] do shine as gold,
> Fit monuments for hunters to behold.
>
> At what time Myrrha wickedly proceeds,
> 590 And takes in hand to act her base desire;
> The shameful lust with cursèd hopes she feeds,
> Which quickly sets her heart upon a fire,
> And thereupon resolveth on her shame,
> And not one thought to contradict it came.
>
> At which the sun his glorious face did hide,
> Each planet pulleth in his golden head,
> The other stars out of the heavens glide,
> And Cynthia from her silver palace fled;
> The night is robbèd of her wonted light,
> 600 Each thing turned dark that formerly was bright.
>
> Three times, by stumbling, Myrrha was foretold
> Of bad success if she did not retire;
> Three times the owls like lessons did unfold,

---

[49] southern images] The reference may be to stars of the southern hemisphere which are visible in southern latitudes of the northern hemisphere.

    Whose doleful note do foul mishap require;   *request*
    Yet she crept on, regarding not the same,
    The want of light allayèd much the shame.

    The nurse doth lead her by her own left hand,
    The right doth grope the dark and desert way;   *forsaken*
    As silent as the night they now do stand,
610   To hear the night crows shriek, and goblins play;
    The lich-fowl[50] beats, and at the window cries
    For to come in, to stay the enterprise.

    'Oh gentle nurse', said Myrrha, 'tell to me,
    What may these screams and doleful shrieks portend?'
    The nurse replied, 'My child, no hurt to thee,
    They are but servants that on night attend;
    These goblins, lich-fowls, owls and night crows too,
    At murders rail, with love have naught to do.'

    And then the beldame leads the lady on,
620   Through many rooms and other turning ways,
    As in a labyrinth they two had gone;
    And as they go, she to the lady says,
    'Now cheer you up, and get a jocund mind
    In thinking of the pleasures you shall find.'

    At last she brings her to the chamber door,
    Which softly she did ope and led her in;
    The lady falls to trembling more and more,
    Her very heart did to relent begin;
    The nearer to the wickedness she went,
630   The more to quake and shiver she was bent.

    Look how you see a blind man on the way,
    Led by another through some desert place,
    Stagger and grope, and at each trifle stay,
    For fear lest he should fall; even in like case
    The wretched nurse the fearful lady leads,
    Who shakes and starts at every step she treads.

    And now she doth her enterprise repent,
    And wish she might unknown return again;
    Unto his bed the pausing nurse then went,
640   And called the king and told him thus much plain:
    'Dread king, awake, of pleasures take thy fill,
    This lady's thine, then use her as you will.'

    The cursèd father then his bowels takes   *offspring*
    Into his bed, O filthy blob and stain!   *pustule*

---

[50] lich-fowl] the screech owl, whose cry was supposed to portend death

His daughter shivers in his arms and quakes,
This being done, the nurse returns again
And said, 'Make much of her; to weep forbear,
Anon you'll[51] weep for that which you now fear.'

The king then cheers his daughter in his arm:
650 'Why dost thou weep? Be still, my sweet, be still,
Come clip thy love, I mean to do no harm;
My kingly bed with pleasures shall thee fill,
And to hide all that idle heads may move,   *foolish, stir up*
Henceforth I call thee daughter and not love.'[52]

Come kiss thy father, gentle daughter then,
And learn to sport thee in a wanton bed.'   *amuse yourself*
'Is this the tricks', she softly said, 'of men?'
And counterfeiting speech unknown, she said:
'A daughter's name, methinks, doth not agree;
660 Is't well with your own child in love to be?'

The king, not deeming who lay by his side,
Replies, 'What hurt, dear lady, can it be?
No ill I know by that means can betide,
The love more firm thereby we common see;
It is not ill though men the same not crave,
For we want daughters till a wife we have.

She did reply, and said: 'Why put the case
That I were Myrrha, for as men do say
My countenance resembleth much her face,
670 Wer't not offence, think you, with me to play?'
Misdeeming nought, again he doth reply: *suspecting*
'No more than 'tis with thee, sweet wench, to lie.'

'O would', quoth Myrrha, 'you could likewise prove,
Whereby I might but know some reason why,
It were not ill to grant to you my love,
That love should then alone to you apply;
Were I your daughter I might well consent,
Say half so much, for me, I am content.'

The king replies, 'My sweet, my will's a law,
680 And may command my subjects when I will;
Besides all this, you furthermore do know
You must obey; I call you daughter still,
Then talk no more.'[53] She said, 'I do agree,
Thy daughter and thy subject yields to thee.'

---

[51] Anon you'll] *1613* 'None wold'. It seems that the nurse now addresses Myrrha, and tells her she'll weep with longing for that which now makes her weep with fear.

[52] I call thee daughter and not love] There is only a brief reference to the fact that Cinyras and Myrrha call each other 'father' and 'daughter' in Ovid.

[53] Then talk no more] It is possible that it is Myrrha who says 'then talk no more'.

O, now the father his own child doth take,
And of his own he doth his own beget;
Of his own loins another child doth make,
Repugnant to the law that nature set;
May one's own seed to procreation move?
690 No sure, unless it doth a monster prove.

Their music is the shrieking of the owls,
As if the fiends came for to sunder them;
The raving dogs affright them with their howls,
As all the fiends came forth to injure them;
The stars behind the clouds, a great way hence,
Like spies lie peeping to disclose the offence.

Their bed doth shake and quaver as they lie,   *tremble*
As if it groaned to bear the weight of sin;
The fatal night-crows at their windows fly,
700 And cries out[54] at the shame they do live in;
And that they may perceive the heaven's frown,
The pucks and goblins pull the coverings down.   *evil spirits*

The pillow that her cursèd head doth bear,
Which is a castle of accursèd ill,
The weighty burden of the same doth fear,
And therefore shrinketh inwards from her still;
Whilst both the ends high swelling with disdain,
Like angry foemen raise themselves amain.[55]   *vehemently*

The bed, more kind than they religious[56] are,
710 Doth seek to shroud their foul defilèd act,
And therefore lets them fall into it far,
As in some vale for to conceal the fact;
Like bulwarks rising to defend their names,
Or swelling mountains to obscure their shames.

O there they lie and glut themselves with sin,
A jocund sin that doth the flesh delight,
A filthy flesh that can delight herein,
A silly joy that 'gainst the soul doth fight,
A fading sport, a pleasure soon forgot,
720 That bringeth shame with an eternal blot.

Thrice happy now had wicked Myrrha been,
If some foul swelling ebon cloud would fall,   *dark*

---

[54] cries out] The subject here is clearly the night-crows even though grammatically the verb requires a singular subject.
[55] 707–08] Lucrece's pillow is similarly affronted (*The Rape of Lucrece*, l. 387), although for a different reason — it has been deprived of a 'lawful kiss' by her hand, and swells on either side of her head with anger (ll. 388–89).
[56] 709] This may be glossed 'the bed is kind to a greater degree than the pillows are religious'.

> For her to hide herself eternal in,
> Or had the bed been burnt with wild fire all,[57]
> And thereby moult the heavens' golden frame,   *melted*
> That all things might have ended with her shame.
>
> And now revenge, a soldier unto lust,
> Comes scouring in as it had been beguiled,   *questing*
> Accompanied with fame and foul distrust,
> 730   And with disgrace, black luxure's basest child;   *lust's*
> These threaten them and blaze abroad the fact,
> And like to trumpets thunder out the act.
>
> Not many nights they spending in this sort,
> But Cinyras at length desired to know
> Who 'twas afforded him this pleasant sport,
> And freely did the courtesy bestow;
> And having done this task used every night,
> Forth he doth steal and goes to seek the light.
>
> O hide thee Myrrha, 'tis not time to sleep,
> 740   A thunderbolt[58] is levelled at thy head;
> Unclose thy eyes, prepare them for to weep,
> With fire and sword thou art betrayed in bed;
> Awaken wench, the day of doom bewray,
> And see the father his own child betray.
>
> And whither steals thou, furious Cinyras?
> Why seek'st a light to open thy own shame?
> Who hop'st to find in this accursèd place?
> Make not such haste to spy thy ignoble game,
> Stay, stay thy feet, thou wilt repent too late,
> 750   Mischief itself comes in with speedy gait.
>
> What, sleep'st thou Myrrha? Why then, sleep thou long,
> Or else awake and welcome in thy woes,
> Another happy day will never come,
> Pale misery thy pleasure overgoes;
> Dream sleeping thou did'st with thy father lie,
> Or wake, and see him revenge the villainy.
>
> Confound thy head and all thy parts with fear,
> And think the fiends encompass thee about,
> Striving with burning tongs thy flesh to tear,
> 760   Pulling thy tongue and eyes with tortures out;
> O think with razors they do flay thy skin,
> Adding new tortures unto every sin.

---

[57] 724] The poet may have stories such as that of Apollonius of Tyre in mind. There a thunderbolt destroys the incestuous pair.
[58] thunderbolt] Cf. note 57.

Now comes the father, being fully bent
For to disclose his love with his fair light;
Sleep Myrrha, thou hast time for to repent,
Arise in cares, pass many a weary night;
Look Cinyras, and spy disgrace too soon,
Myrrha awake, see what thy lust hath done.

Blush, lustful king, and see the end of lust,
770 Behold thy own dishonour and disgrace;
Learn what it is to use thy wife unjust,
And lay a strumpet in her princely place;
Shame follows then, revenge hangs o'er their head,
That basely do defile their marriage bed.

It's like a tender flower, nipped with frost,
That ever after hangs his drooping head,
And hath her wonted prime of glory lost,[59]
Or like the cup that hath his nectar shed;
Crack you the richest pointed diamond,
780 And all his prize and glory's lost and gone.

Old Cinyras, his daughter knowing well,
For very anger could not speak a word,
But into most outrageous fury fell,
And would have killed the lady with a sword,
But nimbly she, by help of cloudy night,
Conveys herself out of her father's sight.

Most like a lion, ranging for a prey,
Each corner of the house he madly looks;
No bar or stop doth hinder him, or stay,
790 He rifles chambers, beds and secret nooks;
This lion seeks for her the dart did throw,[60]
And quickly[61] lets all the other go.

By this the lady's in the Arabian fields,
And fearfully doth range about the same,
Which plenteously the bearing date tree yields;
At length she also through Panchaia came,
Her father's rage being something overpast,
At Saba land she doth arrive at last.

The king, not finding her, begins to fret,
800 And vex himself with anguish, care and grief;
He scolds with fortune, that this trap did set, *wrangles*

---

[59] 775–77] The flower seems to change sex here.
[60] 791] In this stanza Myrrha seems to function both as the lion's hunter and its prey.
[61] quickly] *1613* 'quietly'. A word, perhaps 'hunters', has perhaps been omitted after 'other'. J. Payne Collier who, like Grosart, had no access to *1613* assumes that 'quietly' in *1620* is a revision and sees it as an improvement (*A Bibliographical and Critical Account of the Rarest Books in the English Language*, 2 vols (London: Joseph Lilly, 1865), II, p. 471).

And chides the fates for yielding no relief;
Small sorrows grew till they to greater came,
Like little sparks increasing into flame.

Even as a river, swelling o'er her bounds,
By daily falling of small drops of rain,
Likewise his care continually abounds,
By hourly thinking of his fault again;
Content were found soon in calamity,
810   The thought thereof razed out of memory.

'Daughter', quoth he, with eyes full fraught with tears,
'What hast thou done? O foul accursèd child!
Why hast deceived my aged blossomed hairs?
Why did'st thy princely father so beguile?
Alas! I err, thou art no child to me,
Nor longer I'll thy loving father be.

Go seek some hole eternal to lie in,   *forever*
And nevermore behold the heavens' light;
Thou hast disgracèd all thy name and kin,
820   Then hide thee everlasting from my sight;
Thou hast not only brought us both to shame,
But made thy father actor of the same.

How will thy mother think herself abused,
That hast made her a cuckquean shamefully;   *female cuckold*
Of filthy incest I do thee accuse,
That leman-like did'st with thy father lie;   *lover*
Then hie to hell, haste to the Furies there,
When raging parents witness 'gainst thee bear.

O but the fault thy own[62] was most of all,
830   Poor Myrha thou did'st mean no hurt to me;
I wot,[63] thou said'st (myself I witness call)
'Twas ill with your own child in love to be,
And urged again, 'What if she Myrrha were?'
I basely said there was no fault in her.

Then rent thy brains with terror of the deed,
Confusèd thoughts burst thine accursèd breast,
As if thou did'st on deadly poison feed,
And in Elysium let thy soul ne'er rest;
Roar seas, quake earth, till you devour him
840   That hath defiled his daughter with foul sin.

Yet she did know I was her father dear,
What meant she then to seek me in such sort?
I did not know my daughter to be there,

---

[62] thy own] He now addresses, and blames, himself.
[63] I wot] *1614* 'it wot'

And therefore wishèd her no kind of hurt;
She sinned, and knew her father she abused,
I sinned, uncertain who it was I used.'

By this the sun near passed the Zodiac o'er,
And thrice three signs had fully overrun,
Returning toward the point he was before,
850   Ninety degrees wanting thereto to come;
He had the cliptic[64] save one quarter gone,
And in that space the child ripes in the womb.

When Myrrha, weeping much her burn to bear,   *burden*
Tired with wand'ring in the wood so long,
Weary of life, beginneth for to fear
What shall hereafter of herself become;
Now she perceives the folly lust did bring,
And may take time of penitence to sing.

Things done in haste have time for to repent,
860   A hasty brain is never wanting woe;
Youth with decorum seldom is content,
Young years and lust associate-like do go,
Youth has no wit till it be dearly bought,
And often times then it is good for nought.

'Alas', quoth Myrrha, bursting out with cries,
'What shall I do that have so vilely erred?
Let bellowing groans pierce up unto the skies,
That all the gods to pity may be stirred;
O let some trumpet's voice from thee be driven,
870   To waken mighty Jupiter in heaven.

You gentle gods, that wonted were to hear
The suppliant prayers of distressèd souls,
Now open wide your gracious listening ear,
That I may win some pity with my howls;
O let it stand with your omnipotence,
For to remit the sorrowful's[65] offence.

I do confess my wickedness is much,
And there's no hope that I should favour win,
Yet your still-pardoning clemency is such,
880   That undeservèd you forgive our sin;
We run in errors every day most ill,
Yet you are apt to grant us pardon still.[66]

What have I gained? My father's foul disgrace,
My own dishonour, and my friends' disdain.
What have I won? An imputation base,

---

[64] cliptic] The great circle of the celestial sphere which is the apparent orbit of the sun
[65] sorrowful's] The adjective is used without a modified noun here.
[66] 877–82] Her prayer, particularly its emphasis on abounding mercy, is strongly Christian in tone.

My mother's curse, and a perpetual stain;
I seldom see one mischief to arise,
But it brings others at her heels likewise.

And since my fault into such height is driven
890   That I deserve not in the earth to rest,
Nor have a place amongst the stars in heaven,
You nightly powers, grant me this request:
That neither with the dead nor live I do remain,
And so no place in earth or heaven gain.'

To this, her last request, the gods consent,
And so the ground her feet did cover o'er,
Out from her toes the scrawling roots were sent,   *crawling*
Which by her travel she had bruisèd sore;
These twining roots most plenteously abound,
900   Till they had fixed her body to the ground.

Where be the walls that thou wast wont to have,
The shady groves pavèd with camomile?
The rosy bowers that heat of sun did save,   *preserve*
And yielded to thy sense a pleasant smile?
Where be the pleasant rooms thou solaced in?[67]
Thou art despoiled thereof by thine own sin.

Thou shalt no more within thy chariot ride,
Gazing upon the people kneeling down;
No more will come to woo thee for a bride,
910   Lust hath defiled the type of thy renown;
Those feet of thine, that to offence did lead,
Imprisoned are, and not allowed to tread.

By this the growing tree so far had passed,
That her fair bones to timber turnèd were;
Her marrow did convert to pith at last,
And all her blood the name of sap doth bear;
Her arms to boughs, her fingers branches be,
Her skin to bark, and so she made a tree.

Where is the face that did all faces stain,
920   But shrunk within a hard consolid[68] bark?   *solid*
No one will sue to kiss it once again,
But must be hid perpetually in dark;
That snow-white neck that men desired to touch,
Now they refuse to handle it as much.

Where are those eyes, those glassy eyes of thine,
That lent the glorious sun his chiefest light?
Where is that angel's voice, that voice divine,

---

[67] solace in] *1614* 'solast's in'
[68] consolid] The only instance of this word which is listed in the *OED*

Whose well-tuned tongue did all the gods delight?
What, are they gone? Doth time thy glory rust?
930 No, they be spoiled with incestuous lust.

Farewell thy arms, made kindly to embrace,
But now a bough for birds to perch upon,
Farewell thy pretty fingers in like case,
The curious lute ordained to quaver on;[69]
Your wonted glory you shall see no more,
Your filthy lust hath thrust you out of door.

Nor with her shape she lost her senses quite,
For that and for her fault she weepeth still,
Which tears are held in honour, price and might,
940 And daily do out of the tree distil;
And from the gummy bark doth issue myrrh,
Which evermore shall bear the name of her.

At last the swelling womb divides the tree,
The infant seeking for same passage out;
No nurse nor midwife could the baby see,
The use of speech his mother is without,
And could not therefore beg Lucina's aid,
She might done well could she one prayer said.[70]

And therefore sighs and groans most heavily,
950 Bending most humbly to the ground below,
Shedding from every bough tears plenteously;
At length the gods some favour did bestow,
And so Lucina laid her hand thereon,
And, speaking words, received the child anon.

The wat'ry nymphs this pretty child did take,
And on soft-smelling flowers laid him down,
Of which a curious cradle they did make,
The herbs perfumèd were for more renown;
The nymphs this boy affected more and more,
960 And with his mother's tears still washed him o'er.

As years increase, so beauty doth likewise,
And he's more fair tomorrow than today;
His beauty more and more did still arise,
That envy did delight in him bewray;
As Venus fell in love with him at last,
Who scourged him[71] for his mother's lusting past.[72]

FINIS.

---

[69] 931–34] There is perhaps an echo of Marcus's address to the mutilated Lavinia in *Titus Andronicus* here. He compares her arms to branches (II. 4. 18–20) and notes the way her fingers used to 'tremble [. . .] upon a lute' (II. 4. 45).
[70] 948] 'Have' is to be understood before both verbs in this line.
[71] scourged him] See note 11.
[72] Who scourged him for his mother's lusting past] *1613* 'Who did revenge his mother's lusting past'

JAMES GRESHAM
THE PICTURE OF INCEST (1626)

JAMES GRESHAM
THE PICTURE OF INCEST (1626)

[*Metamorphoses*, X. 287–528]

Sprengius, *Metamorphoses Ovidii* (1563), p. 127ʳ

This version of the story of Myrrha is an expansive but broadly faithful translation of Ovid's tale. It does not seem to have been a widely read or influential text, and it has only once been reprinted. No other works by James Gresham have survived and nothing is known for certain of his life or circumstances. The brief *ODNB* entry for Gresham speculates that he may be the same James Gresham who is recorded as having married a brewer's widow in 1631, and who petitioned the king for clemency after getting into difficulties with his creditors.

Many of Gresham's additions and adjustments have a rather English accent, and he is particularly fond of metaphors relating to ships and the sea. Myrrha wishes that fortune might 'bring me to his bed with wind and sail' (l. 88) and later, when her desires are fulfilled, we are told that 'she attains the port' (l. 479). When she learns that she will gain her desire her conflicting feelings lead to mingled smiles and tears which are likened to an April which is clearly English: 'And therefore weeps, and yet, like April weather, | Again straight smiles, and so in truth doth neither' (ll. 423–24).

One detail in the poem may point to a debt to the slightly earlier *Scourge of Venus*. In that poem, H. A.'s description of the transformed Myrrha (ll. 931–36) seems to echo Marcus's lament for the mutilated Lavinia in *Titus Andronicus* (II. 4. 11–57). Gresham too was apparently influenced by this speech, although he draws on a different detail. Perhaps he was prompted by the example of H. A., yet at the same time wanted to avoid simply copying his predecessor's Shakespearean borrowing:

> Her fair enclasping arms, which but erewhile
> Were snares for amorous lovers to entoil
> Their lust-rapt senses in, were now estranged
> From what they were, and to great branches changed (ll. 607–10)

Although Gresham sometimes seems to misunderstand Ovid's Latin, he can reveal an intelligent critical appreciation of his source material. His apparent engagement both with the context in which Myrrha's story appears in the *Metamorphoses* and with Shakespeare's earlier response to the sequence in *Venus and Adonis* is discussed in the introduction. However, *The Picture of Incest* cannot be said to be an unqualified success; Gresham is a better reader of Ovid than he is a poet. Grosart rates him lower than both H. A. and Barksted,[1] and Flinker dismisses Gresham's 'dull, plodding lines'.[2] The poem is treated slightly more kindly by Elizabeth Haresnape in the *ODNB* — she describes it as a 'competent performance' — and it is hard to argue that it merits any higher praise. Sometimes, for example, one feels aware of Gresham casting around for a rhyme. The word 'surquedries', meaning acts of great arrogance, hardly fits the sense at line 26, and surely only the wish to find a rhyme for 'wooer' could have led Gresham to describe Myrrha beset by 'suers' (pursuers) rather than the expected 'suitors' (l. 35). Gresham makes heavy use of elisions, including some less usual examples such as ''njoy', which have been retained for the sake of the metre. Another of Gresham's quirks is his fondness for hyphenated compounds such as 'sense-delighting-rare-deliciousness' (l. 410). As these are a feature of his style they have also been preserved.

Only two copies of the poem survived, one in the British Library and one in the Beinecke Library, Yale University. The poem was reprinted in 1876 by Alexander Grosart, who based his edition on the British Library copy. The second copy, which was bound in with a selection of other rare printed texts, including a copy of the 1612 edition of Shakespeare's 'Passionate Pilgrim', did not come to light until a few years later.[3]

EDITIONS

James Gresham, *The picture of incest. Liuely portraicted in the historie of Cinyras and Myrrha* (London: [n. pub.] for R. A[llot], 1626), STC 18969.

James Gresham, *The Picture of Incest*, ed. by Rev. Alexander B. Grosart ([Manchester]: [C. E. Simms], 1876).

FURTHER READING

Sarah Carter, *Ovidian Myth and Sexual Deviance in Early Modern English Literature* (London: Palgrave Macmillan, 2011).

Noam Flinker, 'Cinyras, Myrrha, and Adonis: Father-Daughter Incest from Ovid to Milton', *Milton Studies*, 14 (1980), 59–74.

John Loveday, 'A Literary Discovery', *Notes and Queries*, 6 (1882), 124–25.

M. A. Palmatier, 'A Suggested New Source in Ovid's *Metamorphoses* for Shakespeare's *Venus and Adonis*', *Huntington Library Quarterly*, 24 (1961), 164–69.

---

[1] James Gresham, *The Picture of Incest*, ed. by Rev. Alexander B. Grosart ([Manchester]: [C. E. Simms], 1876), p. v.
[2] Flinker, 'Cinyras, Myrrha and Adonis', p. 66.
[3] This discovery is described in John Loveday, 'A Literary Discovery', *Notes and Queries*, 6 (1882), 124–25.

THE PICTURE OF INCEST

    Of strange disasters shall my Muse now sing,
Fathers approach not you my carolling,
Nor you, fair daughters, that in virtue glory,
To taint your chaste ears with my lustful story;
Or if my poor unpolished lines have power
To yield delight unto those hearts of your,   *yours*
Let me not be believed, nor this my tale
Be thought of any credible avail.   *benefit*
Or if to so much truth they gain consent,
10   Yet with the fact believe the punishment.
And sith Dame Nature hath so far transgressed
To suffer such a deed to be confessed,
I'm glad Ismaria[4] and our Orphean Thrace
Are not polluted with an act so base,
And that our native soil so distant lies,
From those wherein there are such villainies.
    Let sweet Panchaia[5] be with riches spread,
And fragrant flowers rarely diaprèd;   *patterned*
May there the taste-delighting cinnamon,
20   Scent-pleasing costus,[6] and the dainty gum   *precious*
Of sweet extracted frankincense there grow,
Whilst that alone can only Myrrha show.
    But sure that tree could not enforce a deed
So bad, from so much goodness to proceed.[7]
No, Myrrha, no — Cupid himself denies
To lend his aid unto such surquedries,[8]
And vindicates his flames from the least wrongs
That to such bestiality[9] belongs;
No, rather have some Stygian fate inspired   *infernal*
30   Thee with a wish by none to be desired.
'Tis lewd to loathe the parent thou should'st rate,   *ill-bred, value*
But this thy love doth even exceed that hate,
Making thee odious and unfit to own
That good the gods upon thee have bestown.
On each hand art thou round beset with suers,   *pursuers*
Both home nobility and foreign wooers,
That both in wit and arms contend and say   *assay*
How to bear thee, the wishèd prize, away.
Of these then, Myrrha, choose thee one to be
40   Thy happy spouse, and let thy sire be free.   *father*

---

[4] Ismaria] Mount Ismarus in Thrace was associated with Orpheus.

[5] Panchaia] (meaning 'all good things') a fabulous island in the 'utopian' tradition, sited somewhere in the Erythrœan Sea, east of Arabia (i.e. an undiscoverable part of *Arabia Felix*), rich in precious stones, incense, myrrh, etc. See Virgil, *Georgics*, II. 139; *Met.*, X. 307–10.

[6] costus] a fragrant root, *saussurea lappa*

[7] 23–24] These confusing lines suggest that Gresham has misunderstood the Latin. Ovid states that the advantage of having a new tree was far outweighed by the terrible crime at its root (*Met.*, X. 310).

[8] surquedries] acts of arrogance. See headnote.

[9] bestiality] indulgence in beastly instincts

        Hereon she ponders, and her lust opposes,
And, to herself, 'What fury', says, 'discloses
My frantic mind? What can I better do?
You sacred gods, and laws parental too,
As you prohibit such a deed's commission,
Resist in me this lawless disposition,
If it at least be lawless. But such favours
Pity[10] forbids to be thought misbehaviours,
Since other creatures, without censuring crime,
50   Do freely couple in their own due time.
      The little heifer, scarce yet aged a year,
Her own begetter on her back may bear,
Yet not be turpious,[11] and the lusty steed   *depraved*
Cover the mare which sprung from his own seed;
The lecherous goat, too, leaps the female she
From whom himself was gendered, and that he
Proceeding from them both, by carnal use,
Oft tups the dam that did himself produce.[12]
Birds with each other too do mate, and by
60   The so up-hatchèd do like fructify,
And I no reason see but we as well
May freely do, when nature doth compel;
O happy they, that have this freedom's bliss,
To couple where they list without amiss,
But most unhappy we that must obey
Such laws as human care provides for stay.   *prevention*
And that whereto our natures most do ply us,   *incline*
That only should those envious laws deny us.
Yea, there are nations too, 'tis said, wherein
70   The bearing mother with her son doth sin,
And the engendering sire his daughter prove,
And by this course ingeminate their love;   *double*
Accursèd I, that, loving as I do,
'Twas not my fortune to be born there too,
But by this island's too too happy[13] fate,
Even seeking love must seem degenerate.
      But why revolve I thus? What help accrues   *ponder*
To my desires by the words I use?
Hence therefore you forbidden thoughts, and fly
80   The troubled breast wherein you lurking lie.
'Tis true my father hath a power to move
An icy disposition unto love,
But yet in me can love nor like no beauty,

---

[10] Pity] This translates *pietas*, a word which does not map simply on to any single English word, but signifies duty and devotion to family, country, and the gods.

[11] turpious] 'Turpious' is not in the *OED* but is clearly related to 'turpid' and 'turpitudinous'.

[12] 56–58] The further incestuous layer here is Gresham's addition.

[13] happy] It is possible that Gresham is using 'happy' to mean simply 'chance', rather than 'fortunate', or that his Myrrha is being ironic.

That aims at aught beyond a filial duty.[14] *anything*
Were my fate such that I were not his daughter,
My wish would then be no such heinous matter;
A smiling fortune might so far prevail
To bring me to his bed with wind and sail.
But now, so ill hath destiny ordained, *unkindly*
90 That though he's mine there's nothing therein gained,
Since that proximity which should combine,
Denies me to be his, or make him mine.
O would I therefore were some other sire's,
That I on him might satiate my desires,
And lose myself amidst those pleasing charms
Which live within the circle of his arms;
Or that 'twere possible for me, by flight,
Leaving these confines and my country's sight,
To fly my destinated woe, and shun *fated, avoid*
100 The shelf[15] that threatens my confusion; *ruin*
But a preposterous-burning-lust restrains *perverse*
My power from doing so, in amorous chains,[16]
Permitting me thus far to reach at bliss,
To hear, and see, and touch, and sometimes kiss,
Though beyond that he grant me nothing more
T'enrich my wish, or make his virtue poor;
"Beyond",[17] said I, fie on thee wretched maid!
Can'st thou even hope for more than th'ast enjoyed?
Or so beguile thy thoughts to think that he,
110 Though thou should'st crave't, would act such villainy? *perform*
Dost thou not weigh that further grants will cause
Both loss of name and breach of human laws,
And make ensuing ages, that shall read
Thy hapless story, blush at thee though dead?
What? Would'st thy mother's rival be, yea more,
Thy father's foul adulterated whore?
Or thy own daughter's sister, and a mother
To that abortive birth thou should'st call brother?
Dost thou not dread those hair-snaked furies' ires,[18]
120 That do not only see thy foul desires,
But can and will, unto thy deed's extent,
Add a condign ensuing punishment?
O quake to think on't, and whilst yet th'art free,
Taint not thy virtuous mind, nor let there be

---

[14] This seems an awkward and unclear translation of 'sed ut pater, est', 'yet is [he worthy of love only] as a father' (*Met.*, X. 337).

[15] shelf] a dangerous sandbank. The word is often used, as here, metaphorically. This is one of Gresham's many maritime figures of speech. Cf. ll. 349–50.

[16] chains] This idea of Myrrha in metaphorical chains is an addition to Ovid and seems, confusingly, to imply that the chains work both to stop her escaping and to prevent her from getting any closer to her father.

[17] Beyond] She picks up on her own use of this word two lines earlier.

[18] 119] Cf. *Met.*, X. 349: 'nec metues atro crinitas angue sorores' (Have you no fear of the sisters with hair of black snakes).

A base pollution of that nature's hests *commands*
Which quite prohibits such unjust requests,
And which, though thou should'st, as thou crav'st, obtain,
Would even at best be but a fleeting gain.
    My father too is pious and precise
130 In due observing of his country's guise, *custom*
And one that by no fascinating art
Will be seduced to render up his heart,
Though, O, I wish, and fervently desire,
There burnt in him the selfsame ardent fire,
That as my heart on his perfections dote,
So he of me and mine would take like note.
But deep and strange must that art be can lure
A mind so good to aught that's so impure.'
    Thus to herself she said. But stupid he, *stupefied*
140 Whom plenty of great suitors made to be
Ambiguous what to do, little supposing *uncertain*
Her thoughts bent to a fact of so much loathing, *deed*
With secret scrutiny assays to know,
By iterating such as did her woo,
Towards whose desert her best affection stands,
To link herself in matrimonial bands. *bonds*
    To this at first she locks her lips, as grieving
To think how far her wish was from relieving,
But after looking with transpiercing eyes
150 Upon her sire, whose love 'twas did surprise
Her heart with lust, vents from her troubled breast
Vollies of sighs, the symptoms of unrest,
And from her rosy cheek a dew let glide
Of pearly tears, like those in summer tide
Falling on the ripe cherries, which the sun
After exhales from lying thereupon,
And with this tear-distillèd shower doth shroud
Her star-like eyes within her apron cloud,[19]
Which strange distemperature of hers, her father, *disorder*
160 Deeming of fear, not lust, yet knowing neither,
Forbids her weeping, and with gentle touch
Wipes her wet eyes, then kisses her as much,
With which she seems to be so much o'erjoyed,
That she even wishes to be still thus cloyed
With the ambrosiac nectar of his lips,
And never to be out of this eclipse.[20]
    He, thinking now if ever had his carriage
Won a wished time to win her unto marriage,
Consults again with her desires, to find
170 What kind of man it was would please her mind,
To whom, as glad by this means to express

---

[19] 153–58] This extended simile is Gresham's invention.
[20] eclipse] Here apparently indicating an embrace which conceals her from sight

The white[21] she levelled at in this distress,
  She thus replies:[22] 'The man that must obtain
  The conquest of my heart, and my bed gain,
  Must in all parts, dear sire, resemble thee,
  Or never look to be embraced by me.'
  Whilst he, not knowing her close thoughts, applauds   *secret*
  Of this her liking, and with lavish lauds
  Says, 'Daughter, may'st thou be thus duteous still,
180 And evermore obey thy father's will;
  The gods will sure reward thee for't, and crown
  Thy duty with perpetual renown.'
     No sooner was that word of 'duty' spoken,
  But straight her countenance with a change was stroken,   *struck*
  As conscious to herself of that foul fact
  Which with her agèd sire she sought to act,
  And grieving that those words, which she intended
  To break the ice,[23] should be misapprehended.
     It now was midnight, and a silent sleep
190 Did cares from mind and toils from body keep,
  When watchful Myrrha, too too hapless maid,
  Is to her former enemy betrayed,
  And so pursued by her unquiet thoughts,
  That night no sleep unto her eyes allots,
  But doth again retract[24] that lewd desire
  Which blew the coals to this incestuous fire,
  And one while timorously despairs to try,
  And yet again resolves it by and by.
  Shaming to ask, she covets what she shames,
200 And these unwilling willing motions blames;
  On every side is her attempt beset
  With hope to forward and with fear to let,   *hinder*
  And in this conflict, what her heart should do,
  Cannot resolve or give consent unto.
     But as the tree, hewn by the sharp-edged steel,
  After a many wounds[25] begins to reel,
  Tremblingly doubtful on which hand to fall,   *side*
  And is on every side much feared of all,
  So stood she, shaken with a various passion,
210 By her too temerous timorous inclination.   *reckless*
  That which dissuades seems light, and what allures

---

[21] white] a white target on a butt in archery

[22] 173–76] It is characteristic of Gresham's expansive mode of translation that he stretches Myrrha's effectively laconic 'similem tibi', 'one like you' (*Met.*, X. 364), to three and a half lines.

[23] To break the ice] As Grosart notes, this is an early use of a now common idiom.

[24] 195–210] Gresham is following the Latin verb *retracto* (*Met.*, X. 370) at this point, which may mean either to 'withdraw' or 'renew'. This atmosphere of paradox is compounded by 'unwilling willing' and 'temerous timorous' and by the phrase 'with fear to let'. The ultimate meaning of the phrase is clear but we can reach that meaning either by deciding that 'let' means 'prevent' or its opposite, 'allow'. Is she beset by the emotion of fear, working to prevent, 'let', her passion? Or is she frightened to allow, 'let', herself be overcome?

[25] a many wounds] The phrase 'a many' followed by a plural noun is common in the period.

As great and just a punishment procures,
And nothing can her thoughts intend, but straight
One change or other on those thoughts do wait.
Much like the billows of the boiling sea,
In a tempestuous and cloudy day,
Where one wave following the first amain,   *with full force*
Comes straight a third that breaks them both in twain.
   No mean nor ease can her distempers find,
220 But that which death affords the love-sick mind,
And that indeed she hugs and straight resolves
To put in execution; then involves
Her fair neck with her zone, tied to that heighth,   *girdle*
That falling thence she so might climb to death.
   And having thus prepared herself to run
On her own woeful, sad confusion:
'Farewell dear father', cries she, 'when I'm dead
Let yet my death's cause be rememberèd,
And since my life durst not my love make known,
230 Let my desires by this my death be shown.'
And therewith apts her girdle's knot t'enchain   *prepares*
Her azure-veinèd neck, to ease her pain.
   'Tis said the mournful murmur of her tears
And sorrow's tones, came to her nurse's ears,
Who then, full little dreaming what a fact   *deed*
Her foster charge was now about to act,
Of self-contriving death, was not far laid
From the sad stage whereon this scene was played,
And, hearing her, straight rises, and with speed
240 Opening the doors, and guessing at the deed
By what she saw provided, first expresses
Her wonder by her cries, tearing her tresses,
And miserably lacerating[26] with her knife
Her age-ploughed bosom, then, to save her life,[27]
Breaks from her tender neck that hard knot tied,
By which so sweet a beauty sought t'have died,
And with soft, kind embraces bids her clear
Those heavens, her eyes, that weeping clouded were,
Earnestly craving what the cause might be,
250 That dragged her thoughts to this self tragedy.
Whilst she, as one dumb stricken, stands at gaze,[28]
With a dejected look, and nothing says,
But grieves that by her death's too slow dispatch,
Her too kind nurse should her so tardy catch.

---

[26] The inappropriateness of the word 'macerating' in the original text suggests a misreading or mishearing by the typesetter, which has been emended here.
[27] her life] i.e. Myrrha's life.
[28] at gaze] The phrase 'at gaze' is most often used of a cornered deer, and this lends an extra significance to the fact that she is 'dumb stricken' and may well remind the reader of the many unfortunate characters in Ovid, Actaeon and Io for example, who are unable to speak following metamorphosis into an animal.

      She, good old nurse, conjures her still with love,   *beseeches*
To show what did these tears' effusion move,
And with her nak'd and wrinkled breasts displayed,
Which hoary age had dry and withered made,
Entreats her by her infant swathlings, and   *swaddling clothes*
260   The food she first receivèd from her hand,
When in her now exhaust and shrivelled nipple   *exhausted*
There then was pleasant milk for her to tipple,
That unto her she would those griefs impart,
Which seemed so much to overload her heart,
Persuading her that "griefs oft kill concealed,
But find redress when th'are in time revealed."
To all which Myrrha, still with silent gaze,
Turning aside, sighs, but yet nothing says,
As one whose thoughts presaging no relief
270   Would rather die than utter forth her grief.
      The gentle nurse, as yet in knowledge blind
What these distempers moved, but bent to find
The fount from whence they flowed, with promise made
Both of her secrecy and utmost aid
(To her best age-worn strength) in aught that might
Assuage these passions, or her heart delight,
Again thus woos her: 'Sweet child, let me know
What sudden grief this is torments thee so,
And what my aged experience can redress,
280   My willing power shall speedily express.
Be't a distracting frenzy, I've a charm
Of sovereign herbs to cure thee of that harm;   *supremely excellent*
Or be'st thou hurt by some malignant fate,
I've yet a spell shall shield thee from that hate;
Or dread'st thou some incensèd god, lo, I
With sacred rites that ire can pacify.
What should I more suggest? Good fortune, she
Sweetly smiles on thee, and as yet we're free
From all incursions; yea, thy sire and mother
290   Are living too, and nightly 'njoy each other.'[29]
      Myrrha no sooner hears the name of sire
Fall from her nurse's lips, but all on fire,
'Like the dry flax to which the smallest coal
Serves as a taper to enflame the whole';
She breathes forth many a sigh, whilst still th'old crone
The cause conceives not of her heavy moan,
But yet suspects she loves, and therefore still
Sticks to her former purpose, and doth will
That, whatsoever 'twere, she yet would please
300   To let her know't, and try her age's ease,[30]
And therewith takes the tear-distilling maid

---

[29] 290] The nurse's rather curious assurance that Myrrha's parents enjoy each other every night is an addition to Ovid.

[30] age's ease] This might be glossed 'the comfort and experience which she can provide because of her age'.

Into her lap, and with weak arms displayed,	*extended*
Impaling³¹ her fair corpse, says, 'Come, I know	
The troubled spring from whence these streams do flow;	
Thou art in love, and either sham'st to say	
With whom, or doubt'st lest I'll the same bewray.	
But credit me, my aid shall serve t'express	
How far I am from such perfidiousness,	
Nor shall my tongue one word thereof reveal	

310 Unto thy father, but the same conceal.'
At which, her ill concluding words, enraged,   *bounds*
Breaking the pale wherein she was encaged,
And with her face pressing the neighbour bed,
As one more grieved than joyed by what she'd said,
Cries, 'O depart, and spare a further quest
Of that which shame constrains me to detest,
And either leave me to myself alone,
Or cease to question more my rueful moan;
For what you crave, t'enrich your knowledge by,

320 Is but a lewd incestuous villainy.'
    Hereat th'old beldame starts, and, what with fear   *aged woman*
And bedrid age, of many a hoary year,
With trembling hands upheaved, doth grovelling lie,
To gain the cause of this her misery;
And one while with delusive flattery sues
To screw it out, another while doth use
The sharp compulsive menaces of death,
By showing her the means to do it with,³²
Adding withal to these her mixed persuasions,

330 All her officious help t'assuage her passions.
    Heart-grievèd Myrrha at those words erects
Her downcast looks, and with such sad effects
As showed how deep sh'was hurt, with briny tears
Bedews her nurse's bosom, and still fears
To let her know't, and yet was oft about
To make it known, yet would not let it out.
But with her vesture clouding those fair skies   *garment*
Wherein there shone at once two sun-like eyes,
"And by these words, like little sparks foreshowing

340 What kind of fire 'twas in her breast was glowing",
Says, 'Happy, O thrice happy art thou sped,
Dear mother, that enjoy'st my father's bed.'
And therewith sighing, shuts her lips, ashamed
To utter more, and therefore leaves't unnamed.
The agèd nurse hereat, with tremor filled,

---

³¹ Impaling] To impale, in this context, means to surround with pales, to fence in. Cf. l. 312 where the image of confinement is continued. This may also pick up on the earlier implied comparison between Myrrha and a desperate hunted animal (l. 251), and also strongly echoes *Venus and Adonis* (ll. 229–32) in which Venus describes Adonis as a deer, herself as a park, and her clutching fingers as an 'ivory pale' preventing him from escaping.

³² 326–28] This seems to represent a misunderstanding of the Latin. In Ovid the nurse simply threatens to reveal her attempted suicide.

Is almost to a jelly pale distilled,
And with her snow-white hairs bristled upright,
Showing how much these words her heart affright,
Strives with request to make her shun that shelf
350 By which she sought to shipwreck her fair self,
And, if 'twere possible, to quench that flame
Which seemed to kindle such a fire of shame.
But she, though knowing what her nurse advised
Was friendly counsel, not to be despised,
And on what dangerous seas her lust must sail
Before it could arrive where't might avail,
Resolves, for sure, that if she did not reap
The fruit sown with so many tears, to heap
Upon her lust self-murder, and thereby
360 To end at once both life and misery.
Her loving nurse, fearing this resolution
Might prove indeed her beauty's dissolution,
If not prevented, to her wounds applies
Sage sovereign oils of age-taught subtleties,
And bids her live, and rather than destroy
So sweet a fabric, fully to enjoy   *body*
Her so much loved — but durst not father name,
For fear to move in her both grief and shame,
And to these words of comfort swears to join
370 Her best endeavour to content her mind.
'Twas now the ripening autumn, the wished time,
Wherein the agèd matrons of that clime,
With snow-white vestures o'er their bodies spread,
And each a corn-made garland on her head,
Did use to celebrate the annual feasts
Of sacred Ceres with their corn and beasts,
'Gainst which solemnity, for nine nights' space,
All venial acts of manly sweet embrace
Were quite prohibited. Unto this throng
380 Comes the ag'd wife of Cinyras among,
Willing to act the secret mysteries
Of those commanding sacred deities,
And to omit no service which might show
The great respect she to those gods did owe.
Whilst therefore by these rites the nuptial bed
Was of its lawful charge disburdenèd,
The ill-seducing nurse, whom age had made
A sound proficient in this kind of trade,   *reliable expert*
Having with wine and fascinating art
390 Bereft the weak-brained Cinyras of his heart,
And brought him to her lure, by cunning gloze,   *deceit*
Doth Myrrha's love in a forged name disclose,
Flattering his fancy with a feignèd lie,
That such a virgin loved him, whose bright eye
Reflected rays of wonder, and should he
Deny her what she sought, 'twould doubtless be

	Her life's consumer, therefore craves with speed	
	That he'd accept her proffer in this need,	*proposition*
	Adding such further praises to her feature	
400	As she best thought might move a yielding nature.	
	He, rapt with wonder, straight desires to know	
	How old that beauty was, that loved him so,	
	To whom she, sense-deluding-crone, replies,	
	'Her years and Myrrha's do just sympathize,	*agree*
	And through my life's long course I cannot tell	
	That e'er I saw a nearer parallel.[33]	
	Hereat he forthwith loves, and craves with speed	
	To bring her to his bed, the mark indeed	*goal*
	At which she aimed, that so he might possess	
410	That sense-delighting-rare-deliciousness.	
	No sooner did his words his wish impart,	
	As lust still speeds when it is helped by art,	
	But back returns the old trot, to discover	*beldame, reveal*
	To her sad charge how she had won her lover,	
	And thus begins, 'Rejoice child, the thing's done,	
	And that great difficulty's overthrown,	
	Which thou thought'st so impossible, and he	
	To whom thou late wert thralled 's now slave to thee.'	
	Ill did th'unhappy virgin entertain	
420	This hapless knowedge of her father's gain,	*unfortunate*
	As one whose heart too truly did presage	
	The sad events of her lust-fired rage,	
	And therefore weeps, and yet, like April weather,	
	Again straight smiles, and so in truth doth neither,	
	But as the current of her passions wind,	*twist*
	So do the various discords of her mind.	
	Now posts swift-wingèd time towards night with speed,	*hurries*
	Making the same as black as was the deed,	
	And with a death-like silence hath possessed	
430	Whatever might disturb a quiet rest;	
	And even now hath Charleswain-chariot[34] run	
	His midway journey from the setting sun,	
	When on she goes to perpetrate that fact	
	Which none but such a minotaur[35] would act.	
	The pale-faced moon, thereat ashamed, doth shroud	*conceal*
	Her silver rays in an obscuring cloud,	*darkening*
	And those bright stars, which nightly used to blaze	
	Their glorious splendour to the world's amaze,	
	Are with black curtains so close overspread,	

---

[33] 404–06] Like H. A., Gresham seems to want to make Cinyras more culpable than in Ovid. Although the nurse in Ovid declares that the girl is the same age as Myrrha, the assertion that she never saw 'a nearer parallel' is Gresham's own addition.

[34] Charleswain-chariot] Gresham seems not to realize that 'Charles' Wain' means Charles's wagon — and prints Charleswaine as one word before adding the superfluous 'chariot'.

[35] minotaur] As well as being a monster, the minotaur was the product of an unnatural liaison between Queen Pasiphaë and a bull.

440	That not the least can be discoverèd.	
	The night itself[36] too wants that wonted light	*lacks, accustomed*
	Which usually it had before that night,	
	And each thing so prodigiously seems bent,	
	As if they justly feared a sad event.	
	Thrice did her stumbling feet seem to foreshow	
	How swiftly she was posting to her woe,	
	And thrice th'ill-boding screech-owl with harsh throat	
	Croaks out an ominous and fatal note,	
	Divining what that foul act's end would be,	
450	That in each scene had so much prodigy.	*abnormality*
	But on she trudges, shrouded by the dark	
	From the least lustre of a shameful spark,	
	With one hand holding her lust-guiding mother,[37]	
	And groping out the blind way with the other.	
	At last, "as oft bad actions hit their aim,	
	Though in the end they perish with the same",	
	She finds the chamber door, and without din,	
	Opening the same, with soft pace enters in,	
	When straight an aspen tremor doth so shake	*immediately*
460	Her feeble-timbered joints, and therewith make	
	Her legs so falter, that with fatal luck	
	Did she the fruit from that forbid tree pluck,	
	The milk-dipped rose vermilion in her cheek	
	Fled from its seat, some safer place to seek,	
	And that angel-like face, in which before	
	There sat a godlike beauty to adore,	
	Did nothing but a bloodless pale retain,	*pallor*
	To link both deed and issue in one chain.[38]	
	Her wonted courage leaves her too, and still	
470	The nearer she approaches to her ill,	
	The more she trembles, and abhors to think	
	How nigh she'was[39] brought unto her wish's brink.	
	It irks her now that e'er she was so unwise	
	To undertake so hard an enterprise,	
	And only wishes to retire, so none	
	Might either[40] see her, or she pass unknown.	
	But after long delay, still steered by	

---

[36] The night itself] The translation is rather awkward here, as Gresham seems to imply that the night might naturally be lit by something other than the moon and stars. Ovid's own 'nox caret igne suo', 'night lacks its light' (*Met.*, X. 450), is more clearly a summary of the effects of the eclipsed moon and stars rather than a new piece of information.

[37] lust-guiding mother] The reference to the nurse being a 'mother' to Myrrha is bleakly ironic.

[38] 459–68] This section is much more elaborate than it is in Ovid, and the precise force of some of the details isn't fully clear. It is perhaps possible that Gresham intends the comparison between Myrrha and a tree to be extended over the course of the passage. Thus when he describes her plucking fruit from the forbidden tree, the tree must be understood, slightly confusingly, as Myrrha herself, and the lost 'fruit' is symbolized by the loss of colour in her face. The case for such a reading is strengthened if we see it as a prolepsis of Myrrha's imminent literal metamorphosis into a tree.

[39] she'was] The apostrophe signals the need to elide the two words as a monosyllable.

[40] either] 'Either' is delayed here, making the sense at first unclear. She hopes either not to be seen at all, or to be mistaken for someone else.

	Her age-experienced nurse's policy	
	In these distractions, she attains the port,	
480	Her father's bed, so longed for in this sort,	
	Whom when her nurse bequeaths to his desires,	
	'Here', says she, 'Cinyras, quench thy lustful fires,	
	And ravel out thy thread of life in pleasure,	
	With that which thou account'st thy age's treasure.[41]	
	Here may'st thou satiate without surfeit, and	
	Enjoy more riches than thy realm command.'	
	And with this heart-delighting-music joins	
	Their destinated breasts for amorous twines,	*embraces*
	Such as indeed are only free for those	
490	That in a lawful marriage bed repose.	
	Her sense-deluded-sire, with arms displayed,	*outspread*
	As one not dreaming to be thus betrayed,	
	Receives into his dark and wanton bed	
	The tender bowels he so fosterèd,	*offspring*
	And with his nectar-candied-words assays	*attempts*
	To drive the damsel from her virgin maze,	*amazement*
	Adding unto these words such pleasing action	
	As he best thought might give her satisfaction,	
	And to complete and make this tide of pleasure	
500	Flow to a greater height and fuller measure.	
	Because her age so justly did resemble	
	Myrrha's, whom she both was and did dissemble,	*imitate*
	They interchange their names, as being nather,	*neither*
	He her sweet daughter calls, she him kind father.	
	Th'incestuous game thus ended, and she, full	
	Of that adulterate fruit she came to pull,	
	Departs, and leaves her new beguilèd sire	
	To guess what sweet thus pleased his fond desire,	
	Bearing within her wretched womb that seed	
510	Which nature made, but lust did merely breed,	
	And the next night returns to clear the score	
	Which both had jointly left unpaid before,	
	Pursuing her desires in that swift sort,	
	As if she wished no end to such sweet sport.	
	At length, when after many nights' exchange	
	Of kind embrace betwixt these lovers strange,[42]	
	And equal intermixture of such sweets	
	As are there used, where love with like love meets,	
	His mind began to crave one happy sight	
520	Of that obscured fuel of delight,	
	Which he so oft had locked within his arms,	
	And freed from rougher handlings and worse harms,	
	But never viewed, and only in obscurity	

---

[41] 484] This rather pointed characterization of the supposedly unknown girl again implies that Cinyras ought to have guessed, and perhaps subconsciously realizes, that she is Myrrha.

[42] 516] This line opposes 'kind' and 'strange' to provide interplay between their meaning as, respectively, 'of kin' and 'not of kin'.

>   Had cropped the sweet flower of her virgin purity;
>   He forthwith craves accordingly to see
>   What this same peerless paragon might be,
>   Whom when apparently his eyes beheld   *manifestly*
>   To be indeed his own and only child,
>   And therewith weighed what an abyss of sin
> 530 His sordid bestial lust had plunged him in,
>   "For vice as till't be acted's ever blind,
>   So when 'tis done it leaves a sting behind",
>   Distracting rage then so possessed his heart,
>   And grief his organ speech, that up he start,   *leapt*
>   And in his fury drawing forth the blade
>   Which fate for this her fault had ready laid,
>   Thought to have sheathed it in that tender breast
>   In which but now his chief'st content did rest.
>   But what with fear of this attempt, and stung
> 540 With the remembrance of that horrid wrong
>   Which she, as in a crystal mirror true,
>   The veil uncovered, did now plainly view,
>   "For perpetrated vice seen after action
>   Appears so foul it oft drives to distraction",[43]
>   Away she flies, and by the help of night
>   Avoids the tragic end of her affright,
>   And ushered by her thoughts, at random roves   *led*
>   Among the large and solitary groves,
>   Leaving the sweet Arabia, and those fields
> 550 Of rich Panchaia which rare odour yields,
>   And nine moons wanders in this careless race,   *journey*
>   Before her fear can find a resting place;
>   Till in the end, not able to sustain
>   A longer durance of her gravid pain,   *pregnant*
>   She seats her in Sabaea,[44] where a while
>   She strives her lust-bred sorrows to beguile,
>   But can scarce longer make her burdened womb,
>   Th'incestuous load therein enclosed entomb;
>   With grief thereof, even ignorant of prayer,
> 560 And almost brought unto a foul despair,
>   By a heart-wounding and afflicting strife
>   Between a feared death and wearied life,
>   She thus in doleful and soul-grieving plaints
>   Bewails the discord of these combatants:
>   'O you all-sacred-deities', quoth she,
>   'That rule the world with sovereign majesty,
>   And guide the heavenly motions of the spheres
>   With supreme power, if you have any ears
>   To hear the woeful, sad and mournful moans
> 570 Of poor, distressèd, wretched, mortal ones,
>   Such as with hearts unfeignèd do confess

---

[43] 539–44] This description of Myrrha's state of mind is Gresham's elaboration.
[44] Sabaea] *1626* 'in a Sabra'. As Grosart notes, this is almost certainly an error for *Sabaea* (*Met.*, X. 480).

       Their soul-deep ulcerated wickedness,
       Hearken, O hearken then, unto my cry,
       Who, as I have deserved, desire to die,
       And will not your dread powers invoke to shun   *avoid*
       The smarting rod of your correction.
       Pour down your angry vengeance on my head,
       That against nature have thus trespassèd,
       And let me now no longer live to shame
580   The lovely sex and root from whence I came.
       But lest my lingering life may be offence,
       To such as shall survive my impudence,
       And my dead corpse those neighbour graves distain,   *stain*
       By whose offenceless sides they must be lain,
       Let me partake neither of life or death,
       To grieve the one, or soil the other with.
       But so transformèd be, that I of either
       May seem possessed, but yet indeed have neither.'
       No sooner were these words effused, but straight   *poured out*
590   A strange effect upon her wish did wait,   *attend*
       Wrought by some certain deity whose ear
       Was bent her pity-moving moan to hear,
       And give redress to. For whilst yet her prayer
       Was uttering, but not quite dissolved to air,
       Those goodly pillars,[45] which but erst did grace   *recently*
       Her stately moving fabric, in their pace
       Were so involved within the humid earth,   *intertwined*
       As if they only there had had their birth,
       And from her flesh-transformèd[46] nails and toes,
600   An[47] outstretched, crooked, winding root there grows,
       From whence the long trunk of the lofty tree
       Receives its prime foundation and degree.
       Her body sweet, so comely in each part,
       Doth to the middle of the tree convert,
       Within whose metamorphosed sapphire veins,
       The life-maintaining marrowy-sap remains.
         Her fair enclasping arms, which but erewhile
       Were snares for amorous lovers to entoil   *entrap*
       Their lust-rapt senses in, were now estranged
610   From what they were, and to great branches changed,
       Through whose each little spray her blood, like juice,
       Dispreads itself with profuse avarice.
       Her dainty fingers too, not hereto borne,   *hitherto*
       Into sun-shading little boughs do turn,
       And finally her snow-white silk-smooth-skin
       Becomes a rough hard bark of what't had bin,

---

[45] 595–96] The words 'fabric' and 'pillars' both associate Myrrha with a building. See introduction, p. 12.

[46] flesh-transformèd] There is no hyphen in *1626*, but the sense seems to demand that these two words are read as a compound epithet, qualifying 'nails and toes'.

[47] An] *1626* 'And'. The sense of the sentence seems to demand 'An'. 'And' was perhaps introduced because this was the first word of the previous line.

```
             Serving to shield her, as her clothes had done,
             Both from the winter's rage and piercing sun.
             In this wise 'gins th'uprising tree t'entomb
620          Within its hollow grave her painful womb,
             And hath, with quicker speed than thought, o'erpressed          crushed
             Those love-delighting hillocks of her breast,
             And with swift change is hastening to enshrine
             Her stately neck within its rugged rine;                       rind
             All which she shuns not, but, as to her fate,
             With willing mind herself doth subjugate
             To the surcrescent⁴⁸ bark, which gliding over
             Doth, as a cloud the sun, her fair face cover;
             And though with this, her body's just correction,
630          She lost both light of reason and affection,                   feeling
             Yet still she weeps, in sign whereof her tears
             On the tree's rind in lukewarm drops appears,
             Wherein a sweet and odoriferous smell
             Of sense-delighting fragrancy doth dwell,
             Which for its worth a semblable name we give,                  similar
             That no age shall forget, nor time outlive.
             But now begins th'incestuous birth to grow
             Unto its full maturity of woe,
             Within the bark-walled limits of the tree
640          Wherewith she was enclosed in misery;
             Striving to burst a way through the dark tomb
             Of her transformed, incarcerating womb,
             Her gravid belly swells unto that heighth,
             That each small throb seems now to threaten death,
             Making her stretch and struggle with the pain
             Which her ripe birth did urge her to sustain.
             Words she hath none to utter or express
             The unknown measure of her wretchedness,
             Nor to invoke a gracious help from those
650          Whose sacred powers help women in their throes,
             But still expects delivery from that sorrow,
             Which as it had no mean,⁴⁹ no help could borrow.
             The bending tree seems with sad hollow tones
             To echo forth her many ruthful groans,                         exciting pity
             And with a flood of tears, gushed from her eyes,
             Bedews and wets itself in piteous wise,
             Whereat the tender-hearted Juno,⁵⁰ grieved
             To see so much distress, so unrelieved,
             Standing as then close by the mourning sprays,⁵¹
```

---

⁴⁸ surcrescent] *1626* 'surcrescent'. Grosart asserts that the word is unknown, but seems to derive from the Latin *succrescere*, 'to spring up, to grow from under'. The *OED* notes this spelling but identifies this as the only instance of the word 'surcrescent', to grow upon or over.

⁴⁹ mean] instrument, here presumably a mouth; could also mean 'intermediary', hence the idea of borrowing.

⁵⁰ Juno] It is Lucina who helps Myrrha in Ovid. Lucina is an epithet of Juno.

⁵¹ sprays] This word might refer either to the tears or to the branches. Such wordplay is characteristically Ovidian — Ovid exploits the fact that *medulla* means both pith and marrow when describing the metamorphosis of Myrrha, for example (*Met.*, X. 492).

660 Puts to her helping hand, and then assays *puts forth*
  With words of child-bed comfort to delude *beguile*
  The wounding sense of this, her solitude.
   Forthwith the womb-swoll'n-tree-begins to crack,
  And through the cleaving bark doth passage make,
  For nine months' growth to enter at, when lo,
  She straight yields up the burden of her woe,
  Which had no sooner birth, but, as allied
  Unto its mother's misery, it cried.
  The neighbouring naiades, whose cells not far *dwellings*
670 From her distressed delivery distant were,
  Hearing the cry, approach, and in their arms
  First taking the young babe, yet free from harms,
  And then, with tender touch, laying him down
  Upon the new-grown, smooth and soft-grassed ground,
  Embalm him with the sweet-myrrh-trickling tears
  Which on his tree-changed-mother's-bark appears.
  Swift posting time had not long run his race
  Before this birth began to wax in face, *child, develop*
  And each part else so lovely, that his feature
680 Grew nature's wonder in a so born creature,
  And envy's self delight. For such as was
  That beauty of the world, which did surpass
  All others, whom the curious artists paint
  In tables naked, and do call love's saint,
  Even such was he, and in a just compare
  Each way as lovely-sweet, as young, as fair;
  And taking from the first his bow and arrows,
  Wherewith he heals by love, and wounds with sorrows,
  Or adding but the like unto the t'other,
690 You'd swear that this were Cupid and no other,[52]
  So fair in matchless beauty did his fate
  Conspire to make him, though unfortunate.

 FINIS.

---

[52] 689–90] The use of an identical rhyme may reflect the perfect resemblance between Cupid and Adonis.

DUNSTAN GALE
PYRAMUS AND THISBE (1617)

DUNSTAN GALE
PYRAMUS AND THISBE (1617)

[*Metamorphoses*, IV. 55–166]

Sprengius, *Metamorphoses Ovidii* (1563), p. 48ʳ

This adaptation of the story of Pyramus and Thisbe from Book IV of the *Metamorphoses* is the only known work of Dunstan Gale. Although the earliest surviving edition dates from 1617, the title page is dated November 1596, and it seems highly likely that it was first published in 1596 or 1597. Although the subject matter of the poem prompts critics to invoke it as a context for *A Midsummer Night's Dream*, it remains a work largely overlooked. Moreover, the dates of the two works make it difficult to determine the direction of influence. Ritson suggests that it might have been the 'butt of Shakespeare's ridicule' in the mechanicals' interlude.[1] However, other commentators, including Malone, believe Gale's poem post-dated Shakespeare's play.[2] There are few close parallels, and it is perhaps most likely that these two near-contemporaneous works were written quite independently. But there are some temperamental affinities between the two versions. Gale's poem has a strong element of burlesque, although not all critics have acknowledged the self-conscious nature of its many absurdities — the odd disjuncture between the elaborate passages of conceited artificiality and the moments of simplicity shading into bathos. Kenneth Muir, for example, dismisses Gale's poem as simply 'dull and bad'[3] and William Keach describes it as

---

[1] Joseph Ritson, *Remarks, Critical and Illustrative, on the Texts and Notes of the Last Edition of Shakespeare* (London: J. Johnson, 1783), p. 47. See also A. B. Taylor, 'Golding's Ovid, Shakespeare's "Small Latin", and the Real Object of Mockery in "Pyramus and Thisbe"', *Shakespeare Survey*, 42 (1990), 53–64.
[2] *The Plays and Poems of William Shakespeare with the Corrections and Illustrations of Various Commentators*, ed. by Edmond Malone, 21 vols (London: Printed for R. C. and J. Rivington *et al.*, 1821), IV, p. 193.
[3] Kenneth Muir, 'Pyramus and Thisbe: A Study in Shakespeare's Method', *Shakespeare Quarterly*, 5 (1954), 141–53 (p. 146).

'ludicrous'.[4] Matthew Steggle's life of Gale, in the *ODNB*, by contrast, describes it as an extreme example of the 'deliberately comic and self-destructively parodic aspects of the [epyllion] form'. Without speculating about any possible direct influence, there is something rather Bottom-like here, for example, in the narrator's helpful anxiety to clarify a point for his apparently clueless readers:

> The town's forgot, and with the town, the name;
> Within which town (for then it was a town)
> Dwelt two commanders of no small renown. (ll. 4–6)

The poem's overwrought and mannered style may partly reflect a straightforward pleasure in patterned repetition. For example, Gale is particularly attached to the polyptoton (the use of words with the same stem but different forms) such as blush(ed) and start(ed) in these lines:

> And spying Thisbe, Thisbe made him start,
> And he her blush, so tender was her heart;
> She blushed, because another was so near,
> He started, for to find another there. (ll. 31–34)

But although it may be assumed that Gale enjoyed crafting such patterns, it would seem that he was also aware of the potential for absurdity in overly elaborate rhetorical devices. The lovers are very childish — they are described as 'brattish elves' (l. 86) by Venus. Their adolescent passion is suggested when Gale describes their erotic suspense, asserting that they 'both did sit on briars' (l. 145). The dramatization of a split between a character's different faculties or attributes was a common device in the poetry of the period — the battle between the red and white in Lucrece's cheeks is described as a battle between her beauty and her virtue for example (*The Rape of Lucrece*, ll. 50–77) — but Gale is surely deliberately engineering absurdity in his own elaborately staged dispute between Pyramus's different body parts and faculties (ll. 311–46).

Assuming that the first edition was indeed first published in the late 1590s, *Pyramus and Thisbe* was reprinted three times in the seventeenth century, twice in conjunction with Robert Greene's *History of Arbasto King of Denmark* (1584), another love story which blends absurdity with pathos. However, despite this initial modest success, it has only once been reprinted in recent years, in Paul W. Miller's *Seven Minor Epics of the English Renaissance* (1967). The 1617 edition which includes only this poem (STC 11527) is here used as the copy text.

EDITIONS

Dunstan Gale, *Pyramus and Thisbe* (London: [John Beale] for Roger Jackson, 1617), STC 11527.

Robert Green, *The history of Arbasto King of Denmarke* [. . .] *Wherevnto is added a louely Poem of Pyramus and Thisbe* (London: J[ohn] B[eale] for Roger Jackson, 1617), STC 12221.

—, *The historie of Arbasto King of Denmarke* [. . .] *Wherevnto is added a louely Poem of Pyramus and Thisbe* (London: [T. Purfoot] for Francis Williams, 1626), STC 12222.

Paul W. Miller, *Seven Minor Epics of the English Renaissance* (Gainesville, FL.: Scholars' Facsimiles & Reprints, 1967).

---

[4] William Keach, *Elizabethan Erotic Narratives: Irony and Pathos in the Ovidian Poetry of Shakespeare, Marlowe and their Contemporaries* (New Brunswick, NJ: Rutgers University Press, 1977), p. 122.

FURTHER READING

Jim Ellis, *Sexuality and Citizenship: Metamorphosis in Elizabethan Erotic Verse* (Toronto: University of Toronto Press, 2003).

Kenneth Muir, 'Pyramus and Thisbe: A Study in Shakespeare's Method', *Shakespeare Quarterly*, 5 (1954), 141–53.

Rufus Putney, 'Venus and Adonis: Amor with Humor', *Philological Quarterly*, 20 (1941), 533–48.

Goran R. Stanivukovic, 'Shakespeare, Dunstan Gale, and Golding', *Notes and Queries*, 239.1 (1994), 35–37.

PYRAMUS AND THISBE

To the worshipful, his very[5] friend, D. B. H., Dunstan Gale wisheth all happiness. The worthiness, good captain, of your demerits,[6] with the benefit of your friendly courtesies, incites me to make proffer unto you of this my unpolished pamphlet, humbly entreating you to vouchsafe it acceptance, in that amongst many whom I have known I could find none more meet for the patronizing it than yourself. Which, if it please you, I hope it will be the better welcome to others for your sake, and if unconstant fortune do but once more enable me for better, then shall you find a grateful mind, ready to requite you with a double guerdon[7] for your former kindness. Thus craving pardon for this my rash attempt, I humbly take my leave this 25 of November, 1596.

Your Worship's ever devoted, Dunstan Gale.

    Near to the place where Nilus' channels run,
    There stood a town, by love long since undone;
    For by a chance that happened in the same,
    The town's forgot, and with the town, the name;
    Within which town (for then it was a town)
    Dwelt two commanders of no small renown,
    Daughter to one was Thisbe, smooth as glass,
    Fairer than Thisbe never woman was;
    Son to the other, Pyramus the bright,
10   Young Thisbe's playfere, Thisbe his delight;   *playmate*
    Both firm in love, as constant and were any,
    Both crossed in love, as proud love crosseth many.

    For in the pride of summer's parching heat,   *height*
    When children play and dally in the street,
    Young Thisbe, severed from the common sort,
    As gentle nurture loathes each rustic sport,
    Went to an arbour — arbours then were green —

---

[5] very] true
[6] demerits] merits
[7] guerdon] reward

      Where all alone, for fear she should be seen,
      She gathered violets and the damask rose,
20   And made sweet nosegays from the which she chose
      One of the sweetest. Sweet were all the rest,
      But that which pleased her wanton[8] eye the best.
      'And this', quoth she, 'shall be my true love's favour';
      Her tender nonage did of true love savour.   *youth*

      No sooner spake, but at her speech she blushed,
      For on the sudden Pyramus in rushed,
      Having but newly cropped the spreading pine,
      And other branches that were green and fine,
      Of which, to pass his idle time away,
30   The boy made wreaths and garlands that were gay,
      And spying Thisbe, Thisbe made him start,
      And he her blush, so tender was her heart;
      She blushed, because another was so near,
      He started, for to find another there;
      Yet looking long, at last they know each other,
      For why, they loved like sister and like brother.

      When they left looking — for they looked awhile —
      First Pyramus, last Thisbe, 'gan to smile.
      'I was afraid', thus Thisbe straight began,
40   Faint he replied: 'A maid, and fear a man?'
      'I feared', quoth she, 'but now my fear is past.'
      'Then welcome me', quoth Pyramus at last.
      'Welcome', quoth she, and then she kissed his lips,
      And he, from her, sweet nectar drops out sips.
      She pats his lips, he pats her milk-white skin.
      Thus children sport, and thus true love begins,
      But they as children, not as lovers, gamed,
      For love, alas, 'twixt them was never named.

      Oft would he take her by the lily hand,
50   Circling her middle, straight as any wand,
      And cast her down, but let her lie alone,
      For other pastime Pyramus knew none.
      Then up she starts, and takes him by the neck,
      And for that fall gives Pyramus a check,
      Yet at the length she chanced to cast him down,
      Though on the green she never gained a gown,[9]
      But rose again, and hid her in the grass,
      That he might tract the place where Thisbe was,   *track*
      And finding her, as children use, embrace her,
60   For, being children, nothing could disgrace her.

---

[8] wanton] The word had many different shades of meaning. 'Lively' or 'unrestrained' is probably closer to the intended meaning here than 'lewd', although 'amorous' (in a more neutral, less judgemental sense) is also possible.
[9] 56] A gown was a traditional prize for village sports.

But mark the issue of their sportive play,
As this sweet couple in the cool shade lay;
Fair Venus, posting whom to Paphos isle,   *Cyprus*
Spièd their sports, nor could she choose but smile,
Wherefore she straight unyoked her silver team,
And walked on foot along the crystal stream,
And envying that these lovers were so bold,
With jealous eyes she did them both behold.
And as she looked, casting her eye awry,
70   It was her chance, unhappy chance, to spy
Where squint-eyed Cupid sat upon his quiver,
Viewing his none-eyed body in the river.[10]

Him straight she called, being called he made no stay,
But to his mother took the nearest way.
Yet ere he came, she marked the t'other two,
Playing as oft tofore th'er[11] wont to do,   *previously*
And then she swore young Pyramus was fair,
Thisbe but brown, as common women are;
Anon she wished young Pyramus was near,
80   That she might bind love in his golden hair,
And love him too, but that she called to mind
That young Adonis provèd so unkind.[12]
But Cupid came, his coming caused her hate them,
And in a heat, proud Venus 'gan to rate them.   *berate*

'See'st thou, my son', quoth she, and then she frowned,
'Those brattish elves[13] that dally on the ground?
They scorn my kingdom, and neglect my mind,
Contemn me as inconstant as the wind.
Then shoot', quoth she, 'and strike them so in love,
90   As nought but death their love-dart may remove.'
At this he looked, the boy was loth to shoot,
Yet struck them both so near the heart's sweet root,
As that he made them both at once to cry.
Quoth he, 'I love'; 'for love', quoth she, 'I die.'
Of this both Venus and her blind boy boasted,
And thence to Paphos isle in triumph posted.

Now was the time when shepherds told their sheep,   *counted*
And weary ploughmen ease themselves with sleep,
When love-pricked Thisbe nowhere could be found,
100   Nor Pyramus, though servants sought them round.
But news came straight, that Pyramus was seen
Sporting with Thisbe lately in the even;[14]

---

[10] 71–72] Cupid is often depicted wearing a blindfold.
[11] th'er] they were
[12] 82] *Met.*, X. 519–739.
[13] elves] children, often (as here) with pejorative connotations
[14] even] evening. The established contraction 'e'en' would improve the rhyme here.

Like news to both their parents soon was brought,
Which news, alas, the lovers' downfalls wrought.
For though they loved, as you have heard of yore,
Their angry parents' hate was ten times more,
And hearing that their children were together,
Both were afraid lest each had murdered other.

When they came home, as long they stayed not forth,
110 Their storming parents frowned upon them both,
And charged them never so to meet again,
Which charge to them, God knows, was endless pain;
For years came on, and true love took such strength,
That they were well-nigh slain for love at length,
For though their parents' houses joined in one,
Yet they, poor peats, were joined to live alone.   *pets, enjoined*
So great and deadly was the daring hate
Which kept their moody parents at debate,   *angry*
And yet their hearts, as houses, joined together,
120 Though hard constraint their bodies did dissever.

At length they found, as searching lovers find,
A shift, though hard, which somewhat eased their mind,   *expedient*
For lo, a time-worn crevice in the wall,
Through this the lovers did each other call,
And often talk, but softly did they talk,
Lest busy spy-faults should find out their walk,[15]   *fault-finders*
For it was placed in such a secret room,
As thither did their parents seldom come.
Through this they kissed, but with their breath they kissed,
130 For why the hindering wall was them betwixt;
Sometimes, poor souls, they talked till they were windless,
And all their talk was of their friends' unkindness.

When they had long time used this late found shift,
Fearing lest some should undermine their drift,
They did agree, but through the wall agreed,
That both should haste unto the grove with speed,
And in that arbour where they first did meet,
With semblant love each should the other greet.   *similar*
The match concluded, and the time set down,
140 Thisbe prepared to get her forth the town,
For well she wot her love would keep his hour,   *knew*
And be the first should come unto the bower;
For Pyramus had sworn there for to meet her,
And like to Venus' champion there to greet her.

Thisbe and he, for both did sit on briars
Till they enjoyed the height of their desires,
Sought out all means they could to keep their vow,

---

[15] walk] 'resort', or perhaps 'course of conduct'

	And steal away, and yet they knew not how.	
	Thisbe at last, yet of the two the first,	
150	Got out; she went to cool love's burning thirst.	
	Yet ere she went, yet as she went, she hied,	*hastened*
	She had a care to deck her up in pride,	
	Respecting more his love to whom she went,	
	Than parents' fear, though knowing to be shent,	*disgraced*
	And tricked herself so like a willing lover,	*adorned*
	As purblind[16] Cupid took her for his mother.	
	Her upper garment was a robe of lawn,	*fine linen*
	On which bright Venus' silver doves were drawn;	
	The like wore Venus, Venus' robe was white,	
160	And so was Thisbe's, not so fair to sight,	
	Nor yet so fine, yet was it full as good,	
	Because it was not stained with true love's blood.[17]	
	About her waist she wore a scarf of blue,	
	In which by cunning needlework she drew	
	Love-wounded Venus in the bushy grove,	
	Where she entreated,[18] Adon scorned her love.	*Adonis*
	This scarf she wore, Venus wore such another,	
	And that made Cupid take her for his mother.	
	Nymph-like attired (for so she was attired)	
170	She went to purchase what true love desired,	
	And as she trod upon the tender grass,	
	The grass did kiss her feet as she did pass,	
	And when her feet against a flower did strike,	
	The bending flowers did stoop to do the like,	
	And when her feet did from the ground arise,	
	The ground she trod on kissed her heel likewise.	
	Tread where she would, fair Thisbe could not miss,	
	For every grass would rob her of a kiss,	
	And more the boughs would bend for joy to meet her,	
180	And chanting birds with madrigals would greet her.	
	Thus goes this maid-like nymph, or nymph-like maid,[19]	
	Unto the place afore appointed laid,	
	And as she passed the groves and fountains clear,	
	Where nymphs used[20] hunting, for nymphs hunted there,	*carried out*
	They swore she was Diana, or more bright,	
	For through the leafy boughs they took delight,	

---

[16] purblind] Here apparently used to mean short-sighted, rather than completely blind.

[17] In Marlowe's *Hero and Leander*, Hero's gown depicts Venus and Adonis (ll. 11–16). Venus's own kirtle is said by Marlowe to be stained 'by the blood of wretched lovers slaine'.

[18] entreated] *1617* 'inheated'. As neither 'inheated' nor 'enheated' appears in the *OED*, it seems likely that 'entreated' was intended, although it is possible that Gale used the nonce word 'inheated' to signify 'inflamed'. If this is the case, a comma is required after 'Where'.

[19] 181] Compare Ovid's description of the minotaur: 'semibovemque virum, semivirumque bovem' ('half bull-like man, half man-like bull', *Ars Am.*, II. 24).

[20] used] This construction involving a present participle was fairly common at this time.

	To view her dainty footing as she tripped,	*moved lightly*
	And once they smiled, for once fair Thisbe slipped,	
	Yet though she slipped, she had so swift a pace,	
190	As that her slipping wrought her no disgrace,	
	For of the nymphs, whose coy eyes did attend her,	
	Of all was none of all that could amend her.	*surpass*

When she had passed Diana's curious train,
The crooked way did bending turn again,
Upon the left hand by a forest side,
Where, out alas, a woe chance did betide;   *woeful*
For love-adoring Thisbe was so fair,
That brutish beasts at her delighted are,
And from the rest as many beasts did roam;
200   A lamb-devouring lion forth did come,
And having lately torn a silly lamb,
The full-gorged lion sported as it came,
To him a sport, his sport made Thisbe hie her,
For why, she durst not let the beast come nigh her.

Yet still it came, to welcome her it came,
And not to hurt, yet fearful is the name,
The name more than the lion her dismayed,
For in her lap the lion would have played,
Nor meant the beast to spill her guiltless blood,
210   Yet doubtful Thisbe, in a fearful mood,   *fearful*
Let fall her mantle, made of purest white,
And, tender heart, betook her straight to flight,
And near the place where she should meet her love
She slipped, but quickly slipped into a grove;
And lo, a friendly cave did entertain her,
For fear the bloody lion should have slain her.

Sprengius, *Metamorphoses Ovidii* (1563), p. 47ʳ

Thisbe thus scaped, for thus she scaped his force,
Although, God wot, it fell out farther worse;
The lion came, yet meant no harm at all,
220 And coming found the mantle she let fall,
Which now he kissed, he would have kissed her too,
But that her nimble footmanship said no.
He found the robe, which quickly he might find,
For being light, it hovered in the wind,
With which the gamesome lion long did play,
Till hunger called him thence to seek his prey;
And having played, for play was all his pleasure,
He left the mantle, Thisbe's chiefest treasure.

Yet ere he left it, being in a mood,
230 He tore it much, and stained it o'er with blood,
Which done, with rage he hasted to his prey,
For they in murder pass their time away.
And now time-telling Pyramus at last,
For yet the hour of meeting was not past,
Got forth; he would have got away before,
But fate and fortune sought to wrong him more,
For even that day, more fatal than the rest,
He needs must give attendance at a feast,
Ere which was done swift time was shrewdly wasted,   *severely*
240 But being done, the lovely stripling hasted.

In haste he ran, but ran in vain, God wot;
Thisbe he sought, fair Thisbe found he not,
And yet at last her long love robe he found,
All rent and torn upon the bloody ground,
At which suspicion told him she was dead,   *slight indication*
And only that remainèd in her stead,
Which made him weep; like mothers, so wept he,
That with their eyes their murdered children see,
And gathering up the limbs in piecemeal torn,
250 Of their dear burden murderously forlorn,   *child*
So Pyramus, sick-thoughted[21] like a mother,
For Thisbe's loss, more dear than any other.

Or who hath seen a mournful doe lament
For her young kid, in piecemeal torn and rent,
And by the poor remainders sit and mourn,
For love of that which, out alas, is gone?
Let him behold sad Pyramus, and say,
Her loss, his love, doth equal every way.
For as a man that late hath lost his wits,
260 Breaks into fury and disaster fits,   *disastrous*
So Pyramus, in grief without compare,

---

[21] sick-thoughted] Venus is described as 'sick-thoughted' in *Venus and Adonis* (l. 5).

Doth rend his flesh, and tear his golden hair,
Making the trees to tremble at his mourning,
And speechless beasts to sorrow with his groaning.

'Alas', quoth he, and then he tore his flesh,
'Gone is the sun that did my zone[22] refresh,
Gone is the life by which I, wretch, did live,
Gone is my heaven, which hopeful bliss did give;
To give me heat, herself lies nak't and cold,
270 To give me life, to death herself she sold,
To give me joy, she bale, alas, did gain,
My heat, life, joy, procured her death, bale pain.   *evil*
Had I been here, my love had not been dead,
At least the beasts had torn me in her stead,
Or would they yet tear me for company,
Their love to me would slack their tyranny.[23]

And then he cast his eyes upon the ground,
And here and there, where bloody grass he found,
'Sweet blood', quoth he, and then he kissed the blood,
280 And yet that kiss, God wot, did little good,
'Could'st thou, being poured into my half-slain breast,
Revive again, or purchase Thisbe's rest,
This hand should tear a passage through the same',
And yet that blood from Thisbe never came.
And then he gathered up the bloody grass,
And looking grieved, and grieving cried, 'Alas,
Where shall I hide this blood of my dear lover,
That neither man nor beast may it discover?'

Then in the mantle he the grass up tied,
290 And laid it close unto his naked side.
'Lie there', quoth he, 'dear to me as my heart,
Of which thy mistress had the greater part.
Tut, she is dead', and then he vowed and swore
He would not live to murder love no more,
Which spoke, he drew his rapier from his side,
Of which the love-slain youth would then have died,
But that he thought that penance too too small,
To pacify fair Thisbe's ghost withal,
Wherefore he raged, and ragingly exclaimed,
300 That he true love, and true love him had maimed.

And then his rapier up again he took,
Then on the mantle cast a grievous look.
'For me', quoth he, 'fair Thisbe lost this blood,
She dead, my life would do me little good.'
And well he thought he could endure the smart

---

[22] zone] region between two latitudes. Pyramus imagines himself as a landscape warmed by the sun of Thisbe.
[23] 275–76] With Thisbe dead, Pyramus would see being killed by wild beasts as an act of love rather than tyranny.

Of death, and yet he could not harm his heart,
For why his hand being guiltless of the deed,
Denied to make his harmless heart to bleed,
And like a trembling executioner,
310　Constrained to kill a guiltless prisoner,
His hand retired still further back and further,
As loathing to enact so vile a murder.

But Pyramus, like to a raging judge,
Seeing his executioner flinch and grudge
To do the duty he enjoined him do,
Replied, 'Dispatch, or I'll cut thee off too',[24]
At which the trembling hand took up the blade,
But when the second proffer it had made,
It threw it down, and boldly thus replied,
320　'He was not cause that lovely Thisbe died,
Nor would I slay thee, knew I she were dead,
Then be the blood upon thy guilty head.'[25]
Of these last words young Pyramus dispenses,[26]
And called a synody of all his severed senses.[27]　　　*assembly*

His conscience told him he deserved not death,
For he deprived not Thisbe of her breath;
But then, suspicion thought, he caused her die,
But conscience swore suspicion told a lie;
At this suspicion prompted love in th'ear,
330　And bade him show his verdict, and come near,
Which soon he did, and sat among the rest,
As one whom Pyramus esteemèd best,
For when proud love gave in his faulty plea,
He asked if he were guilty, love said yea,
And with the youth, fond youth, by love entangled,
Agreed his guiltless body should be mangled.

Resolved to die, he sought the pointed blade,
Which erst his hand had cast into the shade,
And see, proud chance, fell murder's chiefest friend,
340　Had pitched the blade right upwards on the end,
Which being loath from murder to depart,
Stood on the hilt, point-blank against his heart;
At which he smiled, and checked his fearful hand,
That stubbornly resisted his command.
'And though', quoth he, 'thou scorned to do my will,
What lets me now my mind for to fulfil?　　　*prevents*

---

[24] 313–16] There is a humorous illogic here. The threat of the 'judge' makes little sense when the prisoner and the executioner are the same person.
[25] 321–22] The relationship between the narrative and the courtroom comparison becomes particularly confusing here.
[26] dispenses] Perhaps used here in the sense to mete or deal out, rather than to forego.
[27] 324] The hypermetrical line reflects the disorder of Pyramus's mind.

Both fate and fortune to my death are willing,
And be thou witness of my mind's fulfilling.'

With that he cast himself upon the sword,
350 And with the fall his tender breast through gored;
The angry blood, for so his blood was sheed, *shed*
Gushed out to find the author of the deed,
But when it none but Pyramus had found,
Key-cold[28] with fear it stood upon the ground,
And all the blood, I mean that thus was spilt,
Ran down the blade and circled in the hilt,
And presently congealed about the same,
And would have called it by some murderous name,
Could it have spoke, nor sought it any further,
360 But did arrest the rapier of the murther.[29]

And as the child that seeth his father slain,
Will run, alas, although he run in vain,
And hug about the shedder of his blood,
Although, God wot, his hugging do small good,
Even so his blood, the offspring of his heart,
Ran out amain, to take his father's part,
And hung upon the rapier and the hilt,
As who should say, the sword his blood had spilt,
Nor would depart, but cleave about the same,
370 So dear it loved the place from whence it came,
For sure it was poor Pyramus was murthered,
Nor by pursuit could his poor blood be furthered.

When this was done, as thus the deed was done,
Begun, alas, and ended too too soon,
Fair Thisbe, strucken pale with cold despair,
Came forth the cave into the wholesome air,
And as she came, the boughs would give her way,
Thinking her Venus in her best array.
But she, alas, full of suspicious fear,
380 Lest that the late feared lion should be there,
Came quaking forth, and then start back again,
Fearing the beast, and yet she feared in vain.
She feared the lion, lions then were feeding,
And in this fear her nose gushed out a-bleeding.

---

[28] Key-cold] a fairly common epithet at this time
[29] murther] murder. 'Murther' is Gale's usual spelling of the word, but it has only been retained where an adjustment would affect the rhyme.

Lodovico Dolce, *Le trasformationi* (1553), p. 85

>   Her sudden bleeding argued some mischance,[30]
>   Which cast her doubtful senses in a trance,
>   But of the lion troubled Thisbe thought,
>   And then of him, whom fearfully she sought,
>   Yet forth she went, replete with jealous fear,   *watchful*
> 390 Still fearing, of the lion was her fear;
>   And if a bird but flew from forth a bush,
>   She straightways thought she heard the lion rush.
>   Her nose left bleeding, that amazed her more
>   Than all the troublous fear she felt before,
>   For sudden bleeding argues ill ensuing,
>   But sudden leaving is fell fear's renewing.
>
>   By this she came into the open wood,
>   Where Pyramus had lost his dearest blood,
>   And round about she rolls her sun-bright eyes
> 400 For Pyramus, whom nowhere she espies;
>   Then forth she tripped, and nearly too she tripped,[31]
>   And over hedges oft this virgin skipped.
>   Then did she cross the fields and new-mown grass,
>   To find the place whereas this arbour was,
>   For it was seated in a pleasant shade,
>   And by the shepherds first this bower was made.
>   Fair Thisbe made more haste into the bower,
>   Because that now was just the meeting hour.

---

[30] 385] Nosebleeds were sometimes seen as an ill omen, a sign that a friend or relative had died.

[31] 401] The obtrusive play on the two meanings of 'trip' — to step lightly and to stumble — reflects Gale's playful attitude towards the tale.

	But coming thither, as she soon was there,
410	She found him not, which did augment her fear;
	But straight she thought, as true love thinks the best,
	He had been laid down in the shade to rest,
	Or of set purpose hidden in the reeds,
	To make her seek him in the sedgy weeds,
	For so of children they had done before,
	Which made her thoughts seem true so much the more.
	But having sought whereas she thought he was,
	She could not find her Pyramus, alas,
	Wherefore she back returned unto the arbour,
420	And there reposed her after all her labour.

	To one that's weary, drowsy sleep will creep;
	Weary was Thisbe, Thisbe fell asleep,
	And in her sleep she dreamt she did lament,
	Thinking her heart from forth her breast was rent,
	By her own censure damned to cruel death,
	And in her sight bereft of vital breath.
	When she awaked, as long she had not slept,
	She wept amain, yet knew not why she wept,
	For as before her heart was whole and sound,
430	And no defect about her could be found;
	She dreamt she hurt, no hurt could she discover,
	Wherefore she went to seek her late lost lover.

	Suspicious eyes, quick messengers of woe,	
	Brought home sad news ere Thisbe far could go;	
	For lo, upon the margent of the wood,	*margin*
	They spied her love lie welt'ring in his blood,	*saturated*
	Having her late lost mantle at his side,	
	Stainèd with blood; his heart blood was not dried.	
	Wistly she looked, and as she looked did cry:	*closely*
440	'See, see, my heart, which I did judge to die,	
	Poor heart', quoth she, and then she kissed his breast,	
	'Wert thou enclosed in mine there should'st thou rest,	
	I caused thee die, poor heart, yet rue thy dying,	
	And saw thy death as I asleep was lying.	

	Thou art my heart, more dear than is mine own,
	And thy sad death in my false sleep was shown.'
	And then she plucked away the murderous blade,
	And cursed the hands by whom it first was made,
	And yet she kissed his hand that held the same,
450	And double kissed the wound from whence it came.
	Himself was author of his death, she knew,
	For yet the wound was fresh, and bleeding new,
	And some blood yet the ill-made wound did keep,
	Which when she saw she freshly 'gan to weep,
	And wash the wound with fresh tears down distilling,
	And viewed the same, God wot, with eyes unwilling.

She would have spoke, but grief stopped up her breath.
'For me', quoth she, 'my love is done to death,
And shall I live —', sighs stopped her hindmost word,
460 When speechless up she took the bloody sword,
And then she cast a look upon her love,
Then to the blade her eye she did remove,
And sobbing cried, 'Since love hath murdered thee,
He shall not choose but likewise murder me,
That men may say', and then she sighed again,
'I him, he me, love him and me hath slain.'
Then with resolve (love her resolve did further)
With that same blade herself herself did murther.[32]

Then with a sigh she fell upon the blade,
470 And from the bleeding wound the sword had made,
Her fearful blood ran trickling to the ground,
And sought about, till Pyramus it found,
And, having found him, circled in his corse,[33]
As who should say, 'I'll guard thee by my force'.
And when it found his blood, as forth it came,
Then would it stay, and touch, and kiss the same,
As who should say, 'my mistress' love to thee,
Thou dead in her, doth still remain in me.'
And for a sign of mutual love in either,
480 Their ill-shed blood congealèd both together.

---

[32] 478] There is another possible echo of *Venus and Adonis* here: 'Narcissus so himself himself forsook | And died to kiss his shadow in the brook (ll. 161–62).

[33] Jim Ellis notes a possible echo of the description of Lucrece's blood circling her corpse in Shakespeare's *The Rape of Lucrece* (*Sexuality and Citizenship*, pp. 141–42).

THOMAS HEYWOOD
JUPITER AND CALLISTO
from
TROIA BRITANICA (1609)

THOMAS HEYWOOD
JUPITER AND CALLISTO
from
TROIA BRITANICA (1609)

[*Metamorphoses*, II. 401–65]

Lodovico Dolce, *Le trasformationi* (1553), p. 46

This extract is taken from Cantos 2 and 3 of *Troia Britanica*, Thomas Heywood's epic 'history' of the world. *Troia Britanica*'s combination of new material, adaptation, and near translation reflects the great permeability between original poetry and translation in this period, and several other translations from the *Metamorphoses* besides that of 'Jupiter and Callisto' are included in the poem.

Thomas Heywood (*c*. 1573–1641) enjoyed a long and very varied literary career, which opened with a translation from Ovid's *Heroides*, 'Oenone to Paris' (1594). His other translations included the complete *Ars Amatoria* and works by Sallust. He also wrote prose works, including *An Apology for Actors* (1612) and *Gynaikeion* (1624), a study of illustrious women. His dramatic output was extremely wide-ranging, and included romances, such as *The Four Prentices of London* (1599–1600), tragedies, most notably *The Woman Killed with Kindness* (1603), domestic comedies, and the more pageant-like mythological 'Age' plays. And it was from Heywood's own slightly earlier *Troia Britanica* (1609) that these plays, beginning with *The Golden Age* (first published in 1611), were adapted.

The ultimate source for this extract is the second book of the *Metamorphoses*, in which Ovid tells how Lycaon offered Jupiter human flesh to test his divinity and was cast out of his palace by the furious god, and eventually metamorphosed into a wolf.[1] However, much of the material in *Troia Britanica* is derived from Raoul Lefèvre's *Le Recueil des Histoires de Troyes* (1464)

---

[1] Lycaon is also mentioned in *Met.*, I. 216–39.

which was translated into English by William Caxton in 1473 as the *Recuyell of the Historyes of Troy*. Heywood follows the *Recuyell*'s version of the Callisto story quite closely, although the atmosphere of his adaptation is very different from that of his source, and far more Ovidian in spirit. Caxton's translation is formal and courtly, as is his Jupiter. Whereas Heywood emphasizes Jove's youth and amorousness, and his first words to Callisto are those of a shameless flatterer, in Caxton the god's first emotion for her is pity and his words are calmly reassuring. Another apparent source for Heywood's treatment of the myth is William Warner's *Albion's England* (1589). The salacious tone of Warner's adaptation, in particular, seems to have influenced Heywood:

> He feeleth oft her ivory breasts, nor maketh coy to kiss,
> Yet all was well, a maiden to a maiden might do this.
> Then ticked he up her tuckèd frock, nor did Callisto blush[2]

Although Warner's narrative is broadly similar to Caxton's, it is possible to establish that Heywood was almost certainly familiar with both texts, for he includes some elements which can be found only in Caxton, and others which are peculiar to Warner.

Heywood's dramatic treatment of the story of Callisto, in *The Golden Age*, is rather better known than the version included in *Troia Britanica*. In outline, Heywood's two treatments of the myth are very similar, although he varies the details considerably. The Callisto episode reflects the way *Troia Britanica* combines mythical material with references to recent history and current events. Diana is likened to Elizabeth I, for example, as both are apt to banish any erring females from their courts. A longer contemporary digression occurs at the beginning of Canto 3, when Heywood breaks into the story of Callisto to praise the peaceful reign of James I and celebrate the victory of England over the Spanish Armada.

Although Thomas Heywood is one of the better known writers included in this volume, the influence of *Troia Britanica* has been comparatively slight. Its length, its lack of consistent 'originality' — Frederick Boas criticises the poem for being 'derivative' and for having 'recourse to translation'[3] — and its adherence to a recondite view of world history[4] may have contributed to its obscurity. Felix E. Schelling observed that 'this work has more merit than has usually been accorded it'.[5] Although some extracts from the poem were included in William Jaggard's 1612 edition of *The Passionate Pilgrim*, it was 1972 before the entire poem was reprinted. Its first edition had been marred by many errors, but the printer, Jaggard, refused to correct these, prompting Heywood to include a public letter of complaint to the printer Nicholas Okes in his 1612 *Apology for Actors*, noting all 'the misquotations, mistaking of syllables, misplacing half lines, coining of strange and never heard of words' which marred *Troia Britanica*.

EDITIONS

Thomas Heywood, *Troia Britanica: or, Great Britaines Troy A Poem Deuided into XVII. seuerall Cantons, intermixed with many pleasant Poeticall Tales. Concluding with an Vniuersall Chronicle from the Creation, vntill these present Times* (London: W. Jaggard, 1609), STC 13366.

Thomas Heywood, *Troia Britanica, or Great Britain's Troy* (Amsterdam: Theatrum Orbis Terrarum; Norwood, NJ: W. J. Johnson, 1974).

---

[2] William Warner, *Albion's England* (London: George Robinson [and R. Ward] for Thomas Cadman, 1586), p. 45.
[3] Frederick S. Boas, *Thomas Heywood* (London: William & Norgate, 1950), pp. 61, 65.
[4] See introduction, p. 14.
[5] Felix E. Schelling, *The English Chronicle Plays* (New York: Macmillan, 1902), p. 38.

FURTHER READING

Jonathan Bate, *Shakespeare and Ovid* (Oxford: Oxford University Press, 1993).

Frederick S. Boas, *Thomas Heywood* (London: William & Norgate, 1950).

Allan Holaday, 'Heywood's *Troia Britannica* and the *Ages*', *Journal of English and Germanic Philology*, 45 (1946), 430–39.

Kathleen Wall, *The Callisto Myth from Ovid to Atwood: Initiation and Rape in Literature* (Kingston and Montreal: McGill-Queens University Press, 1988).

JUPITER AND CALLISTO

King Jupiter had not yet reigned an hour,	
But with his trusty followers searcheth round	
About the palace royal for the power	*army*
Of king Lycaon, but he no man found —	
Death spares the king that doth his folk devour.	
Yet jealous of his state, like kings new crowned,	
To abide all future garboils and assaults,	*prevent, disturbances*
He searcheth all the cellars, nooks and vaults.	*Jupiter*

     And breaking up a strong barred iron door,
10 He spies a goodly chamber richly hung,
     Where he might see upon the careless[6] floor,
     A discontented lady rudely flung;
     Her habit suiting with her grief she wore,
     Her eyes rained tears, her ivory hands she wrung;
        Her robes so black were, and her face so fair,
        Each other graced, and made both colours rare.

The virgin looked out of her sad attire,	
Like the bright sun out of a dusky cloud,	
Her first aspect[7] set the king's heart afire,	
20 Who, vailing first his bonnet, he low bowed,	*tipping*
And to have seized her fingers presseth nigher;	
But she at sight of strangers weeps aloud,	
Her drownèd eye she to the earth directeth,	
And no man[8] save her own sad woes respecteth.	

The youthful prince, whom amorous thoughts surprise,	
With comfortable[9] words the lady cheers,	*reassuring*
Supports her by the arm, entreats her rise,	
And from her bosom to remove her fears;	
Yet will not she erect her downcast eyes,	

---

[6] careless] The floor, fancifully, is supposed to be indifferent to her suffering.
[7] aspect] stressed on the second syllable
[8] no man] This phrase rather confusingly implies that her woes are a 'man', a rival to Jove.
[9] comfortable] The scansion demands that all four syllables be sounded.

30	Nor to his smooth-sweet language lend her ears,	
	Till from the earth he raised her by the arm,	
	And thus with words begins her grief to charm.	*assuage*

'Bright damsel, did you know the worth of all
Those precious drops you prodigally spill,
You would not let such high prized moisture fall,
Which from your heart your conduit[10] eyes distil;
Oh spare them, though you count their value small!
To have them spared I'll give you, if you will,
    Although not in full payment, yet in part,
40   A prince's favour, and a soldier's heart.[11]

You dim those eyes that sparkle fire divine,   *emit*
By whom this melancholy room is lighted,
The place were dark, and but for their bright shine,
We in this dungeon should be all benighted;
Oh save your beauty then, and spare your eyen,   *eyes*
Why should you at our presence be affrighted?
    We come not with our weapons drawn to fear you,   *frighten*
    But, with our comfortable words, to cheer you.

But say our hostile weapons were all bent
50 Against your breast; yet why should you be mated?   *overcome*
Beauty's sword-proof, no forcible intent
But by a face so fair is soon rebated;   *driven back*
Your beauty was unto your body lent,
To be her secretary, where instated,   *minister*
    It is as safe as if a wall of iron,
    Impregnable, your person should environ.'[12]

With that the woeful maid uplifts her eye,
And fixed it first upon the prince's face,
But there it dwelt not long, for by and by
60 It wandered wildly round about the place;
Yet coming to herself, when she 'gan spy
Herself 'mongst strangers, with a modest grace,
    Having her raging grief a while restrained,
    Thus blushing, she her sad estate complained.

---

[10] conduit] pipe or channel. Occasionally used adjectivally, as here, to form a kind of compound noun.

[11] 33–40] Parallels can be drawn with wooing scenes in Shakespeare's plays *Richard III* and *Henry V*, where the man is faced with a comparably hard task. Richard III woos Anne, whose husband and father he has recently killed. Like Jupiter he pays elaborate compliments, even praising the spit directed at him by Anne (I. 2. 146). When wooing Katharine, the young French princess, Henry V has also to overcome a girl's natural resistance towards her father's foe; like Jupiter, he invokes both his martial and his royal credentials (V. 2. 165–69). The adroitness, eloquence and opportunism, common to all three wooers, are not present in Caxton, who emphasises instead Jupiter's leadership and nobility.

[12] 51–56] His words are illogical, for beauty (as is of course demonstrated later in this tale) increases a woman's vulnerability to attack.

'My father, oh my father, where is he,
To whom these subjects should of right belong?
You are the limbs, the head I cannot see,[13]
Oh, you have done the king some violent wrong!
What stranger's this that doth solicit me?   *disturb*
70   How dare you thus into my chamber throng,
    And fright me, being a princess, with your steel?
    Or where's the king, that to this youth you kneel?

If King Lycaon live, why do you bow
Unto a stranger, he surviving still?
If he be slain, why am I hindered now
Upon his corse my funeral tears to spill?
I may lament by law, no laws allow
Subjects, by treason, their liege lords to kill;
    My tears are natural, and come in season,
80   Your treacherous act is mere unnatural treason.'

By these her words, the amorous prince doth gather
This lady to be King Lycaon's daughter;
It grieves him now he hath exiled her father,
And once again of favour he besought her,
But she, all sorrow, now entreats him rather
To leave the chamber, since his coming brought her
    Nothing but news of death, and words of care,
    Her father's ruin, and her own despair.

By many fair persuasions the prince moves her,
90   To stint her passion, and to stop her tears;   *cease*
He whispers in her ear how much he loves her,
But all in vain, his tongue he idly wears;   *wearies*
By all rhetoric and art he proves her,   *tests*
Which makes her at the length lend her chaste ears,
    And thus reply: 'I cannot love, until
    You one thing grant me'. The prince swears he will.

'Remember', quoth the lady, 'you have sworn;
Being a prince, to break an oath were base;
Wer't in a peasant, it were hardly borne,   *endured*
100   But in a prince it seems a worse disgrace;
The greater y'are, the greater is your scorn
If you should taint your honour in this case;
    'Tis nothing if a poor star's beams be clouded,
    But we soon miss the moon in darkness shrouded.

Princes are earthly gods,[14] and placed on high,
Where every common man may freely gaze;

---

[13] 67] Comparisons between different parts of the body and different elements in the body politic were commonplace. Menenius's account of Aesop's fable of the belly at the beginning of *Coriolanus* is a well-known example (I. 1. 96–141).

[14] 105] Jove is of course a god, although the euhemerizing text deemphasizes his divinity.

> On them the people's universal eye
> Is hourly fixed, to scan their works and ways;
> They look through spectacles your deeds to spy,
110   Which makes the letters of your shame or praise   *records*
>   Grosser to be discerned, and easier scanned;   *perceived*
>   A king should be a light to all his land.'

> These words sighed out have fanned the amorous fire,
> Which did the breast of Saturn's son enflame;
> He that at first her beauty did admire,
> Now wonders at the wisdom of the dame,
> And museth how from such a devilish sire
> As King Lycaon, such an angel came;
>   Now he entreats her ask, with spirit undaunted,
120   For as he is a prince, her suit is granted.

> 'Be it', quoth he, 'the fortunes of this day,
> Be it myself, myself, sweet saint,[15] am thine,
> Be it this kingdom, and this sceptre's sway,
> Behold, my interest I will back resign;
> We have no power to say such beauty nay,
> Being but mortal,[16] and that face divine;
>   What's your demand, sweet saint?' 'It is', quoth she,
>   'That I a consecrated maid may be.'

> Oh, had she asked more gold than would have filled
130   Her father's palace, packed up to the roof,
> Or in her sad boon had the lady willed
> Of his resolvèd spirit to see large proof,
> Monsters he would have tamed, and giants killed,
> And from no stern adventure kept aloof,
>   In hope to have won her love; but being thus coy,
>   This one request doth all his hopes destroy.

> The prince is bound by oath to grant her pleasure,
> Yet from her will he seeks her to dissuade;   *wish*
> 'Hoard not', quoth he, 'unto yourself such treasure,
140   Nor let so sweet a flower ungathered fade;
> Nature herself hath took from you fit measure,
> To have more beauteous creatures by you made;
>   Then crop this flower before the prime be past,
>   Lose not the mould that may such fair ones cast.

> Let not a cloister such rare beauty smother,
> Y'are Nature's masterpiece, made to be seen;
> Sweet, you were born that you should bear another,

---

[15] sweet saint] an example of the strongly Christianized atmosphere and vocabulary of the poem
[16] Being but mortal] This statement should probably be read as a reflection of the poem's lack of emphasis on Jove's divinity rather than a lie.

      A princess, and descended from a queen,
      That you of queens and princes might be mother;
150   Had she that bare you still a virgin been,
         You had not been at all; mankind should fade
         If every female lived a spotless maid.[17]

      You ask, what you by no means can defend,
      In seeking a strict cloister to enjoy;
      Ye wish to see the long-lived world at end,
      And in your heart you mankind would destroy;
      For when these lives no further can extend,
      How shall we people th'earth? Who shall employ
         The crowns we win, the wealth for which we strive,
160   When, dead ourselves, we leave none to survive?

      You might as well kill children, as to hold
      This dangerous error; nay, I'll prove it true,
      For infant souls that should have been enrolled
      In Heaven's predestined book, begot of you,
      Are, by your strangeness, to oblivion sold,   *coldness*
      You might as well your hands in blood imbrue,   *stain*
         Nay better too, for when young infants die
         Their angel souls live in eternity,[18]

      And so the heavens make up their numbers full;
170   You, lady, heaven and earth's right disallow,
      What gods conclude, shall mortals disannul?   *abolish*
      So many as you might have had ere now,
      So many angels from Heaven's throne you pull,
      From earth, so many princes by your vow;
         Now could I get a son, but you, being coy,   *beget*
         Fair murderess that you are, have killed the boy.'

      Much more,[19] but all in vain; the amorous youth
      Thinks in his smooth, sweet language to dissuade her,
      But nothing that he pleads she holds for truth,
180   Though by all gentle means he sought to have stayed her;   *detained*
      She urgeth still his oath, he thinks it ruth   *a pity*
      To have such beauty cloistered, and had[20] made her
         Virginity for Venus' sweets to have changed,
         Had not his oath that purpose soon estranged.   *eschewed*

      Now fair Callisto, by Jove's grant, is free
      To be admitted one of Dian's train,
      Dian, a huntress; the broad shadowy tree,

---

[17] 139–52] The theme of *carpe diem* ('seize the day') was commonplace in the literature of the period. Marvell's rather later 'To his Coy Mistress' is a well-known and extended treatment of this motif.
[18] 161–68] Vowed celibacy was generally viewed with disapproval by Protestants.
[19] Much more] 'He said' should be understood at the beginning of the line.
[20] had] would have

The house beneath whose roof she doth remain;
Venison her food, and honey from the bee,
190   The flesh of elks, of bears, and boars new slain; *deer*
     Her drink the pearlèd brook; her followers, maids; *pearl-like*
     Her vow, chaste life; her cloister, the cool shade.[21]

Her weapons are the javelin and the bow,
Her garments, angel-like, of virgin white;
And tucked aloft, her falling skirt, below
Her buskin meets, buckled with silver bright; *calf-high boot*
Her hair behind her, like a cloak, doth flow,
Some tucked in rolls, some loose with flowers bedight; *arrayed*
     Her silken veils play round about her, slack,
200   Her golden quiver falls athwart her back. *across*

She was the daughter of an ancient king
Called Jupiter,[22] that swayed the Attic sceptre;
To her, as suitors, many princes bring
Their crowns, which scorning, she a virgin kept her;
Yet as her beauty's fame abroad doth ring,
Her suitors multiply; therefore she stepped her
     Into the forest, meaning to exempt her[23]
     From such as to their amorous wills would tempt her.

This new religion, famous, in a queen
210   Of such estate and beauty, drew from far
Daughters of princes; they that late were seen
In courts of kings, now Dian's followers are,
Where they no sooner sworn and entered been,
But against men and love they proclaim war;
     Many frequent the groves, by Dian's motion, *urging*
     For fashion some, and some too for devotion.[24]

Stanzas 63–74 have been omitted. Here Heywood describes the construction of the temple to Diana in Ephesus and its destruction by fire at the hands of Herostratus, before returning to an account of Jove's growing passion for Callisto.

---

[21] 192] In Caxton's *Recuyell* the sense that Diana and her ladies have formed a religious order rather than a virginal band of huntresses is far more clearly and consistently articulated, although this idea is also present, intermittently, in Heywood.

[22] Jupiter] In his notes to the first canto of *Troia Britanica* Heywood notes that 'There were two *Iupiters*, the first *Iupiter Belus*, from whom *Nilus* descended and first Idolatrised to him: the second *Iupiter* of *Creet*, who was after instiled *Olimpian Iupiter*, and supreame king of the Gods'.

[23] 203–08] The obtrusive repetition of 'her', sometimes signifying herself, has a jaunty, even lightly mocking effect, and is a reflexive example of what was already being termed a 'feminine' rhyme — a rhyme which matches two syllables, and where the final syllable is unstressed.

[24] 209–16] Diana's popularity invites comparisons with contemporary courts, such as that of Elizabeth I.

At length he thus concludes: 'I am but young,
No downy hair upon my face appears,
I'll counterfeit a shrill, effeminate tongue,
220 And don such habit as the huntress wears;
When my gilt quiver cross my breast is hung,
And boar-spear in my hand such as she bears;
    My blood being fresh, my face indifferent fair,   *tolerably*
    Modest my eye, and never shorn my hair,[25]

Who can discover me? Why may not I
Be entered as an ancress 'mongst the rest?   *nun*
This is the way that I intend to try,
Of all my full conclusions held the best;
My habit I'll bespeak so secretly,
230 That what I purpose never can be guessed,
    My lords assemble, and to them show reason,
    Why I of force must leave them for a season.'   *necessity*

Th'excuse unto the nobles current seems,   *genuine*
He takes his leave and travels on his way,
Of his intended voyage no man deems;
Now is he brisked up in his brave array,   *smartened, splendid*
So preciously his mistress he esteems,
That he makes speed to where the virgins stay,
    And by the way his womanish steps he tried,
240   And practised how to speak, to look, to stride,

To blush and to make honours and, if need,   *curtsey*
To pule and weep at every idle toy,   *whimper, trifle*
As women use; next to prepare his weed,   *clothing*
And his soft hand to char-works[26] to employ;   *chores*
He profits in his practice — heaven him speed,
And of his shape assumèd grant him joy;
    Of all effeminate tricks (if you'll believe him)
    To practise tears and sempstry did most grieve him.   *needlework*

Yet did he these 'mongst many others learn,
250 He grows complete in all things, saving one,   *accomplished*
And that no eye can outwardly discern —
Unless they search him, how can it be known?
But come unto the place, his heart doth earn,   *tremble*
Twice it was in his thought back to have gone;
    'But I am Jove', quoth he, 'and shall I then
    Of women be afraid, that fear no men?'

---

[25] In the *Metamorphoses* Jove changes shape rather than simply disguises himself. Comparisons may be drawn between Jove's cross-dressing and the disguise of Pyrocles as an Amazon in Sidney's *Arcadia*.
[26] char-works] In William Warner's *England's Albion* (1586), Jove also has to turn his hand to 'womans Chares'.

> With that he boldly knocks, when to the gate
> A royal virgin comes to know his will;
> This lady after was a queen of state,
> 260 And in Arcadia the fierce boar did kill;
> Atlanta[27] was she called, admitted late,
> Who, thinking to have there remainèd still,
>   King Meleager in Achaia reigned,
>   And to his nuptial bed this queen constrained.
>
> 'Fair virgin', quoth Atlanta, 'what's your pleasure?'
> Jove, after bows and curtseys, thus bespake her:
> 'Bright damsel, if you now retain that measure
> Of grace, you have of beauty from your maker,
> Pity a maid that hath nor gold, nor treasure,[28]
> 270 And to your sacred order would betake her;
>   Know from a noble house I am descended,
>   That humbly pray to be so much befriended.
>
> Prefer me to the mistress of these shades,   *Recommend*
> Diana, whom I reverence, not through folly,
> But as divinest goddess of all maids,
> To whose chaste vows I am devoted wholly.'
> Atlanta says she will, and straight invades[29]
> Diana thus: 'Oh thou adorèd solely[30]
>   Of virgins, fairest Cynthia,[31] will you deign,
> 280   To make this stranger lady of your train?'
>
> Diana takes her state,[32] about her stand
> A multitude of beauties; 'mongst the rest,
> As Jove about him looks, on his right hand
> He spies Callisto, Dian's new-come guest,
> She for whose sake he left th'Epirian land;[33]
> At sight of her, fresh fires inflame his breast,
>   And as he stands, walled in with beauteous faces,
>   He most commends Callisto for her graces.
>
> So many sparkling eyes were in his sight,
> 290 That hedged the sacred queen of virgins round,
> That with their splendour have made noon of night —
> Should all at once look upward, the base ground
> Might match the sky, and make the earth as bright,

---

[27] Atlanta] Cf. *Met.*, VIII. 316–44, X. 560–707.
[28] 269] an apparent allusion to the practice of giving dowries to girls who entered nunneries
[29] invades] *OED* only gives meanings of this verb which relate to attack or intrusion. 'Inveigh' (in the sense of allure or assault with words) seems to fit better into the sense but not the rhyme.
[30] solely] Presumably Atlanta is saying that virgins adore Diana alone, not that only virgins adore her.
[31] Cynthia] As well as being an epithet for Diana, 'Cynthia' helps to signal possible connections with Elizabeth I, for the name was often associated with her.
[32] takes her state] assumes an air of grandeur and dignity
[33] th'Epirian land] a region of north-western Greece

  As in that even, when Ariadne³⁴ crowned   *evening*
   Was through the Galaxia in pomp led,   *galaxy*
   Millions of stars all burning o'er her head.

  Diana Jove in every part surveys,
  Who simpers by himself, and stands demurely,
  His youth, his face, his stature she doth praise,
300 A brave virago she supposed him surely.
  'Were all my train of this large size', she says,
  'Within these forests we might dwell securely,
   'Mongst all that stand or kneel upon the grass,
   I spy not such another manly lass.'³⁵

  So gives her hand to kiss; Jove grace doth win   *approval*
  With Phoebe and Atlanta, who suppose
  Him what he seems, and now receivèd in,
  With all the maids he well acquainted grows,
  They teach him how to sew, to card, and spin.   *comb (wool)*
310 Callisto for his bedfellow he chose;
   With her all day he works, at night he lies,
   Yet, every morn, the maid a maid doth rise.³⁶

  For if he glanced but at a word or two   *alluded obliquely*
  Of love, or grew familiar (as maids use),   *are accustomed to do*
  She frowns, or shakes the head (all will not do),
  His amorous parley she doth quite refuse;   *speech*
  Sometime by feeling touches he would woo,
  Sometime her neck and breast, and sometime choose
   Her lip to dally with: what hurt's in this?
320 Who would forbid a maid, a maid to kiss?

  And then amidst this dalliance he would cheer her,
  And from her neck decline unto her shoulder,
  Next to her breast, and thence descending nearer
  Unto the place where he would have been bolder;
  He finds the froward girl so chastely bear her,
  That the more hot he seemed, she showed the colder,
   And when he grew immodest, oft would say:
   'Now fie for shame, lay by this foolish play'.³⁷

  Alas, poor prince, thy punishment's too great,
330 And more than any mortal³⁸ can endure,

---

³⁴ Ariadne] Ariadne is often depicted with a starry crown, and sometimes associated with an apotheosis into stars.
³⁵ There is some additional humour at this point in *The Golden Age* when Jupiter is sternly commanded to swear never to lie with a man and only to take women as bedfellows. He complies very readily.
³⁶ 311–12] The *Recuyell* lacks these titillating details and Caxton's Jupiter is much more modest and reticent than Heywood's.
³⁷ 328] In *The Golden Age* Jove slyly reinforces his identity as a woman: 'I would the gods would shape thee to a boy, | Or me into a man' (f. E3ᵛ).
³⁸ mortal] See note 16 above.

  To be kept hungry in the sight of meat, *food*
  And thirsty in the sight of waters pure;
  Thou seek'st the food thou most desir'st to eat,
  Which flies thee most, when most thou think'st it sure;
   'Tis double want 'mongst riches to be poor,
   And double death, to drown in sight of shore.[39]

  Besides, the prince too boldly dares not prove her,
  As ignorant, how she may take his offer;
  Nor dare he tell her he is Jove, her lover,
340 Though she at first might deem the prince did scoff her;
  Yet if she should his secrecy discover, *reveal*
  He fears what violent force the queen might proffer
   To one, that with such impudence profane,
   Should break the sacred orders of her train.

  He therefore a convenient season watched,
  When bright Diana the wild stag would chase;
  The beauteous virgins were by couples matched,
  And as the lawns they were about to trace, *glades, pass through*
  Their pointed javelins in their hands they latched; *grasped*
350 About their necks, in many a silken lace,
   Their bugles hung, which as the groves they trip,
   Were oft-times kissed by every lady's lip.

  And in their ears the shrilling music tingled,
  Which made the echoing hills and vales resound;
  Jove and Callisto 'mongst the rest was mingled,
  Until the youthful prince occasion found
  To shrink behind; him fair Callisto singled, *took to one side*
  And throws herself by Jove upon the ground,
   And says: 'How comes it you so soon are tired?'
360 Oh Jove, now thou hast what thou long desired!

  He chose a place thick set with broad-leaved boughs,
  Which from the grassy earth screened the bright sun;
  Here never did the wanton he-goat browse,
  Nor the wild ass for food to this place run;
  This seat as fit for pastime he allows,
  And longs, withal, until the sport be done, *moreover*
   For whilst the game flies from them, here he lags,
   Covered with trees, and hemmed in round with flags. *reeds*

  Nor are they within hearing of the cries
370 Of the shrill bugles th'huntress virgins wear,
  When the bold prince doth 'gainst Callisto rise,
  Resolved to act what he did long forbear;
  Nothing to hinder his attempt he spies,

---

[39] 330–36] An apparent echo of Ovid's account of Narcissus, in particular the famous paradox 'inopem me copia fecit', 'plenty makes me poor' (*Met.*, III. 466)

Being alone, what should the bold youth fear?
   Now with his love he once more 'gins to play,
   But still she cries, 'Nay, prithee, sweet, away.'

He 'gins t'unlace him, she thinks 'tis for heat,
And so it was for heat, which only she,
And none but she, could qualify; his seat   *moderate*
380 He changed, and now his dalliance grows more free,
For as her beauty, his desire is great,
Yet all this while no wrong suspecteth she;
   He heaves her silk-coats,[40] that were thin and rare,   *lifts*
   And yet she blushed not, though he see her bare.

Jove takes th'advantage, by his former vow,   *in spite of*
And force perforce,[41] he makes her his sweet prize;
Th'amazèd virgin (scarce a virgin now)
Fills all the neighbour groves with shrieks and cries;
She catches at his locks, his lips, his brow,
390 And rends her garments, as she struggling lies,
   The violence came so sudden and so fast,
   She scarce knew what had chanced her, till 'twas past.

As when a man, struck with a blast of thunder,[42]
Feels himself pierced, but knows not how, nor where,
His troubled thoughts confused with pain and wonder,
Distracted 'twixt amazèdness and fear,   *torn*
His foot removes not, nor his hands doth sunder,
Seems blind to see, and being deaf to hear,
   And, in an ecstasy, so far misled,   *stupor*
400   That he shows dead alive and living dead.

Even so this new-made woman, late a maid,
Lies senseless after this her transformation,[43]
Seeing in vain she had implored Heaven's aid
With many a fearful shriek and shrill oration;
Like one entranced upon the ground she's laid,
Amazed at this her sudden alteration,
   She is she knows not what, she cares not where,
   Confounded with strange passion, force and fear.

Jove comforts her, and with his princely arm
410 He would have raised her from the settled grass,
With amorous words he fain her grief would charm,
He tells her what he meant, and who he was,
But there is no amends for such shrewd harm,   *severe*

---

[40] silk-coats] A coat can mean a skirt or tunic.
[41] force perforce] by dint of force, or perhaps 'using force, of necessity'
[42] thunder] Thunderbolts are particularly associated with Jove.
[43] transformation] Heywood employs the language of (Ovidian) metamorphosis, depicting Callisto's loss of virginity as a radical transformation.

Nor can he cheer the discontented lass,
   Though he oft swore, and by his life protested,
   She in his nuptial bed should be invested.

But nothing can prevail; she weeping swears
To tell Diana of his shameful deed,
So leaves him, watering all her way with tears;
420   Young Jove to leave the forest hath decreed,
He would not have it come to Dian's ears,
And therefore to the city back doth speed,
   She to the cloister, with her cheeks all wet,
   Alone, as many, as when first they met.   *had sexual intercourse*

Notes[44]

Iasius[45] reigned in Italy, at whose marriage the famous Egyptian Io was present. This was in the year of the world 2408. It was just six years after that Moses, at the age of forty, having slain the Egyptian, fled from the sight of Pharaoh.

Eleven years after Moses departed out of Egypt the two brothers, Dardanus and Iasius, waged wars in Italy. Iasius was assisted by the Ianigenes (so called of Janus), Dardanus was aided by the Aborigines, so called by Sabatus Saga,[46] who succeeded Comerus Gallus,[47] the Scythian, in certain conquered provinces of Italy.

At this time Lusus[48] reigned in Spain, Allobrox[49] in France, Crothopus[50] the 8th king of the Argives now reigned; Craunus the second king of Athens, and at this time Aaron[51] was consecrated high priest among the Israelites.

Iasius was slain in the year of the world 2457, in whose place Coribantus, his son, succeeded. Dardanus sojourned certain years in Samothracia and erected his city Dardan, called Troy, in the 31st year of the dukedom of Moses, receiving that province where his city was erected from Atho, prince of Moenia.

About the same time, by equal computation, Arcas[52] and Callisto, subduing the Pelasgians[53] (by the help of Jupiter), called the whole province Arcadia.

---

[44] The notes for the whole of the second canto are included.
[45] Iasius] more usually Iasion. In the *Aeneid* it is suggested that Iasion and his brother Dardanus were originally from Italy, although other versions of the story place their origins in Greece. Dardanus is also the mythical founder of Troy whereas Iasion was meant to have settled in Samothrace, an island in the Northern Aegean. Heywood describes the enmity of the two brothers in Book One of *Troia Britanica*.
[46] Sabatus Saga] the nephew of Noah, according to Annius of Viterbo
[47] Comerus] the eldest son of Japeth
[48] Lusus] the legendary founder of Lusitania (Portugal)
[49] Allobrox] The name is associated with the Allobroges, a Celtic tribe in Gaul.
[50] Crothopus] an Argive king
[51] Aaron] the brother of Moses
[52] Arcas] Callisto's son by Jupiter
[53] Pelasgians] pre-Hellenic peoples in Greece

Tantalus[54] ruled the Phrygians, who were before his time called Moeones. This Moeonia is now called Lydia, under which climate Arachne was born, by Pallas turned into a spider.[55]

Diana was thought to be daughter to an ancient king called Jupiter of Attica, which I take to be Jupiter Belus[56] before spoken of. She was the first that instituted a professed order of virginity. The poets call this Diana Cynthia, and Phoebe, figuring in her the moon, and that her brother Phoebus and she were born of their mother Latona, daughter to Caeus[57] the giant in the isle of Delos.

Atlanta was daughter to Iasius,[58] sister to Coribantus; she first wounded the Calydonian boar, and was after espoused to Meleager, son to Oeneus, the king of Calydon, by his wife Althaea.[59]

Lycaon was the son of Pelasgus[60] (the son of Jupiter and Niobe[61]) and of Melibea, or as some think, Cyllene. He had many sons by many wives: Maenalus, Thesprotus, Nectinnes, Caucon, Lycus, Maenius, Macareus. In Arcadia, Menatus that built the city Menatus; Moeleneus that built Moeleneus not far from Megapolis. Acontius that built Acontium. Charisius that gave name to Charisium, and Cynethus to Cynetha. He had besides Psophis, Phthinus, Teleboas, Aemon, Mantinus, Stimphalus, Clitor, Orchomenus, and others.

Some reckon them to the number of fifty, others to many more. Amongst all these, he had but two daughters, Callisto and Dia.[62]

Touching Ariadne's crown, it is thus remembered:

> Atque corona nitet clarum inter sidera signum,
> Defunctae quam Bacchus ibi dedit esse Ariadnae.[63]

Being forsaken of Theseus,[64] in the isle Naxos, whom before she had delivered from the minotaur, she was espoused by the god Bacchus, and by him had Thoas, Oenopion, Staphilus, Exanthes, Latramis, and Tauropolis.

The end of the second canto

---

[54] Tantalus] A number of different stories are associated with Tantalus. He is perhaps most famous for serving his son Pelops to the gods and being punished in Hades by visions of food and drink which he cannot reach.
[55] Arachne] *Met.*, VI. 1–145.
[56] Jupiter Belus] Many different characters are associated with the name Belus. Sometimes, as here, the epithet is associated with Jupiter, but elsewhere Belus is identified as a king of Babylon.
[57] Caeus] a Titan
[58] Iasius] In mythology Atalanta was the daughter of Iasius, but not of the same Iasius who was the father of Coribantus.
[59] Althaea] *Met.*, VIII. 445–525.
[60] Pelasgus] Different traditions are associated with Pelasgus, whose name is linked with the Pelasgians.
[61] Niobe] the daughter of Phoroneus, rather than the more famous Niobe who incurred the wrath of the gods for her hubris
[62] Dia] wife of Ixion and mother of Pirithous, the Lapith whose marriage with a centaur, Hippodamia, was the cause of a battle (*Met.*, XII. 210–535)
[63] Atque . . . Ariadnae] 'And the crown which Bacchus established as an illustrious memorial to the departed Ariadne shines among the stars'. In the original, the marginal note reads 'Arat. in astron', indicating that the Latin verses derive from the Greek didactic poet Aratus's *Phaenomena* (ll. 71–72), a hexameter poem on the constellations and related celestial phenomena. The marginal note suggests that Heywood may have read Aratus in a compilation of ancient astronomical writings, such as the *Astronomica veterum scripta isagogica Graeca et Latina* (Heidelberg, 1589). Aratus influenced, among many others, Ovid, who, like Cicero, translated the work into Latin.
[64] Theseus] Versions of this story can be found in many classical texts including Hesiod's *Theogony*, 947 and Ovid's *Heroides*, X.

BOOK 3

Argumentum

Callisto, known to be with child, is driven
From Dian's cloister; Arcas doth pursue
His mother; unto him Pelage is given,   *Pelasgia*
Now termèd Arcady; when Titan[65] knew
Saturn had sons alive, his heart was riven
With anger; he his men together drew
   To battle; the two brothers fight their fills,
   Jove saves his father, and his uncle kills.

Transformed Callisto, and the giant kings,
Jove's combat with great Typhon, Gama sings.[66]

CANTO 3

When I record the dire effects of war
I cannot but with happy praise admire
The blessèd friends of peace, which smooths the scar
Of wounding steel, and all-consuming fire;
Oh, in what safety then thy subjects are,
430   Royal King James,[67] secured from war's fierce ire,
   That by thy peaceful government[68] alone,
   Studiest divided Christendom t'attone.   *reconcile*

To thee may poets sing their cheerful lays,
By whom their muses flourish in soft peace;
By thee, the swains may tune eternal praise,
By whom they freely reap the earth's increase;
The merchants through the earth applaud thy days,[69]
Wishing their endless date may never cease,
   By whom they through the quartered world may traffic,
440   Asia, Europe, America, and Afric.

Thy liege men thou has placed as on a hill,
Free from the cannons' reach, from far to see
Divided nations one another kill,[70]
Whilst thy safe people as spectators be,

---

[65] Titan] Heywood gives a fuller account of the brothers' background in Book 1, and they also play an important role in *The Golden Age*.
[66] Gama] This is perhaps a reference to Camões's mythologized historical epic *Lusiads* (1572), whose subject is Vasco da Gama.
[67] King James] James VI and I
[68] peaceful government] One sign of James's preference for peace was the 1604 peace treaty he signed between England and Spain.
[69] 437] James promoted international trade. The East India Company was particularly active at this time.
[70] 443–44] Perhaps a reference to the wars between Spain and the Netherlands

Only to take a view what blood they spill;
They near to ruin, yet in safety we,
    Alone in peace, whilst all the realms about us,
    Envy our bliss, yet forced to fight about us.

So did the neuter Londoners once stand   *neutral*
450 On Barnet Heath, aloof, to see the fight[71]
Twixt the fourth Edward, sovereign of this land,
And the great Duke of Warwick,[72] in the right
Of the sixth Henry, in which, hand to hand,
Brave John of Oxford,[73] a renownèd knight,
    Made many a parting soul for life-breath pant,
    And vanquished many a worthy combatant.

So stood the Kentish men[74] to view the main,   *open sea*
In the year eighty eight, when th'English fleet
Fought with the huge Armadas brought from Spain;[75]
460 With what impatience did they stand to see't
On the safe shore, willing to leave the train
Of such faint cowards as think safety sweet
    In such a quarrel, where invaders threat us,
    And in our native kingdom seek to beat us.

Where royal England's admiral, attended
With all the chivalry of our brave nation,
The name of Howard[76] through the earth extended,
By naval triumph o'er their proud invasion;
Where victory on the Red Cross[77] descended,
470 In lightning and earth's thunder, in such fashion,
    That all the sheafèd[78] feathered shafts of Spain,
    Headed with death, were shot them back again.

It showed as if two towns on th'ocean built,
Had been at once by th'heaven's lightning fired;
The shining waters, with the bright flames gilt,
Breathed clouds of smoke which to the spheres aspired;
The blood of Spanish soldiers, that day spilt,

---

[71] fight] This battle took place on 14 April 1471.
[72] Duke of Warwick] Richard Neville, 16th Earl of Warwick (1428–71), known as Warwick the Kingmaker, switched sides more than once during the Wars of the Roses. He was killed at the Battle of Barnet.
[73] John of Oxford] John de Vere, 13th Earl of Oxford (1442–1513), fought on the Lancastrian side.
[74] Kentish men] The bystanders are characterized rather differently in this stanza. As the context involves a direct threat from a foreign power Heywood seems to depict them as men who are spectating because they are prepared to get involved, by contrast with the cowards who have presumably sought safety.
[75] Armadas brought from Spain] Severe storms ensured that the Spanish Armada failed in its mission against England in 1588.
[76] Howard] Charles Howard, 1st Earl of Nottingham (1536–1624), was Lord Admiral of the English fleet.
[77] Red Cross] The context is slightly ambiguous, but this is probably a reference to the cross of Burgundy, used by Spain as a naval ensign, rather than to the English flag.
[78] sheafèd] A sheaf is a bundle or quiverful of arrows.

	Which through the portholes ran, Neptune[79] admired,	*wondered at*
	And took it for the Red Sea, whilst the thunder	
480	Of English shot proclaimed the sea-god's wonder.	

But lest this ordinance[80] should wake from sleep
Our ancient enmity, now buried quite,
The grave of all their shame shall be the deep,
In which these peopled sea towns first did fight;
Yet that I may a kind of method keep,
And some deserving captains to recite,
    Live famous Hawkins,[81] Frobisher[82] and Drake,[83]
    Whose very name made Spain's Armadas quake.

	Now to return unto Pelasgia back,	
490	Which Jove hath made to him and to his seed,	
	Then takes his leave; the people, loath to lack	
	The prince that from a tyrant hath them freed,	
	Who of their lives and honours sought the wrack,	*destruction*
	Would change his purpose, but he hath decreed	
	Pelasgia to forsake, and I must leave him	
	To Epire's king,[84] who gladly will receive him.	

	And to the forest to Callisto turn,
	Whose sorrow with her swelling belly grows;
	Alas, how can the lady choose but mourn,
500	To see herself so near her painful throes?
	'Tis August, now the scorching dog stars burn,
	Therefore the forest queen a set day chose
	For all her train to bath them in the flood,[85]
	Callisto 'mongst them by the river stood.

The queen with jealous eyes surveys the place,[86]
Lest men or satyrs should be ambushed[87] by them,
The naked ladies in the flood to face,

---

[79] Neptune] This reference to Neptune, within a modern context, reflects Heywood's opportunistic approach to myth. For much of the poem Heywood takes a highly euhemerizing approach to Ovidian material; the gods are real and historical figures, but not divinities. Here, by contrast, it is clear that Neptune is a god but only a fictional one, an allegorical ornament, just as he is in Marvell's 'Last Instructions to a Painter'.

[80] ordinance] ordnance. Display of military force here used metaphorically of Heywood's poem itself.

[81] Hawkins] Admiral Sir John Hawkins (1532–95), a merchant and navigator who was also involved in the early slave trade, was knighted for his role in the victory over the Armada.

[82] Frobisher] Sir Martin Frobisher (?1535–94), explorer and privateer, was also knighted for his services against the Armada.

[83] Drake] Sir Francis Drake (1540–96), privateer and navigator, was second in command of the English fleet at the time of the Armada.

[84] Epire's king] Earlier in the first book of *Troia Britanica* Heywood had described the conflict between Lycaon of Pelasgia and Melliseus of Epirus.

[85] 503] Not surprisingly, Heywood prefers to turn back to Ovid's scenario of a bathing party rather than copy the more austere account of an assembly in Diana's chapter-house which Caxton offers in the *Recuyell*.

[86] 505] The scene in which Callisto's pregnancy is discovered is presented as a brief dumb show in *The Golden Age*.

[87] ambushed] lying concealed with the intention of attacking rather than, as now, themselves being the objects of attack

Or in their clotheless beauty to espy them;
Now all at once they 'gin themselves t'unlace —
510   Oh ravishing harmony! Had I been by them,
    I should have thought so many silken strings,
    Touched by such white hands, music fit for kings.[88]

They doff their upper garments; each begins
Unto her milk white linen smock to bare her —
Small difference twixt their white smocks and their skins,
And hard it were to censure which were fairer;   *judge*
Some plunge into the river past their chins,
Some fear to venture whilst the others dare her,
    And with her tender foot the river feels,
520   Making the water's margent rinse her heels.

Some stand up to the ankles, some the knees,
Some to the breast, some dive above the crown;[89]
Of this her naked fellow nothing sees,
Saving the troubled waves where she slid down;
Another sinks her body by degrees,
And first her foot, and then her leg, doth drown;
Some their faint fellows to the deep are craving,   *urging*
Some sit upon the bank, their white legs laving.   *washing*

One only, discontented, shrinks aside,
530   Her faint unbracing idly she doth linger,   *unfastening, delay*
(Full fain the lass her swelling breast would hide)
She pins and unpins with her thumb and finger;
Twice Phoebe sends, and musing she denied   *grumbling*
To bathe her; she commands the rest to bring her,[90]
Who, betwixt mirth and earnest, force and play,
All but her cobweb shadow snatched away.

Dian at first perceives her breasts to swell,
And whispers to Atlanta what she found,
Who straight perceived Callisto was not well;
540   They judged she had her virgin's belt unbound,[91]
But when her veil beneath her navel fell,
And that her belly showed so plump and round,
They little need to ask if she transgressed,
Callisto's guilty blush the act confessed.

---

[88] 511–12] The poet makes a playful comparison between the silken strings securing their dresses and the strings of musical instruments.

[89] some dive above the crown] Presumably this means that some are completely submerged so that even their head (crown) is covered by water.

[90] 533–34] The repetition of 'she' is slightly confusing. Callisto refuses to bathe (herself) so Diana commands the other nymphs to fetch her.

[91] 540] At the end of the canto Heywood provides a note to this stanza: 'It was the custom in those days, the day of every virgin's marriage, to have her girdle loosed, by him that should be her husband'.

    Therefore she banished her, nor suits nor tears
    Can with the queen of damsels aught prevail,
    Who, when by strict enquiry made she hears
    Of Jupiter and his deceitful stale,[92]
    Who seemed so like a virgin, Phoebe swears,
550 Because her judgement thenceforth shall not fail,
    And to avoid occasion of like venter,   *venture*
    To search all such as to her train shall enter.

    Thus is Lycaon's daughter banished now
    The city, by her late assumed profession,
    Banished the cloister by her breach of vow,
    For by no prayers,[93] tears or intercession,
    Diana her re-entrance will allow
    After exilement, for her late transgression,
    Therefore, ashamed, through dark shades she doth run,
560 Till time expires, and she brings forth a son.

    So did our Cynthia chastity prefer,   *Elizabeth I*
    The most admirèd queen that ever reigned;
    If any of her virgin train did err,
    Or with the like offence their honours stained,
    From her imperial court she banished her,
    And a perpetual exile she remained;
    Oh bright Eliza, though thy dated days   *finite*
    Confine, there is no limit to thy praise!

---

[92] stale] Perhaps here used in the sense of lure or bait, to refer to Jupiter's disguise. However it is possible this is a reference to Callisto as a 'stale', an unchaste woman. 'Virgin' may be opposed either to man or unchaste woman.
[93] prayers] a disyllable

GEORGE SANDYS

JUPITER AND CALLISTO

from

THE FIRST FIVE BOOKES OF OVIDS METAMORPHOSIS (1621)

GEORGE SANDYS

JUPITER AND CALLISTO

from

THE FIRST FIVE BOOKES OF OVIDS METAMORPHOSIS (1621)

[*Metamorphoses*, II. 401–534]

Sprengius, *Metamorphoses Ovidii* (1563), p. 25ʳ

George Sandys (1578–1644) was a son of Edwin Sandys, Archbishop of York, a leading member of the Virginia Company. Sandys was admitted to St Mary Hall, Oxford, in 1589, but is thought to have later transferred to Corpus Christi. In 1596 he moved to Middle Temple. No evidence of whether he qualified from either Oxford or the Middle Temple is recorded. His first published work was *A Relation of a Journey Begun an. Dom. 1610* (1615) which narrated his travels to the Ottoman Empire and Levant. His translation of the first five books of the *Metamorphoses*, from which this extract is taken, appeared in 1621. In the same year Sandys was appointed treasurer for the colony of Virginia, and sailed to Jamestown. The remaining books of Ovid's poem were translated on the long voyage, and during Sandys's stay at the colony, which was marked by clashes with the native Virginians. This full translation was published in 1626. A sumptuous second edition of the complete translation, dedicated to Charles I and Henrietta Maria, and including fine engravings and detailed notes, appeared in 1632. In 1636 Sandys published his *Paraphrase upon the Psalms*, and in 1638 a translation of Hugo Grotius's Latin verse drama, *Christus Patiens*.

Sandys is thought to have drawn on a number of different editions and commentaries of Ovid while preparing his translation, including those of Raphael Regius (1493), George Sabinus (1554) and Jacobus Pontanus (1618).[1] Small changes between the different editions published

---

[1] Raphael Lyne, *Ovid's Changing Worlds* (Oxford: Oxford University Press, 2001), p. 203; Deborah Rubin, *Ovid's Metamorphoses Englished: George Sandys as Translator and Mythographer* (New York: Garland, 1985), pp. 175–83.

in his lifetime reflect Sandys's scrupulous attention to detail,[2] and his commentaries, added to the 1632 edition, are in many ways similar to the kind of textual apparatus a reader would expect to find in a modern scholarly edition, although they also demonstrate the tenacity of the interpretative tradition, and in fact provide a unique compendium of the moral and allegorical readings of the *Metamorphoses* still current well into the seventeenth century. However, Sandys's interest in the *Metamorphoses* was not purely literary or antiquarian. Echoing Golding's Christianized attitude towards the pagan poet, he notes that Ovid 'appears in the rest so consonant to the truth, as doubtlesse he had either seene the Books of Moses, or receaved that doctrine by tradition'.

The translation follows Ovid's Latin reasonably closely. Some very minor changes perhaps reveal a slightly censorious attitude. Sandys omits, for example, Ovid's reference to the fire of Jove's love penetrating his bones (II. 410), and, when translating Ovid's comparison between Callisto's beautiful mouth and the ugly jaws of the bear into which she is transformed, adds the detail that these lips 'late to sin | Enticed a god', as though blaming her for the rape. His Juno is still more unforgiving than in Ovid. Sandys picks up her reference to Callisto as 'importuna', 'forward', and makes his own Juno accuse Callisto of having been complicit in a 'willing rape'. One of Sandys's adjustments in the later edition of 1632 was to change the word 'proud' to the more insulting 'wanton' when Juno makes her (insincere) suggestion that Jove restore her body to its former shape (I. 138).

Michael Drayton, in his 'Elegy 123', praised the 'sweetness and unusual grace' of Sandys's translation. It marks a turning point between the traditions of Ovidian translation represented in this volume, and the achievements of later poets such as Milton, Dryden and Pope — all of whom were influenced by Sandys. In particular, Sandys's heroic couplets, his compressed and witty style, anticipate his Augustan successors, as does his Latinate vocabulary, very different from the more homely language of Golding.[3] As a poet who helped shape a new tradition, Sandys contrasts sharply with Heywood, who, although writing only a few years earlier, harks back both to the language and the intellectual culture of an earlier age. Sandys's position as a kind of 'proto-Augustan' is also reflected in the continuing popularity of the translation, which was reprinted several times in the later seventeenth century.

EDITIONS[4]

The First Five Bookes of Ovid's Metamorphosis, trans. by George Sandys ([London]: [n. pr.] for W. B[arrett], 1621), STC 18963.3.

Ovid's Metamorphosis Englished, trans. by George Sandys (London: [William Stansby], 1626), STC 18964.

Ovid's Metamorphosis Englished, Mythologiz'd and Represented in Figures, trans. by George Sandys, ed. by Karl K. Hulley and Stanley T. Vandersall (Lincoln: University of Nebraska Press, [1970]).

Ovid's Metamorphosis Englished, Mythologiz'd, and Represented in Figures. An Essay to the Translation of Virgil's Æneis [Bk I], trans. by George Sandys (New York: Garland, 1976).

---

[2] For a discussion of the changes, see Lee T. Pearcy, *The Mediated Muse: English Translations of Ovid 1560–1700* (Hamden, CT: Archon Books, 1984), pp. 78–82.
[3] For a comparison of the two translators' styles, see Lyne, *Ovid's Changing Worlds*, pp. 201–09.
[4] This is only a selective list. Further editions were published in 1628, 1632, 1669, 1678 and 1690.

FURTHER READING

Gertrude C. Drake, 'Ovid's *Metamorphoses*, the Facsimile of the Caxton MS, and Sandys's 1632 Version', *Papers on Language and Literature*, 7 (1971), 313–15.

Raphael Lyne, *Ovid's Changing Worlds* (Oxford: Oxford University Press, 2001).

Liz Oakley-Brown, *Ovid and the Cultural Politics of Translation in Early Modern England* (Aldershot: Ashgate, 2006).

Lee T. Pearcy, *The Mediated Muse: English Translations of Ovid, 1560–1700* (Hamden, CT: Archon, 1985).

Deborah Rubin, *Ovid's Metamorphoses Englished: George Sandys as Translator and Mythographer* (New York: Garland, 1985).

JUPITER AND CALLISTO

	The Thunderer then walks the ample round	
	Of heaven's high walls, to search if all were sound,	
	When, finding nothing there by fire decayed,	
	He earth and human industries surveyed.	*exertions*
	Arcadia[5] chiefly exercised his cares,	
	There springs and streams, that durst not run, repairs,	
	The fields with grass, the trees with leaves endues,	*covers*
	And withered woods with vanished shades renews.	
	Oft passing to and fro, a Nonacrine[6]	
10	The god enflamed, her beauty more divine!	
	'Twas not her art to spin, nor with much care	
	And fine variety to trick her hair,	*adorn*
	But with a zone her looser garments bound,	*girdle*
	And her rude tresses in a fillet wound;	*headband*
	Now armèd with a dart, now with a bow,	
	A squire of Phoebe's. Maenalus[7] did know	
	None more in grace of all her virgin throng,	
	But favourites in favour last not long.	
	The parted day in equal balance held,	
20	A wood she entered, as yet never felled;	
	There from her shoulders she her quiver takes,	
	Unbends her bow, and, tired with hunting, makes	
	The flowery-mantled earth her happy bed,	
	And on her painted quiver lays her head.	
	When Jove the nymph without a guard did see,	
	In such a posture: 'This stealth', said he,	
	'My wife shall never know, or, say she did,	
	Who, ah, who would not for her sake be chid!'	*scolded*
	Diana's shape and habit then endued,	*clothing, assumed*
30	He said, 'My huntress, where hast thou pursued	

---

[5] Arcadia] region of Greece, in the Peloponnese
[6] Nonacrine] an inhabitant of Nonacris, a town in Arcadia
[7] Maenalus] a town in Arcadia

This morning's chase?' She, rising, made reply:
'Hail pow'r, more great than Jove (though Jove stood by)
In my esteem.' He smiled, and gladly heard
Himself, by her, before himself preferred,
And kissed. His kisses too intemperate grow,
Not such as maids on maidens do bestow.
His strict embracements her narration stayed,   *close, halted*
And, by his crime, his own deceit betrayed.
She did what woman could to force her fate,   *overcome*
40 Would Juno saw, it would her spleen abate;   *ill-humour*
Although, as much as woman could, she strove,
What woman, or who can contend with Jove!
The victor hies him to th'ethereal states,
The woods, as guilty of her wrongs, she hates,   *aware*
Almost forgetting, as from thence she flung,
Her quiver, and the bow which by it hung.
High Maenalus, Dictynna[8] with her train
Now entering, pleased with the quarry slain,
Beheld, and called her; called upon, she fled,
50 And in her semblance Jupiter doth dread,
But when she saw th'attending nymphs appear,
She troops amongst them, and diverts her fear.
Ah, how our faults are in our faces read!
With eyes scarce ever raised, she hangs the head,
Nor perks[9] she now, as she was wont to do,
By Cynthia's side, nor leads the starry crew.
Though mute she be, her violated shame
Self-guilty blushes silently proclaim;
But that a maid, Diana the ill-hid
60 Had soon espied;[10] they say her sly nymphs did.
    Nine crescents now had made their orbs complete,
When, faint with labour, and her brother's heat,[11]
She takes the shades, close by the murmuring
And silver current of a fruitful spring.
The place much praised, the stream, as cool as clear,
Her fair feet glads. 'No spies', said she, 'be here,
Here will we our disrobèd bodies dip.'
Callisto blushed, the rest their fair limbs strip,
And her perforce unclothed, that sought delays,   *of necessity*
70 Who, with her body, her offence displays;
They, all abashed, yet loath to have it spied,
Striving her belly with their hands to hide.
'Avaunt', said Cynthia, get thee from our train,
Nor, with thy limbs, this sacred fountain stain.'
    This knew the matron of the Thunderer,[12]

---

[8] Dictynna] a Cretan goddess, later identified with Diana (Artemis)

[9] perks] To perk means to assert oneself, generally with connotations of jauntiness or self-satisfaction.

[10] 59–60] Diana would have realized the reasons for Callisto's embarrassment if she had not been a virgin herself.

[11] Her brother's heat] Diana's brother was Apollo, god of the sun.

[12] matron of the Thunderer] Juno

Whose thoughts to fitter times revenge defer,
Nor long delays, for Arcas (which more scorn
And grief provoked) was of the lady born.
Beheld with ire, which turned her eyes to flame:
80 'Must thou be fruitful too, to blaze my shame,
And propagate the wrong? And must he be
A living infamy to Jove and me?
I'll not endur't. That so self-pleasing shape,
Which drew my husband to thy willing rape,
I sure shall spoil.' This said, her hair she wound
About her hand, and dragged her on the ground;

Sprengius, *Metamorphoses Ovidii* (1563), p. 26ʳ

Her hands, for pity heaved — so smooth, so fair! —
Grew forthwith rough, and horrid with black hair.   *bristling*
Her dainty hands which, swift, deformity   *swiftly*
90 Converts to paws, the place of feet supply.
The mouth, so praised by Jove, that late to sin
Enticed a god, now horribly doth grin,
And, lest she might too powerfully beseech,
She instantly bereft her of her speech,
Instead whereof, a noise ascends her hoarse
And rumbling throat, which terror doth enforce.
Although a bear, her mind she still possessed,
And with continual groans her grief expressed;
With paws stretched up to heaven, accused her fate,
100 And whom she could not call,[13] she thought ingrate.   *ungrateful*
How oft, afraid to keep the woods alone,
Sought she the house and fields that were her own!

---

[13] whom she could not call] Jove

How often, chased by the pursuing cry,
Th'affrighted huntress from her hounds did fly!
Oft she, the wood's wild foragers espied,[14]
Forgetting what she was, herself would hide;
A bear, yet trembles at the sight of bears,
And wolves, her father[15] then amongst them, fears.
    When, lo, Lycaon's grandchild thither drew,   *Arcas*
110 Thrice five years old, nor of his mother knew;
While he pursues the chase and salvage spoils,   *wild prey*
The Eryrmanthian[16] woods begirt with toils,   *enclosed, nets*
Her he encounters. Arcas seen, she stayed,
And would have ta'ne acquaintance. He, afraid,   *taken*
Stared upon her with a constant eye,   *fixed*
And backward stepped, as she approachèd nigh,
About to wound her undefended breast.
The king of gods, who did the fact detest,   *deed*
With them the crime withdrew, and both conveyed
120 To heaven; now neighb'ring constellations made.
    Saturnia swelled to see her rival shine   *Juno*
Amongst the stars. She stoops to Neptune's brine,
Grey Tethys[17] and the old Oceanus,[18]
Graced by the deities, accosting thus:
    'Ask you why I, the queen of gods, am come
From blessed abodes? Another holds my room.
When night's black mantle shall the world enfold,
My wounds, those honoured stars, you may behold;
There, where the shortest circle, at the end   *orbit*
130 Of all the turning axle-tree[19] doth bend.
Who would not injury the wife of Jove,   *injure*
When our worst punishments preferments prove?
How great our act! How is our power displayed!
Unformed a woman,[20] and a goddess made.
Thus we the guilty scourge! Thus, thus, we our
Revenge advance! Such, and so great, our power!
Let him unbeast the beast (as heretofore
Phoronida[21]) and her proud shape restore.
Why doth he not Lycaon's daughter wed,
140 Rejecting me, and place her in his bed?
But you, who once my careful nurses were,
If my indignities do touch you near,

---

[14] espied] 'having' is understood before 'espied', here a past participle
[15] Jove turned Lycaon into a wolf after he tried to test his divinity by serving him a dish of human flesh. See *Met.*, I. 218–39.
[16] Erymanthian] Erymanthus was a city in Arcadia.
[17] Tethys] titaness and sea goddess
[18] Oceanus] titan and sea god
[19] the end | Of all the turning axle-tree] the uttermost pole
[20] Unformed a woman] Although Juno is preoccupied by Callisto's elevation, the original 'unforming' was her transformation into a bear.
[21] Phoronida] Phoronis is an appellation of Io, who was changed into a heifer, but later restored to human form. See *Met.*, I. 610–746.

Command you that the seven Triones[22] keep
Their lazy wain[23] out of your sacred deep.
From thence, those stars, the price of whoredom, drive,
Nor let th'impure in your pure surges dive.'
    They both assent. Her peacocks to the skies
Their goddess draw, late stuck with Argus' eyes.[24]

Sprengius, *Metamorphoses Ovidii* (1563), p. 27^r

---

[22] Triones] the seven stars of the Great Bear
[23] wain] waggon. The Great Bear was also known as Charles's Wain.
[24] 147–48] See *Met.*, I. 568–746.

TEXTUAL NOTES

T. H., THE FABLE OF OVID TREATING OF NARCISSUS (1560)

l. 25
nymphs] *1560* 'imphes'

l. 50
Why fliest] *1560* 'Whistlest'

l. 70
now] *1560* 'none'

l. 71
thus other] *1560* 'they other'

l. 73
so one] *1560* 'soone'

l. 129
done] *1560* 'dime'

l. 130
shun] *1560* 'shine'

l. 171
hue] *1560* 'heare'

l. 186
Styx] *1560* 'Stype'

l. 224
bend] *1560* 'bends'

l. 270
saving] *1560* 'saying'

l. 277
Daphne] *1560* 'Daphus'

l. 324

them] *1560* 'the'

l. 325

them] *1560* 'the'

l. 421

then] *1560* 'the'

l. 439

Tereus] *1560* 'Terus'

l. 464

uncertain] *1560* 'unsuerties'

l. 504

Which] 1560 'With'

l. 522

fame] *1560* 'shame'

l. 531

deserts] *1560* 'desarties'

l. 541

It] *1560* 'I'

l. 542

ere] *1560* 'or'

l. 599

woos] *1560* 'waves'

l. 636

starve] *1560* 'starne'

l. 663

thereabout to stand] *1560* 'there a bate to stand'

l. 683

the] *1560* 'they'

TEXTUAL NOTES

l. 693

spends] *1560* 'spendeth'

l. 764

Than] *1560* 'them'

l. 796

the] *1560* 'thy'

l. 849

Midas'] *1560* 'Minarnais'

l. 955

low] *1560* 'lost'

l. 969

That thought his shadow to be such a gain.] *1560* 'That through his shadow to be soche agayne'

l. 1006

is] *1560* 'in'

l. 1022

They] *1560* 'The'

l. 1025

their] *1560* 'here'

THOMAS HEDLEY, THE JUDGEMENT OF MIDAS (*c.* 1552)

l. 4

so] *1560* 'lo'

l. 26

Both] *1560* 'but'

ARTHUR GOLDING, SALMACIS AND HERMAPHRODITUS (1565)

l. 51

for to be] *1567* 'to be'

THOMAS PEEND, THE PLEASANT FABLE OF HERMAPHRODITUS AND SALMACIS (1565)

l. 294

swingeing] *1565* 'swinging'

WILLIAM BARKSTED, MYRRHA, THE MOTHER OF ADONIS (1607)

Title page

Nanciscetur] *1607* 'Nansicetur'.

l. 171

fire's extinct at] *1607* 'fire extinct as'

l. 209

love] *1607* 'loves'

l. 244

the] *1607* 'she'

l. 285

she] *1607* 'the'

l. 288

Or one more fair than to deny her suit] *1607* 'or one more farre, then to denie her suite'

l. 295

Many have] *1607* 'Many staue'

l. 392

thy] *1607* 'their'

l. 461

repair] *1607* 'repaide'

l. 508

Venus doth smile] *1607* 'Venus smile'

l. 546

ease] *1607* 'eyes'

l. 554

Cinyr] *1607* 'Cynix'

l. 588

Thought] *1607* 'Though'

l. 756

Annoyed] *1607* 'annoided'

l. 770

ne'er-returnèd] *1607* 'nere-erturned'

H. A., THE SCOURGE OF VENUS (1613)

l. 5

worse] *1613* 'more'

l. 37

wight] *1613* 'night'

l. 87

shame] *1613* 'chance'

l. 93

wax] *1613* 'way'

l. 112

suit] *1613* 'sweet'

l. 131

nearly] *1613* 'sweetly'

l. 163

scribbled] *1613* 'scrambled'

l. 268

To stop her breath most desperately doth vow] *1613* 'And minds to hang herself her love to show'

ll. 463–74

These two stanzas were both added to *1614*.

l. 506

no] *1613* 'that'

l. 544

breasts] *1613* 'breath'

l. 549

Began at length] *1613* 'now did begin'

l. 648

Anon you'll] *1613* 'None wold'

l. 717

delight] *1613* 'rejoice'

l. 719

fading] *1613* 'fasting'

l. 741

Unclose] *1613* 'unless'

l. 776

That] *1613* 'it'

l. 792

quickly] *1613* 'quietly'

l. 851

save] *1613* 'and'

l. 859

time for] *1613* 'leisure'

l. 901

walls] *1613* 'walks'

l. 937.

Nor] *1613* 'now'

l. 944

same] *1613* 'some'

l. 954

child] *1613* 'words'

l. 963

did still arise] *1613* 'continual doth arise'

l. 966

Who scourged him for his mother's lusting past] *1613* 'Who did revenge his mother's lusting past'

JAMES GRESHAM, THE PICTURE OF INCEST (1626)

l. 90

he's] *1626* 'she's'

l. 500

fuller] *1626* 'fullier'

l. 555

Sabaea] *1626* 'in a Sabra'

l. 600

An] *1626* 'and'

l. 627

surcrescent] *1626* 'surrescent'

DUNSTAN GALE, PYRAMUS AND THISBE (1617)

l. 40

Faint he replied: 'A maid, and fear a man?'] *1617* 'Faint (he replied) a maid and feare a man?'

l. 45

pats] *1617* 'pals'

l. 151

she hied] *1617* 'she hide'

l. 166

entreated] *1617* 'inheated'

l. 439

Wistly] *1617* 'Wisty'

THOMAS HEYWOOD, JUPITER AND CALLISTO (1609)

l. 188

whose] *1609* 'who'.

l. 218

appears] *1609* 'appear'.

GEORGE SANDYS, JUPITER AND CALLISTO (1621)

l. 103

Chased by the pursuing cry] *1632* 'chased by the following cry'

l. 138

Phoronida) and her proud shape restore] *1632* 'Phoronis) and her wanton shape restore'

BIBLIOGRAPHY

PRIMARY TEXTS

Alexander, Nigel, ed., *Elizabethan Narrative Verse* (London: Edward Arnold, 1967)

Barksted, William, *Mirrha the Mother of Adonis: or, Lust's Prodegies. Whereunto are added certain eclogues by L. M.* (London: John Bache, 1607)

—, *The Poems of William Barksted*, ed. by Rev. Alexander B. Grosart ([Manchester]: [C. E. Simms], 1876)

Caxton, William, trans., *Six bookes of Metamorphoseos in whyche ben conteyned the fables of Ovyde*, ed. by George Hibbert (London: Shakespeare Press, 1819)

—, *Ovyde, hys booke of Methamorphose Books X-XV*, ed. by Stephen Gaselee and H. F. B. Brett-Smith (Oxford: Basil Blackwell, 1924)

—, *The Metamorphoses of Ovid*, 2 vols (New York: G. Braziller, 1968)

Chaucer, Geoffrey, *The Riverside Chaucer*, ed. by Larry D. Benson (Oxford: Oxford University Press, 2008)

Chiari, Sophie, ed., *Renaissance Tales of Desire: Hermaphroditus and Salmacis* [Thomas Peend], *Theseus and Ariadne* [Thomas Underdowne], *Ceyx and Alcione* [William Hubbard] (Cambridge: Cambridge Scholars Publishing, 2009)

Churchyard, Thomas (et al.), *The Contention betwyxte Churchyeard and Camell, vpon Dauid Dycers Dreame sett out in suche order, that it is bothe wyttye and profytable for all degryes* (London: Owen Rogers for Mychell Loblee, 1560)

Edwards, Thomas, *Cephalus and Procris: Narcissus. From the Unique Copy in the Cathedral Library, Peterborough*, ed. by Rev. W. E. Buckley (London: Nichols, 1882)

Ficino, Marsilio, *Marsilio Ficino's Commentary on Plato's 'Symposium': The Text and a Translation, with an Introduction*, ed. and trans. by Sears Reynolds Jayne, University of Missouri Studies 19.1 (Columbia: University of Missouri Press, 1944)

Gale, Dunstan, *Pyramus and Thisbe* (London: [John Beale] for Roger Jackson, 1617)

Golding, Arthur, trans., *The fyrst fower bookes of P. Ouidius Nasos worke, intitled Metamorphosis* (London: Willyam Seres, 1565)

—, *The xv Bookes of P. Ouidius Naso, entytuled Metamorphosis* (London: Willyam Seres, 1567)

—, *Shakespeare's Ovid: Being Arthur Golding's Translation of the 'Metamorphoses'*, ed. by W. H. D. Rouse (London: De La More Press, 1904)

—, *Ovid's 'Metamorphoses': The Arthur Golding Translation, 1567*, ed. by John Frederick Nims (New York: Macmillan, 1965)

—, *The xv bookes entytuled Metamorphosis by P. Ovidius Naso* (Amsterdam: Theatrum Orbis Terrarum; Norwood, NJ: W. J. Johnson, 1977)

—, *Ovid's 'Metamorphoses'*, ed. by Madeleine Forey (London: Penguin, 2002)

Green, Robert, *The history of Arbasto King of Denmarke* [. . .] *Wherevnto is added a louely Poem of Pyramus and Thisbe* (London: J[ohn] B[eale] for Roger Jackson, 1617)

—, *The historie of Arbasto King of Denmarke* [. . .] *Wherevnto is added a louely Poem of Pyramus and Thisbe* (London: [T. Purfoot] for Francis Williams, 1626)

Gresham, James, *The picture of incest. Liuely portraicted in the historie of Cinyras and Myrrha* (London: [n. pr.] for R. A[llot], 1626)

—, *The Picture of Incest*, ed. by Rev. Alexander B. Grosart ([Manchester]: [C. E. Simms], 1876)

H. A., *The scourge of Venus. Or, The wanton Lady. With the rare birth of Adonis* (London: Nicholas Okes, 1613)

—, *The scourge of Venus: or, The wanton Lady. With the rare birth of Adonis. The second impression, corrected, and enlarged, by H. A.* (London: N[icholas] O[kes] for Robert Wilson, 1614)

—, *The scourge of Venus (1614)*, ed. by Rev. Alexander B. Grosart ([Manchester]: [C.E. Simms], 1876)

Hedley, Thomas, trans., *Of such as on fantesye decree & discuss: on other me[n]s works, lo Ouids tale thus* [Judgement of Midas] (London: Hary Sutton, [1552?])

Heywood, Thomas, *Troia Britanica: or, Great Britaines Troy. A Poem Deuided into XVII. seuerall Cantons, intermixed with many pleasant Poeticall Tales. Concluding with an Vniuersall Chronicle from the Creation, vntill these present Times* (London: W. Jaggard, 1609)

—, *The Brazen Age* (London: Nicholas Okes for Samuel Rand, 1613)

—, *Troia Britanica, or Great Britain's Troy* (Amsterdam: Theatrum Orbis Terrarum; Norwood, NJ: W. J. Johnson, 1974)

Hughes, Ted, *Tales from Ovid* (London: Faber & Faber, 1997)

Jiriczek, O. L., *Specimens of Tudor Translations from the Classics* (Heidelberg: Carl Winter's Universitätsbuchhandlung, 1923)

Jonson, Ben, *The Workes of Benjamin Jonson* (London: William Stansby, 1616)

Miller, Paul W., *Seven Minor Epics of the English Renaissance, 1596–1624* (Gainesville, FL: Scholars' Facsimiles & Reprints, 1967)

Ovid, *Tristia, Ex Ponto*, trans. by Arthur Leslie Wheeler, 2nd edn, rev. by G. P. Goold (Cambridge, MA: Harvard University Press, 1988)

Peend, Thomas, *The Pleasant fable of Hermaphroditus and Salmacis* [. . .] *With a morall in English Verse* (London: Thomas Col[well], 1565)

Sandys, George, trans., *The First Five Bookes of Ovids Metamorphosis* ([London]: [n. pr.] for W. B[arrett], 1621)

—, *Ovid's Metamorphosis Englished* (London: [William Stansby], 1626)

—, *Ovid's Metamorphosis Englished, Mythologiz'd and Represented in Figures*, ed. by Karl K. Hulley and Stanley T. Vandersall (Lincoln: University of Nebraska Press, [1970])

—, *Ovid's Metamorphosis Englished, Mythologiz'd, and Represented in Figures. An Essay to the Translation of Virgil's Æneis [Bk I]* (New York: Garland, 1976)

Shakespeare, William, *The Plays and Poems of William Shakespeare in Sixteen Volumes*, ed. by Edmond Malone (Dublin: John Exshaw, 1794)

—, *The Plays and Poems of William Shakespeare with the Corrections and Illustrations of Various Commentators*, ed. by Edward Malone, 21 vols (London: Printed by F. C. and J. Rivington *et al.*, 1821)

T. H., *The fable of Ouid treting of Narcissus translated out of Latin into English metre with a moral thereunto, very pleasant to read. MDLX* (London: Thomas Hackette, 1560)

Warner, William, *Albion's England. Or Historicall Map of the same Island* (London: George Robinson [and R. Ward] for Thomas Cadman, 1586)

SECONDARY TEXTS

Baldwin, T. W., *William Shakespere's Small Latine and Lesse Greeke* (Urbana: University of Illinois Press, 1944)

Bate, Jonathan, *Shakespeare and Ovid* (Oxford: Clarendon Press, 1994)

Bennett, J. A. W., 'Caxton's Ovid', *Times Literary Supplement*, 2 November 1966, p. 1108

Blake, N. F., *William Caxton* (Aldershot: Variorum, 1996)

Blumenfeld-Kosinski, Renate, *Reading Myth: Classical Mythology and its Interpretations in Medieval French Literature*, (Stanford, CA: Stanford University Press, 1997)

Boas, Frederick S., *Queen Elizabeth in Drama and Related Studies* (London: George Allen and Unwin, 1950)

—, *Thomas Heywood* (London: William & Norgate, 1950)

Boswell, Chris, 'The Culture and Rhetoric of the Answer Poem: 1485–1626' (unpublished doctoral thesis, University of Exeter, 2004)

Braden, Gordon, *The Classics and English Renaissance Poetry: Three Case Studies* (New Haven, CT: Yale University Press, 1978)

—, 'Epic Kinds', in Braden, Gordon, Cummings, Robert and Gillespie, Stuart, eds, *The Oxford History of Literary Translation in English: Volume 2, 1550–1660* (Oxford: Oxford University Press, 2010), pp. 167–93

Brydges, Sir Egerton and Haslewood, Joseph, *The British Bibliographer*, 4 vols (London: T. Bensley for R. Triphook, 1810–14)

Bush, Douglas, *Mythology and the Renaissance Tradition in English Poetry* (New York: Norton, 1963)

Carter, Sarah, *Ovidian Myth and Sexual Deviance in Early Modern English Literature* (London: Palgrave Macmillan, 2011)

Clark, Arthur Melville, 'Thomas Heywood's *Art of Love* Lost and Found', *The Library*, 4th ser., 3 (1922), 210–22

Collier, J. Payne, *The Poetical Decameron, or Ten Conversations on English Poets and Poetry, Particularly of the Reigns of Elizabeth and James I*, 2 vols (Edinburgh: Archibald Constable, 1820)

—, *Extracts from the Registers of the Stationers' Catalogues from 1557 to 1587* (London: The Shakespeare Society, 1853)

—, *A Bibliographical and Critical Account of the Rarest Books in the English Language*, 2 vols (London: Joseph Lilly, 1865)

Dewar, Michael, '*Siquid habent veri vatum praesagia*: Ovid in the 1st –5th Centuries A.D.', in *Brill's Companion to Ovid*, ed. by Barbara Weiden Boyd (Leiden: Brill, 2002), pp. 383–412

Drake, Gertrude C., 'Ovid's *Metamorphoses*: The Facsimile of the Caxton MS, and Sandys's 1632 Version', *Papers on Language and Literature*, 7 (1971), 313–35

Ducke, Joseph, 'Shakespeare's *Macbeth* and the 'Fable of Ovid Treting of Narcissus' by Thomas Hackett' (2007) <http://www.grin.com/e-book/110628/about-shakespeare-s-macbeth-and-the-fable-of-ovid-treting-of-narcissus> [accessed 21 January 2010]

Ellis, Jim, 'Imagining Heterosexuality in the Epyllia', in *Ovid and the Renaissance Body*, ed. by Goran B. Stanivukovic (Toronto: University of Toronto Press, 2001), pp. 38–57

—, *Sexuality and Citizenship: Metamorphosis in Elizabethan Erotic Verse* (Toronto: University of Toronto Press, 2003)

Ellis, Roger, and Oakley-Brown, Liz, eds, *Translation and Nation: Towards a Cultural Poetics of Englishness* (Bristol: Multilingual Matters, 2001)

Ficino, Marsilio, *Commentary on Plato's 'Symposium': The Text and a Translation, with an Introduction'*, ed. and trans. by Sears Reynolds Jayne (Columbia: University of Missouri Press, 1944)

Flinker, Noam, 'Cinyras, Myrrha, and Adonis: Father-Daughter Incest from Ovid to Milton', *Milton Studies*, 14 (1980), 59–74

Forey, Madeleine, '"Bless thee, Bottom, bless thee! Thou art translated!": Ovid, Golding and *A Midsummer Night's Dream*', *Modern Language Review*, 93 (1998), 321–29

Freedman, Luba, *Classical Myths in Italian Renaissance Painting* (Cambridge: Cambridge University Press, 2011)

Fyler, John M., *Chaucer and Ovid* (New Haven, CT: Yale University Press, 1979)

Gilbert, Ruth, *Early Modern Hermaphrodites: Sex and Other Stories* (Basingstoke: Palgrave, 2002)

Gillespie, Alexandra, 'Caxton and the Invention of Printing', *Tudor Literature, 1485–1603*, ed. by Mike Pincombe and Cathy Shrank (Oxford: Oxford University Press, 2009), pp. 21–36

Gosse, Edmund, *The Jacobean Poets* (London: John Murray, 1894)

Halliwell-Phillipps, James Orchard, *An Introduction to Shakespeare's 'Midsummer Night's Dream'* (London: William Pickering, 1841)

Hazlitt, W. C., *Shakespear* (London: Bernard Quaritch, 1902)

Holaday, Allan, 'Heywood's *Troia Britannica* and the *Ages*', *Journal of English and Germanic Philology*, 45 (1946), 430–39

James, Heather, 'Ovid in Renaissance English Literature', in *A Companion to Ovid*, ed. by Peter E. Knox (London: Wiley-Blackwell, 2009), pp. 423–41

Keach, William, *Elizabethan Erotic Narratives: Irony and Pathos in the Ovidian Poetry of Shakespeare, Marlowe and their Contemporaries* (New Brunswick, NJ: Rutgers University Press, 1977)

BIBLIOGRAPHY

Kilgour, Maggie, *Milton and the Metamorphosis of Ovid* (Oxford: Oxford University Press, 2012)

King, John N., *English Reformation Literature: The Tudor Origins of the Protestant Tradition* (Princeton, NJ: Princeton University Press, 1982)

Knox, Peter E., 'Commenting on Ovid', in *A Companion to Ovid*, ed. by Peter E. Knox (London: Wiley-Blackwell, 2009), pp. 327–40

Lewis, C. S., *English Literature in the Sixteenth Century Excluding Drama* (Oxford: Oxford University Press, 1954)

Livingston, Carole Rose, *British Broadside Ballads of the Sixteenth Century* (New York: Garland, 1991)

Loveday, John, 'A Literary Discovery', *Notes and Queries*, 6 (1882), 124–25

Lucas, Scott, 'Diggun Davie and Davy Dicar: Edmund Spenser, Thomas Churchyard and the Poetics of Public Protest', *Spenser Studies*, 16 (2002), 151–65

Lyne, Raphael, *Ovid's Changing Worlds: English Metamorphoses 1567–1632* (Oxford: Oxford University Press, 2001)

Mann, Jenny, 'How to Look at a Hermaphrodite in Early Modern England', *Studies in English Literature*, 46 (2006), 67–91

Maslen, R. W., 'Myths Exploited: The Metamorphoses of Ovid in Early Elizabethan England', in *Shakespeare's Ovid: The 'Metamorphoses' in the Plays and Poems*, ed. by A. B. Taylor (Cambridge: Cambridge University Press, 2000)

McIlwraith, A. K., '"W. B." and Massinger', *Review of English Studies*, 4 (1928), 326–27

Melnikoff, Kirk, 'Thomas Hacket and the Ventures of an Elizabethan Publisher', *The Library*, 7th ser., 10 (2009), 257–71

Moss, Ann, *Ovid in Renaissance France: A Survey of the Latin Editions of Ovid and Commentaries Printed in France before 1600*, Warburg Institute Surveys, VIII (London: The Warburg Institute, 1982)

Muir, Kenneth, 'Pyramus and Thisbe: A Study in Shakespeare's Method', *Shakespeare Quarterly*, 5 (1954), 141–53

Oakley-Brown, Liz, 'Translating the Subject: Ovid's *Metamorphoses* in England, 1560–7', in *Translation and Nation: Towards a Cultural Politics of Englishness*, ed. by Roger Ellis and Liz Oakley-Brown (Bristol: Multilingual Matters, 2001), pp 48–84

—, *Ovid and the Cultural Politics of Translation in Early Modern England* (Aldershot: Ashgate, 2006)

Palmatier, M. A., 'A Suggested New Source in Ovid's *Metamorphoses* for Shakespeare's *Venus and Adonis*', *Huntington Library Quarterly*, 24 (1961), 164–69

Pearcy, Lee T., *The Mediated Muse: English Translations of Ovid, 1560–1700* (Hamden, CT: Archon, 1985)

Pincombe, Michael, 'The Ovidian Hermaphrodite: Moralisations by Peend and Spenser', in *Ovid and the Renaissance Body*, ed. by Goran B. Stanivukovic (Toronto: University of Toronto Press, 2001), pp. 155–70

Pound, Ezra, *An ABC of Reading* (New York: New Directions, 1960)

Putney, Rufus, 'Venus and Adonis: Amor with Humor', *Philological Quarterly*, 20 (1941), 533–48

Ritson, Joseph, *Remarks, Critical and Illustrative, on the Texts and Notes of the Last Edition of Shakespeare* (London: J. Johnson, 1783)

—, *Biographia Poetica: A Catalogue of the English Poets* (London: C. Roworth, 1802)

Rubin, Deborah, *Ovid's Metamorphoses Englished: George Sandys as Translator and Mythographer* (New York: Garland, 1985)

Runsdorf, R. H., 'Transforming Ovid in the 1560s: Thomas Peend's *Pleasant Fable*', *American Notes and Queries*, 5 (1992), 124–27

Schelling, Felix E., *The English Chronicle Plays* (New York: Macmillan, 1902)

Shrank, Cathy, 'Trollers and Dreamers: Defining the Citizen-Subject in Sixteenth-Century Cheap Print', *Yearbook of English Studies*, 32 (2008), 102–18

Silberman, Lauren, 'The Hermaphrodite and the Metamorphosis of Spenserian Allegory', *English Literary Renaissance*, 17 (1987), 207–23

Smith, H. D., *Elizabethan Poetry: A Study in Conventions, Meaning and Expression* (Cambridge, MA: Harvard University Press, 1966)

Stanivukovic, Goran R., 'Shakespeare, Dunstan Gale, and Golding', *Notes and Queries*, 239.1 (1994), 35–37

Swinburne, Algernon Charles, *The Age of Shakespeare* (London: Chatto & Windus, 1908)

Taylor, Anthony Brian, 'Thomas Peend and Arthur Golding', *Notes and Queries*, 16 (1969), 19–20

—, 'Spenser and Arthur Golding', *Notes and Queries*, 32 (1985), 18–21

—, 'Golding's Ovid, Shakespeare's "Small Latin", and the Real Object of Mockery in "Pyramus and Thisbe"', *Shakespeare Survey*, 42 (1990), 53–64

—, 'Lively, Dynamic, but Hardly a Thing of "Rhythmic Beauty": Arthur Golding's Fourteeners', *Connotations*, 2 (1992), 205–22

—, 'Melting Earth and Leaping Bulls: Shakespeare's Ovid and Arthur Golding', *Connotations*, 4 (1994–95), 192–206

—, 'Narcissus, Olivia, and a Greek Tradition, *Notes and Queries*, 44 (1997), 58–61.

—, 'A Note on Christopher Marlowe's *Hero and Leander*', *Notes and Queries*, 16 (1969), 20–21

Tillyard, E. M. W., *The English Epic and its Background* (London: Chatto and Windus, 1954)

Wall, Kathleen, *The Callisto Myth from Ovid to Atwood: Initiation and Rape in Literature* (Kingston and Montreal: McGill-Queens University Press, 1988)

Warton, Thomas, *The History of English Poetry*, 4 vols (London: Reeves and Turner, 1871), IV

Wright, Neil, 'Creation and Recreation: Medieval Responses to *Metamorphoses* I. 5–88', in *Ovidian Transformations: Essays on Ovid's Metamorphoses and its Reception*, ed. by Philip Hardie, Alessandro Barchiesi and Stephen Hinds (Cambridge: Cambridge Philological Society, 1999), pp. 68–84